FOREIGN DIRECT INVESTMENT IN JAPAN

Foreign Direct Investment in Japan presents a detailed examination of recent trends of inward foreign direct investment (FDI) and their impact on the Japanese economy. Historically much less open to foreign trade and investment than other major economies, Japan experienced an unprecedented jump in FDI inflows around the turn of the millennium. This book looks at the profound changes in Japan that made this jump possible and considers the potential contribution of foreign firms to productivity and overall economic growth. Detailed case studies illustrate that in certain sectors the presence of foreign firms already is a key factor shaping industry dynamics. Yet, despite recent changes, resistance to inward FDI remains strong and the government could do much more if it were committed to attracting FDI. Overall, Japan continues to appear reluctant to embrace fully, and therefore seems unlikely to benefit even more substantially from, globalization.

Ralph Paprzycki is a Research Fellow at the Institute of Economic Research, Hitotsubashi University, Tokyo, Japan. He has also taught at Sophia University in Tokyo. Dr. Paprzycki's book *Interfirm Networks in the Japanese Electronics Industry* was published in 2005. He obtained his doctorate in economics from the School of Oriental and African Studies, University of London.

Kyoji Fukao is Professor at the Institute of Economic Research, Hitotsubashi University, Tokyo, Japan, and Director of the Center for Economic Institutions at the Institute. A Faculty Fellow of the Research Institute of Economy, Trade and Industry in Japan since 2001, he also serves as the Chief Research Fellow in the Asia Research Division of the Japan Center of Economic Research and as Science Advisor to the Ministry of Education. Professor Fukao coauthored *Foreign Direct Investment and the Japanese Economy* (in Japanese) with Tomofumi Amano in 2004 and has published articles in journals such as the *Quarterly Journal of Economics*, *Journal of Political Economy*, *Journal of the Asia Pacific Economy*, and the *Journal of the Japanese and International Economies*.

Foreign Direct Investment in Japan

Multinationals' Role in Growth and Globalization

RALPH PAPRZYCKI
Hitotsubashi University

KYOJI FUKAO
Hitotsubashi University

CAMBRIDGE
UNIVERSITY PRESS

CAMBRIDGE
UNIVERSITY PRESS

32 Avenue of the Americas, New York NY 10013-2473, USA

Cambridge University Press is part of the University of Cambridge.

It furthers the University's mission by disseminating knowledge in the pursuit of
education, learning and research at the highest international levels of excellence.

www.cambridge.org
Information on this title: www.cambridge.org/9780521873680

First published 2008
First paperback edition 2012

A catalogue record for this publication is available from the British Library

Library of Congress Cataloguing in Publication data
Paprzycki, Ralph.
Foreign direct investment in Japan : multinationals' role in growth and
globalization / Ralph Paprzycki, Kyoji Fukao.
p.   cm.
Includes bibliographical references and index.
ISBN 978-0-521-87368-0 (hardback)
1. Investments, Foreign – Japan.   2. International business enterprises – Japan.
I. Paprzycki, Ralph.   II. Fukao, Kyoji.   III. Title.
HG5772.P37   2008
332.67'30952 – dc22   2007040091

ISBN 978-0-521-87368-0 Hardback

Contents

List of Figures and Tables

Figures

Tables

Acknowledgments

This book has greatly benefited from the generous cooperation of a large number of people to whom we express our deep gratitude.

To Alison Murray, Executive Director of the European Business Community in Japan (EBC), Jakob Edberg, Policy Director of the EBC, and Don Westmore, Executive Director of the American Chamber of Commerce in Japan (ACCJ), sincere thanks are due for kindly helping to arrange the interviews that informed the industry studies in Chapter 6.

We are also grateful to the following interviewees who all generously gave their time and shared their knowledge and insights with us: Bill Bishop (Director of Corporate Affairs, Wyeth Japan), Richard Colasse (EBC Chairman and President of Chanel Japan), Takeshi Fujiwara (President of Gambro Japan), Guy Harris (Chairman of the ACCJ Health Care Services Committee and President, Digital Medical Communications Corporation), Richard Mason (Chairman of the EBC Human Resources Committee and Associate Director, JAC Japan), A. N. R. Millington (Director General of the Tokyo Office of the European Automobile Manufacturers Association), Jean-Francois Minier (EBC Vice Chairman and Managing Director, Dresdner Kleinwort Wasserstein), Hitoshi Morita (President and CEO of PCA Life Insurance), John Reilly (Director of the International Bankers Association), Thomas Riley (Managing Director, Morgan Stanley Japan), Takashi Takenoshita (Principal at McKinsey & Company), and Akihiro Yamamoto (Managing Director, Japan Medical Devices Manufacturers Association).

Further, we express our thanks to Nicholas Benes, Chairman of the FDI Task Force of the ACCJ, who helped us to understand the intricacies and implications of the triangular merger scheme and other regulations in Japan.

Kyoji Fukao is also grateful to Professor Tomofumi Amano, University of Tokyo, with whom he published an earlier study on FDI in Japan, for his continuing collaboration and stimulating discussions.

Finally, we extend a big thank you to Yumiko Moriyama for the help and support cheerfully provided in a myriad of little ways throughout the work on this book.

ONE

Introduction

The world is moving ever faster toward a truly globalized economy. International trade in goods and services is expanding at exponential rates, financial markets are becoming ever more integrated, and multinational companies with operations around the globe are ubiquitous. Few corners of the world have been left unaffected by these trends, and how nations respond to the opportunities and challenges posed by globalization is a key determinant of their future economic prosperity.

Although globalization has been greeted with a mixture of excitement and apprehension in most places, few developed countries appear as ambiguous toward it as Japan. On the one hand, the island nation has greatly benefited from the opportunities provided by access to world markets. Exports played a significant role in the country's stellar economic rise during the postwar period and external demand propped up the economy when domestic demand collapsed during the 1990s. In addition, Japanese firms have actively invested overseas, purchasing real estate and movie studios in the United States and setting up production facilities in the United States, Europe, and the rest of Asia. Yet, throughout most of its history, Japan has been wary of granting access to its own domestic market. During the early postwar period, government policies placed tight controls on imports and inward investment, and even after many regulations were lifted during the 1960s and 1970s, exports to and investment in Japan continued to face various informal obstacles that severely limited the presence of foreign firms in the Japanese market.

However, as a result of government reforms and structural change triggered by the prolonged recession, many of the informal obstacles to foreign direct investment (FDI) have also recently weakened or vanished. Important service sectors such as finance and telecommunication have been deregulated and measures to facilitate mergers and corporate restructuring introduced; the bank-centered horizontal *keiretsu* (business groups) have all but disappeared as extensive cross-shareholdings were unwound; mergers and acquisitions (M&A), previously almost unheard of in Japan, have become almost commonplace; and the lifetime employment system, another pillar of "Japan Inc.," has been seriously undermined by mass layoffs.

At the same time as these and other fundamental changes in the Japanese economy were gathering pace during the second half of the 1990s, the world was swept by a boom in M&A activity, which saw a series of megamergers in a number of sectors. In the car industry, for example, Germany's Daimler-Benz acquired American Chrysler Corp. in a deal worth US$40 billion, while in the telecommunications industry, Britain's Vodafone bought Airtouch Communications from the United States for about US$60 billion and Mannesmann from Germany for about US$200 billion. With investment barriers vanishing, some of this global M&A boom also reached the shores of Japan, resulting in a large surge in inward FDI. Cross-border mergers and acquisitions with major Japanese firms as the target were headline-grabbing stuff around the turn of the millennium. Prominent cases include the acquisition of a controlling stake in Nissan by French carmaker Renault, the acquisition of Japan Telecom first by British Telecom and AT&T and then Vodafone, and the sale of failed Long Term Credit Bank to foreign investors. Thanks to these megadeals, as well as many smaller ones, FDI flows into Japan during 1999 and 2000 combined outstripped the cumulative total of the entire three preceding decades.

Although FDI inflows have leveled off somewhat since those heady days and remain much lower than in many other countries, these developments and the way they have been received in Japan represent an important break with the past. Both the government and the public at large are increasingly aware that if the country is to achieve sustainable growth in the future, it needs to embrace globalization – and foreign investment – more fully. Foreign multinationals can contribute to Japan's economy in multitudinous ways: through the introduction of managerial expertise and advanced technologies that have been tested in the global market place; by adding a healthy dose of competition in areas that often have seen little so far; and by offering consumers a wider range of products and services to choose from. Yet, whether the country will be able to attract more FDI in the future greatly depends on whether the deregulation and structural change initiated in the 1990s will continue in the years to come.

The purpose of this book is to assess the issues surrounding the recent increase in FDI in Japan in detail. Of interest in particular are the forces underlying the surge in inward FDI and the impact that the growing presence of foreign multinationals is having on the Japanese economy. Specifically, the aim is to examine questions such as: Why was inward FDI in the past so low and why did it increase when it did? How can foreign firms contribute to productivity and growth? How does the entry of foreign multinationals affect the industries in Japan in which they operate? What are the future prospects for FDI in Japan, and what could or should the government do to achieve its ambitious goal of raising the inward FDI stock to 5 percent of gross domestic product (GDP) by 2010?

By looking at the actual impact of inward FDI on the Japanese economy, this book moves beyond much of the existing literature on the topic. Given that, until recently, FDI in Japan has been miniscule, it is not surprising to find that, at least up to the beginning of this decade, most research has concentrated on trying to explain why this is so. There is a long list of studies with titles such as "Why is FDI in Japan so small?" (Wakasugi, 1994); "Japan's low levels of inward direct investment: Causes, consequences and remedies" (Mason, 1995), and "Japan's low levels of inward investment: The role of inhibitions on acquisitions" (Lawrence, 1994). Even the booklength study edited by Yoshitomi and Graham (1996), with a title similar to the present volume and containing contributions by leading scholars and business practitioners, deals almost exclusively with the issue of access to Japan, discussing topics such as "How can theories of foreign direct investment shed light on the small size of FDI into Japan?" "How do Japan's distinctive business practices and trade structure affect FDI into Japan" and "What are the actual experiences of foreign multinational companies in Japan?" with the latter again concentrating on the difficulties faced by foreign firms in the country.[1]

It is only since the beginning of this decade that scholars have started to examine the role of foreign multinationals in the Japanese economy. Much of that research has concentrated on comparing the productivity and profitability of foreign- and domestically-owned firms in Japan.[2] Although FDI may have an impact in various other areas, such as employment or the

---

[1] The list continues. Other studies with indicative titles include "On the causes of low levels of FDI in Japan" (Wakasugi, 1995) and "Tainichi chokusetsu toshi wa naze ka sukanai ka? Keiretsu, kisei ga mondai ka? [Why is FDI in Japan so small? Is it because of the *keiretsu* or because of regulations?]" (Nakamura, Fukao, and Shibuya (1997). The level of and/or barriers to FDI in Japan are also a major concern in Encarnation (1992), Mason (1992), Eaton and Tamura (1994), Weinstein (1996, 1997), Kawai and Urata (1997), and Feenstra (1998).

[2] See, e.g., Fukao and Murakami (2005), Fukao, Ito, and Kwon (2005), and Kimura and Kiyota (2007).

current account balance, the direction and magnitude of that impact are difficult to determine once one attempts to take into account the reverberations in the rest of the economy – such as potential reductions in employment at domestic firms in response to competition from foreign multinationals. For this reason, probably the most important benefit of inward FDI is the contribution it can make to productivity growth as a result of the inflow of managerial resources. Empirical studies along these lines indicate that foreign firms indeed tend to be more productive and profitable than domestic firms.[3] These are important results that suggest FDI can make a potentially significant contribution to overall growth at a time when Japan, despite recovering from stagnation, continues to face serious economic challenges.

Research along these lines represents an important step forward from the focus on the level of and barriers to FDI. However, most of these studies are rather specialized, focus on a single, narrowly defined topic, and often tend to be technical. In addition, some of this research as well as many other materials are available only in Japanese. Against this background, the aim of this book is to provide an overview and synthesis of recent research results, put these results in the wider context of FDI in Japan, and take this as the point of departure for new original research. The next section provides an outline of each of the chapters and the topics they address.

Outline

Following this outline, the remainder of this introductory chapter provides a definition of foreign direct investment and a description of the data sources on FDI in Japan. In the Japanese context, the first challenge facing the researcher is the quest to obtain consistent, reliable, and internationally comparable figures on FDI. Reflecting the country's ambiguous attitude toward inward FDI until the recent past and also partly explaining researchers' concern with FDI *levels*, such data are difficult to come by. What are available instead are a host of different statistical sources of varying usefulness and it is therefore helpful to discuss their characteristics before embarking on the analysis of FDI in Japan.

With these caveats in mind, Chapter 2 begins the analysis by looking at various measures of inward FDI in Japan. Internationally comparable figures, such as the United Nations Conference on Trade and Development's (UNCTAD's) data on inward FDI flows and stocks, for example, indicate that

---

[3] Again, see, e.g., Fukao and Murakami (2005), Fukao, Ito and Kwon (2005), and Kimura and Kiyota (2007).

foreign investment in Japan is indeed substantially lower than in other advanced and many developing economies. This assessment is further supported by statistics of the Organisation for Economic Co-operation and Development (OECD) statistics comparing the share of industrial production or employment accounted for by foreign firms across member countries. However, in conducting such a comparison, the OECD has to rely on national statistics, which in Japan are based on a survey that suffers from a low response ratio and does not include foreign affiliates in the real estate and financial sectors.

To address these shortcomings and to provide a comparison of the extent of FDI penetration in Japan, Chapter 2 presents an alternative measure, the employment share accounted for by foreign affiliates in Japan, using a survey that is compulsory and covers all enterprises in Japan. Comparing these shares with figures for the United States suggests that the employment accounted for by foreign affiliates in Japan in 2001 was about half of the equivalent level in the United States in 1997, suggesting that although FDI penetration in Japan remains much lower than in the United States, the gap may not be as large as is typically assumed.

The second major topic addressed in Chapter 2 is why FDI in Japan is so low. Although geography can partly account for this, there is little doubt that government policy is a main factor. In fact, keeping foreign influences at bay has a long tradition in Japan and this chapter provides an historical overview of government policy toward foreign business. The overview shows that even though there were periods during which foreign investment was welcomed, these tended to be short-lived and for the most part investment inflows were restricted. Even when FDI "liberalization" began in the 1960s, the process was only gradual and, during the 1970s and 1980s, formal restrictions were replaced by informal barriers. It is against this historical background that the surge in FDI in Japan since the mid-1990s and the changes that have made it possible must be viewed.

Yet, as Chapter 2 also shows, although inward FDI has been restricted throughout most of Japanese history, this does not mean that foreign firms have played no part in the country's economic development. On the contrary, during the brief period when the investment regime was relatively liberal during the first three decades of the twentieth century, foreign capital and technology were instrumental in the establishment of some of Japan's most successful industries. This episode thus provides a vivid illustration of the transformative potential of FDI, although, because of the size and level of development of Japan's economy today, any impact is likely to be much less dramatic.

The surge in inward FDI in Japan over the past decade and its underlying causes are the subject of Chapter 3. The analysis suggests that the 1990s were a period of substantial political and economic change in Japan that has significantly reshaped the environment for FDI in the country. Seeking to overcome the economic stagnation that followed the burst of the bubble economy, the government enacted various reforms to deregulate the economy and attract foreign investment. For example, the Large Retail Store Law was revised twice; the telecommunications industry was deregulated and foreign investment allowed for the first time; financial sector reform was implemented; and changes in accounting rules and measures to facilitate mergers and corporate restructuring were introduced.

In addition, structural changes brought about by economic stagnation significantly reduced or even removed many of the informal barriers that had hampered inward FDI. The unwinding of cross-shareholdings, together with the measures to facilitate M&A as well as the rising number of distressed companies, for the first time, made the acquisition of Japanese firms by foreign multinationals a viable proposition. Changes in the labor market, in particular the erosion of the lifetime employment system, made it easier – and cheaper – for foreign firms to hire qualified Japanese staff, and falling property prices and office rents lowered the costs of doing business in the country. Finally, long-term economic stagnation contributed to a change in attitudes toward foreign direct investment among policy makers, the Japanese business community, and society in general.

At the same time, however, the surge in FDI in Japan from 1997 to 2000 coincided with a global boom in M&A activity, and on closer inspection, there is a conspicuous overlap between leading inward FDI sectors in Japan and industries at the forefront of the global FDI boom during that period. This suggests that, rather than the changes in Japan acting as a trigger for an autonomous rise in FDI inflows, they largely opened the gates for the wave of global FDI to lap onto Japanese shores. What is more, following the surge around the turn of the millennium, net inward FDI has been on a downward trend since its peak in 1999. This trend suggests that without significant further deregulation it will be difficult to achieve the government's target of an inward FDI stock equivalent to 5 percent of GDP by 2010.

Leaving trends in FDI inflows behind, Chapters 4 to 6 turn to consider the impact foreign firms have on the Japanese economy. Chapter 4 begins the analysis by examining Japan's recent growth performance. Although the prolonged economic stagnation during the 1990s and early 2000s to a certain extent was a cyclical phenomenon triggered by the collapse of the bubble economy, more fundamental structural factors are at work that play a crucial role in explaining the disappointing growth record. These structural factors include the unfavorable demographic trends and the declining productivity of capital in Japan. Against this background, a key role falls to total factor productivity (TFP) – the efficiency with which factors of production are used – which reflects technological progress in the broadest sense and depends on the rate of innovation, the accumulation of intangible assets, and the degree of competition in the economy. The chapter shows how TFP growth, too, has declined in recent years, highlights some of the reasons, and argues that it is in this area, which is key to achieving sustained economic growth in Japan, that foreign firms can make an important contribution.

Chapter 5 delves deeper into the analysis of the potential growth contribution FDI could make by presenting empirical evidence on the relative TFP level of foreign and domestic firms in Japan. Comparing foreign and domestic firms, it becomes evident that the former tend to show both higher TFP levels and higher TFP growth and, moreover, are ahead of domestic firms in terms of a range of other indicators, such as return on capital, wages, and research and development (R&D) investment per worker. However, most FDI cases in Japan consist of M&As, and on closer inspection, it turns out that foreign firms' superior performance partly owes to the fact that they acquire Japanese firms that already perform better than the average local firm. Nevertheless, further investigation reveals that out–in M&As (i.e., M&As where a domestic firm is acquired by a foreign one) do improve target firms' TFP level and current profit/sales ratio. In other words, the evidence suggests that FDI is indeed helping to raise productivity and thereby contributing to the growth of the Japanese economy.

The second part of Chapter 5 then attempts to quantify the macroeconomic impact of inward FDI in Japan. Because comprehensive and reasonably up-to-date statistical data for a rigorous empirical investigation are unavailable, the analysis instead simulates the impact of FDI by using the results on the improvement in TFP experienced by firms acquired by foreigners and combining these with various assumptions regarding the level of future inward FDI flows. The purpose of the simulation is not so much to provide accurate estimates of the macroeconomic impact of FDI, but to gain an overall impression of the magnitude of the effects under various assumptions. The results suggest that the impact on Japan's GDP ranges from rather modest under a relatively conservative scenario, which probably underestimates the true effect of foreign acquisitions on TFP, to quite substantial under a more optimistic scenario that assumes a fairly large, although unlikely, increase in FDI. The simulation thus supports the view that there is considerable scope for Japan to more fully benefit from inward FDI.

Whereas Chapter 5 attempts to quantitatively assess the impact of FDI on the Japanese economy, Chapter 6 takes a closer look at more qualitative evidence through a series of detailed sectoral case studies. This qualitative approach complements and extends the quantitative analysis in that the case studies provide concrete illustrations of the intangible assets – management skills, business models, the knowledge and technology embodied in products – that foreign firms introduce into the Japanese market and show how their presence shapes the competitive parameters and the degree of competition in their respective industries. In fact, in some of the industries that will be examined, the presence of foreign firms has reached sufficient critical mass to contribute to substantial structural change (although the overall number of such industries is small).

In the automobile sector, for example, foreign acquisitions of Japanese firms, and in particular that of Nissan by Renault, have led to an increased focus on profitability throughout the industry and a reconfiguration of supplier networks in parts of it. In the pharmaceutical and the insurance sectors, foreign multinationals have gained significant market share and are leading the way in overhauling distribution channels and introducing new products hitherto unavailable in Japan, thus increasing consumer choice and forcing domestic firms to raise their game. And in the wholesale and retail sector, by circumventing the traditional multilayered distribution system and introducing new retail business concepts, foreign multinationals have compelled domestic competitors to streamline their own purchasing operations, which, in turn, has resulted in consolidation in the wholesale sector.

However, there are also sectors where, despite substantial FDI inflows, foreign firms have failed to make a tangible and/or lasting impact. Prime examples are retail banking and especially telecommunications. The telecommunications industry played a central role in the increase in FDI around the turn of the millennium; yet, today, only a few years later, no foreign firms are left in Japan that offer telecommunications services to the wider public. Although the specific reasons why foreign multinationals have failed to make an impact differ in these two industries, it appears that certain features they have in common (such as the importance of local knowledge, firm size and concentration, etc.) and possibly regulation continue to form barriers to foreign firms.

What is more, the industries chosen for the case studies represent sectors that have received significant amounts of foreign investment, but large sections of the economy remain that have received hardly any FDI at all – partly as a result of industry structure, partly as a result of regulations that discriminate not necessarily against foreign firms in particular, but against new entrants in general. Yet, as the case studies show, even at the current low levels of FDI penetration, foreign firms can play an important role in reshaping and revitalizing the Japanese economy.

Obviously, though, FDI would have a much more substantial impact if there was more of it, and Chapter 7 sets out to examine the prospects for future investment flows into Japan. To do so, the chapter considers the determinants of FDI in Japan, highlighting that the central motive underlying the majority of foreign investments is to gain access to the Japanese market. Profitability and market growth therefore are likely to be key determinants of Japan's attractiveness as an investment destination. Using data on U.S. multinationals, the available evidence suggests that the profitability of foreign affiliates in Japan has improved in recent years and now is more or less on par with that in other advanced economies such as Germany, France, and the United Kingdom. At the same time, however, both the number and size of FDI withdrawals from Japan have jumped in recent years, suggesting that profits are not guaranteed and many firms have been unable to fulfill their ambitions. The outlook for market growth is also rather mixed. On the positive side, Japan has finally managed to pull out of its decade-long recession and, if all goes well, may continue to enjoy sustainable growth at rates that are more or less on par with those of Western European countries facing similar population dynamics. Yet, Japan's growth prospects pale in comparison with those of most of the rest of the region and it seems unlikely that FDI in Japan is going to benefit much from these regional growth dynamics.

Other aspects considered are political, social, and cultural factors that shape the investment climate in Japan. Compared with only a decade earlier, attitudes toward FDI have certainly changed considerably. Politicians, ministries, and business organizations are much more aware of the potential benefits of FDI and, in principle, have become much more supportive of measures to facilitate greater inflows. Society as a whole is also generally favorably inclined toward foreign multinationals. Surveys indicate, for example, that a majority of Japanese believe that foreign companies had a positive effect on the economy and especially many younger Japanese would be happy to work for one. On the other hand, Japanese society remains much less internationalized than that of most Western countries, meaning that it still remains difficult for foreign multinationals to recruit employees with the right skills, attitudes, and experience, including an international outlook. Moreover, as the economy is regaining strength and confidence in business circles is rising once again, there are also signs of a revival of earlier patterns, such as a renewed increase of cross-shareholdings as a defense against takeovers. Finally, although the government has declared its desire to attract more FDI to Japan, few concrete policy steps have been taken to achieve this goal.

Yet, it seems unlikely that FDI inflows will increase significantly without further government measures. To a large extent, the surge in inward investment in the late 1990s represents the response to deregulation and structural change during that period, which has now largely run its course. But numerous areas remain that the government could address to improve the business environment for foreign multinationals and thus increase FDI inflows. These areas include the policy framework for mergers and acquisitions, where the government needs to ensure that the triangular merger scheme introduced in May 2007 can play its intended role and thereby make it easier for foreign companies to acquire Japanese firms. Also, there remain numerous industries in which regulations hamper FDI not by banning foreign firms but by restricting market access and competition more generally. Creating a level playing field would allow foreign firms to compete and exploit their strengths in such industries and would therefore help to raise Japan's inward FDI potential and benefit the economy as a whole.

The main findings of the study are summarized in Chapter 8 and put into the context of Japan's globalization more generally. It is argued that, despite the recent increase in inward FDI, the country's integration into the world economy remains severely unbalanced. Whereas Japanese firms are pressing ahead with "outer globalization," taking advantage of opportunities overseas, "inner globalization" continues to lag significantly behind. Japan therefore faces a real danger of failing to benefit from the fruits of globalization.

As the country's own experience illustrates, inflows of foreign knowledge and technology have played a historically important role in its economic development. But whereas in the past it may have been sufficient to rely on knowledge and technology that is easily separable from managerial resources – technology that can be obtained through licensing, for example – this is no longer the case. Today, the areas in which Japan would most benefit from foreign knowledge and technology are those that are embodied in people, organizational structures, business processes, and products and come as a "package," that is, in the form of FDI. While this is true for the manufacturing sector, it is especially true for services, which will have to generate most of Japan's future economic growth, but in which the country has produced few internationally competitive companies and productivity lags considerably behind that of other advanced economies. However, for Japan to be able to take advantage of such types of knowledge, it will have to achieve "inner globalization" based on the recognition that the nationality of a firm is of little relevance for a country's economic welfare.

What is Foreign Direct Investment? – Concepts, Definitions, and Data Sources

Before looking at foreign direct investment in Japan, it is useful to discuss a few concepts and definitions. These will help to clarify what is commonly understood by the term FDI; its underlying rationale according to economic theory; and some of the problems associated with the measurement of FDI.

The International Monetary Fund (IMF), in its *Balance of Payments Manual* (Fifth Edition), defines foreign direct investment as follows:

Direct investment is the category of international investment that reflects the objective of a resident entity in one economy obtaining a lasting interest in an enterprise resident in another economy. (The resident entity is the direct investor and the enterprise is the direct investment enterprise.) The lasting interest implies the existence of a long-term relationship between the direct investor and the enterprise and a significant degree of influence by the investor on the management of the enterprise. Direct investment comprises not only the initial transaction establishing the relationship between the investor and the enterprise but also all subsequent transactions between them and among affiliated enterprises, both incorporated and unincorporated.[4]

It is worth elaborating on the various elements of this definition. First, FDI involves a "long-term relationship" and "lasting interest" entailing a "significant degree of influence [...] on the management" of the enterprise. A central aspect of FDI thus is that it involves a management interest, distinguishing it from "indirect" portfolio investment which consists of the acquisition of equity and debt securities or the extension of bank loans without any control in the management of a company and is conducted solely for the purpose of earning a financial return in the form of dividends, interest payments, and other financial claims. Moreover, because FDI involves the acquisition of management control, it tends to be long-term and lasting, which results from the underlying purpose of the investment. From the vantage point of economic theory, this purpose can be described as the maximization of profits based on the utilization of the investor's intangible assets. Such intangible assets may include, for example, the firm's management skills, technologies and technological expertise accumulated through past R&D activities, marketing know-how, an established network of suppliers and/or customers, and a host of other assets that underpin a firm's

---

[4] IMF (1993: 86).

wealth-creating capacity. However, for the parent to bring these assets to bear and maximize their return, it is usually necessary for the foreign affiliate to adapt the organization of its various assets (physical assets, land, labor, supplier networks, etc.) to the requirements of the parent. Such parent-firm-specific adaptations constitute a sunk cost that the parent firm would be unable to recover if it were to sell the affiliate, which explains why direct investments tend to be long-lasting.

The second element of the definition above that deserves elaboration is of a more technical nature and concerns the financial flows associated with FDI. As stated, FDI flows include "not only the initial transaction" between the parent and the foreign affiliate "but also all subsequent transactions." Three components can be distinguished: the first is equity capital (i.e., the foreign direct investor's purchase of shares of an enterprise); the second is reinvested earnings; and the third is intracompany loans or debt transactions (i.e., the borrowing and lending of funds between the direct investor and the affiliate).[5] Note that net inward FDI flows could well be negative – i.e., foreigners are disinvesting in the economy – if at least one of the three components is negative and is not offset by positive amounts of the other components.

In Japan's case, FDI transactions fall under the control of the Foreign Exchange and Foreign Trade Law ("Foreign Exchange Law"), which has been revised several times since its introduction in 1949. The Foreign Exchange Law defines FDI as follows: (1) the acquisition of unlisted stocks or equities; (2) the acquisition of 10 percent or more of listed stocks by a single investor; (3) the transfer of stocks; (4) consent to the alteration of business objectives of a company, one-third or more stocks of which are owned by the consenting party; (5) the establishment of branches, plants, and other business offices; (6) loans of a maturity of more than one year and in excess of ¥200 million or loans of a maturity of more than five years in excess of ¥100 million; (7) the acquisition of corporate bonds; and (8) the acquisition of capital certificates.[6,7]

Turning from definitions to data sources, the analysis of FDI in Japan is complicated by the fact that there is no single dataset that is consistent

---

[5] UNCTAD (2003: 231–2).

[6] Loans of a maturity of more than one year and in excess of ¥200 million or loans of a maturity of more than five years in excess of ¥100 million, the acquisition of corporate bonds, and the acquisition of capital certificates (items 6 to 8) are classified as FDI only if they are conducted by nonbank firms.

[7] *Sources:* METI (N.D.), online: <http://www.meti.go.jp/english/report/data/cFDI101e. html>; UNCTAD (N.D.), *UNCTAD WID Country Profile: Japan* online: <http://www. unctad.org/sections/dite_fdistat/docs/wid_cp_jp_en.pdf> (both accessed January 8, 2007).

over time and provides the kind of information one would wish for. Rather, there are five principal sources for data on FDI in Japan, each with its own particular shortcomings. The first of these is the balance of payments (BOP) statistics as they were published until the end of 2004. The BOP statistics provide the most internationally comparable data on FDI and cover all actual transactions in excess of ¥5 million, including both new investments and additional working capital. These "old" BOP statistics, however, suffer from two serious drawbacks: first, they were published on a net basis, that is, no separate data for investment inflows and withdrawals (investment outflows) were provided; and second, FDI data were published only on an aggregated basis, that is, they provide no breakdown of FDI by industry.

An alternative set of statistics, published by the Ministry of Finance, also until the end of 2004, provides exactly such a breakdown. In contrast with the BOP data, however, the MOF statistics are based on investment notifications under the Foreign Exchange Law, leading to two serious problems. The first is that the statistics only recorded investment inflows, but not withdrawals. Thus, if, for example, a Japanese firm was bought by a foreign investor in one year and then sold to another foreign investor in the next year, and the seller transferred the proceeds abroad, the MOF statistics only counted the inflow. In such cases, the MOF statistics would therefore suggest that foreign direct investment had increased further in the second year, while in fact it had remained unchanged and the only thing that had happened was that the ownership of the Japanese affiliate had changed hands. Thus, the fact that disinvestments are not included in the MOF statistics means that they potentially *over*state inward FDI flows. The second flaw is that the MOF data do not include reinvested earnings, because these do not involve any foreign exchange transactions and therefore do not fall under the Foreign Exchange Law. This omission potentially results in an *under*statement of inward FDI flows. Consequently, whether the MOF statistics over- or understate actual inward FDI depends on the magnitude of the two omissions and may well differ from one year to the next (see below). Finally, a shortcoming that both the BOP statistics and the MOF statistics have in common is that they do not collect data from smaller firms – a source of understatement of inward FDI, however, that is likely to be relatively unimportant.

To address the various shortcomings of these two datasets, the items released in the BOP statistics were recently expanded, while publication of FDI data on a notification basis was discontinued. BOP statistics now offer a breakdown of direct investment in Japan into inflows and outflows, making it possible to identify fresh inflows and withdrawals, and provide a breakdown of FDI flows by industry. The expansion of FDI-related items now covered in the BOP statistics represent a vast improvement and will therefore greatly help to facilitate the analysis of FDI flows in the future. Unfortunately, though, they also complicate the data situation even further: because FDI data on a notification basis are no longer published, but data on a BOP basis by industry have been collected only since 2005, no consistent data on the industry distribution of inward FDI are available.

A fourth dataset on FDI in Japan is published by the Ministry of Economy, Trade and Industry (METI) in its *Gaishikei Kigyo Doko Chosa* [Survey of Trends in Business Activities of Foreign Affiliates], which provides information on foreign firms operating in Japan. However, this publication also suffers from many serious shortcomings. First, the survey is not compulsory and, as a result, the response ratio is no higher than 50 percent and varies considerably from year to year and across industries.[8] Second, the survey covers only firms with 33 percent or more foreign ownership – a percentage far higher than the 10 percent in the definition provided by the Foreign Exchange Law and also used in other major countries. Third, the survey does not cover subsidiaries in real estate, finance, and insurance. Fourth, investments in branches and offices are also not covered. As a result of these problems, the data are an even less reliable measure of the extent of FDI in Japan than those provided by the Bank of Japan and MOF, though this does not mean that they have not been used for that purpose.[9]

The fifth major dataset is the *Gaishikei Kigyo Soran* [Directory of Foreign-owned Companies in Japan] by the private research and publishing firm Toyo Keizai Shinposha. Similar to the METI publication, the *Gaishikei Kigyo Soran* is based on a survey of foreign-owned firms in Japan. However, the survey is supplemented with information on nonresponding firms from additional sources such as financial reports and includes the finance and insurance sector. Nevertheless, although the coverage is much more comprehensive than in the METI statistics, it is not complete because the survey is not mandatory and information is often missing. What is more, there are certain inconsistencies with regard to the inclusion of branches (as opposed to subsidiaries) in some sectors, but not in others.[10]

The various shortcomings of the different statistical sources mean that it is difficult to obtain reliable data on the extent of foreign direct investment in Japan, in a given year and cumulatively, and to measure the role that foreigners play in the Japanese economy. Just how difficult it is to say anything

---

[8] See Weinstein (1997).

[9] See the discussion on this set of data in Feenstra (1998) and Weinstein (1997).

[10] For a more detailed discussion of the shortcomings of METI's *Gaishikei Kigyo Doko Chosa* and Toyo Keizai Shinposha's *Gaishikei Kigyo Soran*, see, e.g., Fukao and Ito (2003).

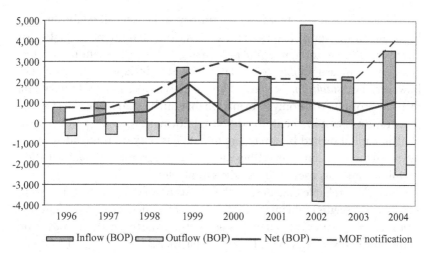

Figure 1.1. Comparison of BOP and MOF notification data on inward FDI (¥ billion)
Source: Ministry of Finance, online: <http://www.mof.go.jp/bpoffice/bpdata/fdi/ efdi2bop.htm> and <http://www.mof.go.jp/english/fdi/reference05.xls> (accessed February 17, 2007).

with certainty about FDI in Japan is shown by a comparison of the MOF statistics on a notification basis and the "new" FDI statistics of the BOP for the period in which their coverage overlaps (1996–2004). In Figure 1.1, the broken line shows the inward FDI reported in the MOF statistics on a notification basis, while the solid line shows *net* inward FDI on a BOP basis. Until the FDI data in the BOP started to also report investments and disinvestments (inward FDI inflows and outflows) separately in 2005, these two were actually the only data series available. As can be readily seen, both the trend indicated by the two lines and the magnitude of inward FDI differ considerably. Following the introduction of the extended FDI coverage in the BOP, a breakdown of inward FDI inflows and outflows going back to 1996 is available, showing that, generally speaking, the MOF data and the BOP data on gross inflows (the columns labeled "Inflow (BOP)"), follow a similar trend, although the magnitudes differ substantially in some years. Finally, the MOF figures are not consistently smaller or larger than the inward FDI inflow on a BOP basis, suggesting that the MOF data overstate inward FDI in some years and understate it in others.

One way in which this study attempts to address the data problems is to provide an alternative estimate in Chapter 2 that gauges the extent of foreign involvement by using data from the Management and Coordination Agency's *Establishment and Enterprise Census*. This census has the considerable advantage that it is compulsory and covers all establishments in Japan. Moreover, it allows the use of various definitions of FDI – for example, different foreign capital participation ratios – to examine how this changes the measured degree of FDI penetration in Japan. Unfortunately, however, the *Establishment and Enterprise Census* does not contain data on sales (or profits), so the only information that can be used to measure foreign penetration is employment. In addition, information on the percentage of paid-in capital owned by foreigners to date has only been included in the 1996 and the 2001 censuses, so these are the only years for which information useful for our purposes in this study is available.

The lack of reliable data despite the profusion of data sources, at least to some extent, seems emblematic of the low significance the Japanese government accorded to inward FDI in the past. By the same token, the introduction of the new FDI statistics in the balance of payments indicate that the importance of FDI for the Japanese economy is increasingly being recognized. For the present study, the data problems mean that the available statistics are often less than ideal and it is necessary to piece together information from a variety of sources. Chapter 2 begins this task to provide an overview of the extent and history of FDI in Japan.

TWO

The Extent and History of Foreign Direct
Investment in Japan

The past few decades have seen rapid advances toward a truly global economy, driven, to a large extent, by the growing role of multinational corporations (MNCs) and their activities around the world. Japanese companies
have vigorously participated in this trend, both through exports and foreign
direct investment. However, when it comes to Japan as a marketplace for
foreign companies, the country has lagged far behind. Generating roughly
10 percent of global GDP, Japan accounts for less than 5 percent of worldwide merchandise imports and, even after the boom in recent years, for just
2 percent of the global inward FDI stock.[1] In most other developed countries, foreign firms have come to play an important part in overall economic
activity, making sizeable contributions to capital formation and employment. This is not the case in Japan: as new calculations in this chapter show,
using employment as an indicator, foreign firms' role in the Japanese economy may be substantially larger than the most frequently cited published
statistics suggest. Nevertheless, compared with countries such as the United
States, Germany, or the United Kingdom, Japan's inward FDI penetration
remains conspicuously low.

One important reason, of course, is geography. An island nation situ-
ated on the edge of a continent of which it is by far the most economically
advanced, Japan has enjoyed none of the natural advantages that have facilitated cross-border trade and investment in other parts of the world such
as Europe, where countries share land borders as well as cultural and linguistic roots. But geography provides only part of the answer. Of similar, if
not greater importance, is Japan's economic and political history over the
past few centuries which has shaped attitudes and policies toward foreign

---

[1] Percentage shares are authors' calculation based on data for 2005 from World Bank, WTO,
and UNCTAD websites.

17

business in the country: with the exception of a few brief interludes, foreign business involvement in the Japanese economy has predominantly been seen as a threat to national aspirations.

Yet, this is not to say that foreign firms have not played their part in Japan's economic development. Quite the contrary; during the brief period at the beginning of the twentieth century when Japan was relatively welcoming to foreign investment, ventures by companies such as Ford, General Motors, Western Electric, General Electric, and Siemens helped to lay the foundations of the Japanese automobile and electronics industries – the country's two most successful export sectors of the postwar period. However, this era provides the exception that proves the rule, and although there are some examples of foreign firms that operated – sometimes quite successfully – in Japan during the 1950s to 1980s, their impact was much more limited as a result of government policies.

The situation of FDI in Japan today can be understood only in a broader, historical context, which the following sections aim to provide. The discussion begins with a brief overview of worldwide trends in FDI and the substantial contribution Japanese firms have made to these trends from a relatively early period onward. This is followed by an examination of the extent of FDI in Japan in international comparison. The discussion then moves on to explaining the low level of FDI in Japan, focusing, in particular, on the history of government policies toward inward foreign investment. Finally, the role of foreign investment that did find its way into Japan up to the 1990s is considered.

Global FDI Trends and Japan's Outward Investment

Although the extent of global economic integration we see today is a new phenomenon, cross-border business activities are not. Trading between different lands can be traced back to the dawn of recorded human history more than 4,000 years ago, and by the first millennium CE, vast networks of commercial exchange spanning Asia, Africa, and Europe had sprung up. International business activities experienced a significant boost when advances in transportation and transborder communications during the sixteenth and seventeenth centuries ushered in the age of merchant capitalism, giving rise to the establishment of such well-known trading firms as the British and Dutch East India Companies. But it was only with the advance of industrial capitalism in the nineteenth century that cross-border activities significantly extended beyond trading and banking to include foreign investments in plantations, mines, factories, and distribution facilities. By the onset of the World War I in 1914, at least US$14.5 billion, according to one estimate, had been invested around the world by nonresident individuals or firms and first-generation migrants.[2] By far the most important home countries of FDI were Britain, the birthplace of the industrial revolution, and the United States, followed by France and Germany. However, even at this early stage, Japanese firms already were playing a not insignificant role, accounting for about 2 percent of global cumulative FDI in 1914.[3] Japanese firms had come to control much of the coastal industries and trade of Eastern China, and trading houses such as Mitsui had set up branch offices as far afield as Shanghai, Paris, New York, and London.

The upheavals following World War I and the collapse of international capital markets in the late 1920s and early 1930s curtailed cross-border investment activities, especially in Europe. Nevertheless, cumulated FDI almost doubled during the interwar period to US$26.4 billion, largely because U.S. firms had escaped relatively unscathed from the war and continued their rapid overseas expansion. Japanese firms more than doubled their overseas investment during this period: cotton spinners and weavers set up production bases in China, so that in Shanghai, for example, they soon surpassed the British in the number of mills erected.[4]

Following the rupture of World War II, international trade and investment expanded once more. However, as a result of the devastation of the war in Europe and Japan, FDI during the 1950s and 1960s was heavily dominated by U.S. firms. Only during the 1970s, after successful reconstruction in Europe and Japan, did firms from these countries once again join the fray in earnest. Finally, rapid economic development in South Korea, Taiwan, and Singapore, among others, has led companies from these countries to become increasingly international in their operations over the past decade or two.

The 1990s, moreover, were a period in which a host of national, regional, and worldwide initiatives – such as the launch of the Common Market in Europe, the North American Free Trade Agreement (NAFTA), the completion of the General Agreement on Tariffs and Trade (GATT) Uruguay Round, the foundation of the World Trade Organization (WTO), and the gradual opening of the Chinese economy – intensified the trend toward global economic integration. In the wake of these developments, worldwide FDI flows accelerated and reached a peak of US$1.4 trillion in 2000.[5]

---

[2] Dunning (1993: 116).
[3] Dunning (1993: 117).
[4] For details on Japanese investment in China during this period, see, e.g., Howe (1996: 410–25).
[5] Global inward FDI flows. Source: UNCTAD, *Key Data from WIR Tables*, Table 21; online: <http://www.unctad.org/Templates/Page.asp?intItemID=3277&lang=1> (accessed January 15, 2007).

A few more figures illustrate the important role that firms' international activities have come to play in the world economy: measured in relation to global capital formation, FDI inflows jumped from 2.2 percent in 1980 to a peak of 20.0 percent in 2000 before dropping again and stood at 9.4 percent in 2005.[6] As a result of this increase, the total worldwide inward FDI stock climbed from 5.3 percent of GDP in 1980 to 22.7 percent in 2005.[7] At the same time, the sales of MNCs' foreign affiliates in relation to global GDP more than doubled from 23.1 percent in 1980 to 49.6 percent in 2005.[8] Moreover, at US$22.2 trillion in 2005, the sales of foreign affiliates worldwide were almost twice the amount of global merchandise and service exports.[9]

It should be noted, however, that to some extent the term "globalization" is a misnomer when it comes to FDI because of the extremely uneven distribution of such flows. Developed countries accounted for almost 90 percent of investment outflows during the past ten years (1996–2005) and roughly 70 percent of inflows, whereas developing countries received only 28 percent (the remaining 2 percent are unaccounted for).[10] But even among developing countries, FDI inflows are highly concentrated in a small number of countries, with China (including Hong Kong) receiving the lion's share (9.6 percent of global inflows during 1996–2005), and a string of other East and Southeast Asian countries together accounting for a further 4.0 percent.[11] Outside Asia, the only developing countries that account for sizeable shares of global FDI inflows are Brazil (2.6 percent) and Mexico (2.1 percent). In contrast, most countries of Sub-Saharan Africa, Central and South America, the Middle East, South Asia, and the Pacific have received only negligible amounts of FDI.

Turning to Japan's outward FDI, a few figures illustrate that the country's firms have actively participated in and contributed to the substantial increase in cross-border business activities. At the end of 2005, Japan's cumulative

---

[6] UNCTAD, *Key Data from WIR Tables*, Table 20; online: <http://www.unctad.org/Templates/Page.asp?intItemID=3277&lang=1> (accessed January 15, 2007).

[7] UNCTAD, *Key Data from WIR Tables*, Table 18; online: <http://www.unctad.org/Templates/Page.asp?intItemID=3277&lang=1> (accessed January 15, 2007).

[8] Based on figures from UNCTAD (2004), Table I.3, and UNCTAD (2006), Table I.2.

[9] Based on figures from UNCTAD (2006), Table I.2.

[10] Based on UNCTAD, *Key Data from WIR Tables*, Tables 12 and 21; online: <http://www.unctad.org/Templates/Page.asp?intItemID=3277&lang=1> (accessed January 15, 2007).

[11] The figure for East and Southeast Asian countries includes South Korea, Taiwan, Singapore, Malaysia, Thailand, and Indonesia. Figures calculated from UNCTAD, *Key Data from WIR Tables*, Table 21; online: <http://www.unctad.org/Templates/Page.asp?intItemID=3277&lang=1> (accessed January 15, 2007).

FDI stock stood at US$386.6 billion, which is 3.6 percent of the world total.[12] These figures put Japan in ninth place, behind the United States, the United Kingdom, Germany, France, the Netherlands, Hong Kong, Canada, and Switzerland. Japan's low rank may be surprising considering that it has the second largest economy in the world. However, compared with the nations of the West, Japan is an economic latecomer, and the country's firms were still busy catching up during the 1960s and 1970s. They therefore possessed little technological or managerial know-how that they could have profitably employed overseas. What is more, even if they had wanted to invest abroad, they would have found it difficult to do so. Reflecting official concern about the country's shortage of foreign exchange, the government restricted outward direct investment until 1968 and liberalization was not complete until 1972.

Even after liberalization, FDI outflows did not amount to much more than a trickle: benefiting from a favorable exchange rate, Japanese companies preferred to serve overseas markets through exports rather than FDI. It was therefore only when growing trade friction with the major trading partners of the West and rapid appreciation of the yen during the second half of the 1980s rendered this strategy increasingly difficult that Japanese firms began to invest abroad in earnest. The "bubble economy" added further fuel, allowing Japanese companies to go on a shopping spree overseas and buy up real estate, banks, and other companies, especially in the United States. As a result, annual Japanese FDI outflows soared by a factor of twenty from US$2.4 billion in 1980 to a peak of US$48.0 billion in 1990.[13]

However, reflecting the burst of the "bubble economy" in the early 1990s and the ensuing recession, Japanese FDI outflows contracted again and only in 2006 again reached levels seen more than a decade-and-a-half earlier. Nevertheless, a considerable number of the largest and best-known MNCs in the world today are Japanese. While the notification data by the Ministry of Finance suggest that the service sector accounts for about two-thirds of all outward FDI, Japan's most conspicuous multinationals in fact hail from the manufacturing sector,[14] and it is Japan's most successful industries –

---

[12] UNCTAD, *Key Data from WIR Tables*, Table 9; online: <http://www.unctad.org/Templates/Page.asp?intItemID=3277&lang=1> (accessed January 15, 2007).

[13] UNCTAD, *Key Data from WIR Tables*, Table 12; online: <http://www.unctad.org/Templates/Page.asp?intItemID=3277&lang=1> (accessed January 15, 2007).

[14] This is, in fact, less contradictory than it might at first seem. Approximately one-fifth of Japan's cumulative outward FDI for the period 1989–2004 is accounted for by the financial sector alone. However, while the financial assets and hence the recorded FDI flows involved in this sector tend to be large, its economic weight in terms of employment or value-added

especially the automobile and electronics industries – that have been most aggressive in investing abroad. As a result, these industries are rapidly becoming as internationally oriented as their counterparts from Europe or the United States. Although the overseas production ratio of the Japanese manufacturing sector as a whole still lags considerably behind that of United States or Germany, the ratios for the electrical machinery and automobile industries at 21.3 percent and 36.0 percent are rapidly catching up.[15]

Much of the outward FDI in the auto and electronics industry consists of the relocation of production to low-cost countries in the rest of Asia. And although such relocation of activities, especially of low-value-added assembly processes, plays an important role in the restructuring of the economy by freeing up domestic resources, which can then be employed in higher-value-added activities, this trend has also led to concerns about the "hollowing-out" of the country's industrial base. This is because it is especially the most

is considerably smaller. What is more, the industry breakdown of FDI flows provided by the Ministry of Finance is on a gross basis, that is, disinvestments – potentially of a similar size – are not taken into account. Most scholars therefore believe that net outflows in the service industry in fact are smaller than those in the manufacturing sector. It should also be noted that much Japanese outward FDI in the service sector during the "bubble period" was real estate related and subsequently encountered huge capital losses, providing another reason why the economic weight of Japanese service-sector FDI is much smaller than manufacturing-sector FDI, even though Ministry of Finance (MOF) figures suggest otherwise. In fact, looking at the industry breakdown of the new FDI data on a balance of payments (BOP) basis, which so far are available only for 2005 and 2006, suggests that in those years the service sector accounted for only 42.8 percent and 31.3 percent of outward FDI, respectively (Bank of Japan, "Industrial/regional breakdowns of direct investment," online: <http://www.boj.or.jp/en/type/stat/boj_stat/bop/diri/index.htm>; accessed May 9, 2007).

[15] In 1997, the last year for which METI provides an international comparison, the overseas production ratio in the Japanese manufacturing sector overall stood at only 12.4 percent, compared with 27.7 percent for the United States and 32.1 percent for Germany. The figures for the electrical machinery industry were: Japan, 20.8 percent; United States, 25.7 percent; Germany, 32.6 percent; while in the transportation machinery industry the rates were: Japan, 30.8 percent; Unites States, 47.3 percent; Germany, 53.9 percent (Source: METI, 2001, *Kaigai Jigyo Katsudo Kihon Chosa Kekka Gaiyo, Dai-29-kai* [Summary of the 29th Basic Survey of Overseas Activities], Table 2-(2)-2–3, online: <http://www.meti.go.jp/statistics/data/h2c410bj.html>). The figures in the text, which are for 2002, mean that in these two sectors, Japan has more or less reached the same levels as the other two countries five years earlier. In contrast, the overseas production ratio for the Japanese manufacturers as a whole, at 17.1 percent in 2002, still remained far below that of the United States and Germany (Source: METI, 2005, *Kaigai Jigyo Katsudo Kihon Chosa Kaigai Jigyo Katsudo Kihon Chosa Kekka Gaiyo, Dai-33-kai* [Summary of the 33rd Basic Survey of Overseas Activities], Figure 5–1, online: <http://www.meti.go.jp/statistics/downloadfiles/h2c402fj.pdf>.) More recent figures are available but not comparable with the 1997 data because of a revision of industry classifications.

productive firms that are taking advantage of the opportunities offered overseas, while the less productive firms are staying at home.

Foreign direct investment – by Japanese firms and companies worldwide –
plays an important part in the deepening of the international division of
labor. However, not all countries have participated in this trend to the
same extent or in the same way. For example, fewer than a dozen countries account for most of the FDI originating from and going to developing
economies. Even among the developed countries, considerable differences
persist, largely as a result of their (economic) history and geographic location. Thus, countries like Britain and the Netherlands occupy shares in global
outward and inward FDI stocks that far outweigh the size of their economies:
both countries were among the earliest nations to industrialize, have been
international in their outlook due to their history as colonial powers, and
are at the heart of an increasingly integrated Europe. In contrast, Japan is
not only a latecomer to industrialization, but also has been inward-looking
for much of its history and finds itself at the periphery of a continent that to
this day is ruled by political and economic regimes of all imaginable shades.
Nevertheless, the level of Japan's outward FDI has been rapidly catching up
with that of other industrialized nations. *Inward* FDI, however, continues
to lag considerably behind.

The Extent and Nature of FDI in Japan

Assertions that inward foreign investment in Japan is extremely low have
become almost axiomatic. No matter which measure of international comparison is chosen, the limited extent of inward FDI, and hence foreign companies' role, in the Japanese economy stands out. A figure often cited in the
late 1980s and early 1990s was that foreign direct investment accounted for
less than 1 percent of the value of assets or of the share of sales or employment
in Japan.[16] However, though based on data published by Japan's Ministry of
International Trade and Industry (MITI; now Ministry of Economy, Trade
and Industry, METI), this figure has been shown to substantially understate
the actual level of inward FDI.[17] The conflicting evidence highlights the difficulties in obtaining reliable data on the extent of FDI in Japan highlighted
in Chapter 1. However, what indicators are available show that the situation is no longer as black-and-white as it used to be: a number of statistics
certainly do show that foreign investment in Japan is much smaller than

[16] See Feenstra (1998).
[17] See, e.g., Weinstein (1997).

(a) Outward FDI stock/GDP (percent)

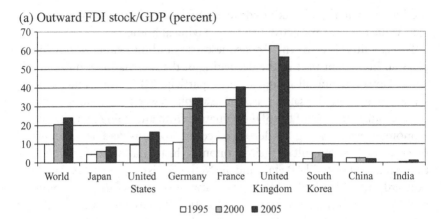

□1995 ▨2000 ■2005

(b) Inward FDI stock/GDP (percent)

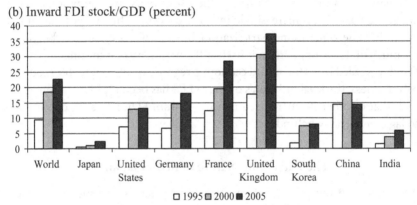

□ 1995 ▨ 2000 ■ 2005

Figure 2.1. Japan's inward and outward FDI position in international comparison
(a) Outward FDI stock/GDP (percent)
Source: UNCTAD, *Key Data from WIR Annex Tables,* Table 9, online: <http://www.
unctad.org/Templates/Page.asp?intItemID=3277&lang=1> (accessed January 10, 2007).

(b) Inward FDI stock/GDP (percent)
Source: UNCTAD, *Key Data from WIR Annex Tables,* Table 19, online: <http://www.
unctad.org/Templates/Page.asp?intItemID=3277&lang=1> (accessed January 10, 2007).

(c) Inward FDI flows/gross fixed capital formation (Average 2000–2005, percent)
Source: Authors' calculations based on UNCTAD, *Key Data from WIR Annex
Tables,* Table 18, online: <http://www.unctad.org/Templates/Page.asp?intItemID=
3277&lang=1> (accessed January 10, 2007).

(d) Share of foreign affiliates in manufacturing and service turnover (2002, percent)
Source: OECD (2005), *Measuring Globalisation: OECD Globalisation Indicators,*
Figures C.1.1 and D.1.1.
* Manufacturing data are for 2001.
** Manufacturing data are for 1999.

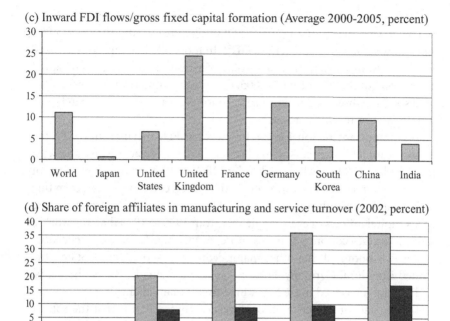

(c) Inward FDI flows/gross fixed capital formation (Average 2000-2005, percent)

(d) Share of foreign affiliates in manufacturing and service turnover (2002, percent)

□ Manufacturing ■ Services

Figure 2.1 (*continued*)

in other comparable countries, but other figures suggest that the gap has substantially narrowed.

There is no shortage of statistics showing that inward FDI in Japan remains conspicuously low (see Figure 2.1). For example, most of the advanced countries are both major foreign investors and major recipients of foreign investment; their ratios of outward to inward FDI stocks consequently typically lie somewhere between one and two. In Japan's case, however, there is a large imbalance and even today the outward FDI stock outstrips the inward FDI stock by almost a factor of four.[18] What is more, measured in relation to GDP, Japan's inward FDI stock in 2005 stood at only 2.2 percent, compared with between 18.0 and 37.1 percent for the three largest European economies – Germany, France, and the United Kingdom – and

[18] 2005. Based on UNCTAD, *Key Data from WIR Tables*, Tables 9 and 19; online: <http://www.unctad.org/Templates/Page.asp?intItemID=3277&lang=1> (accessed January 15, 2007).

13.0 percent for the United States. In fact, even in South Korea, which has not been particularly welcoming to FDI until quite recently, the inward FDI stock now stands at 8.0 percent of GDP. In most other advanced countries, FDI inflows, moreover, make a sizeable contribution to gross fixed capital formation: for the period 2000–2005, the average annual share in the United States and the three largest European economies was 7–25 percent; in Japan, it did not even reach 1 percent.[19]

One important reason for the low level of FDI in Japan has been the almost complete absence of cross-border mergers and acquisitions, at least until the late 1990s. Such cross-border M&As have been the main mode of FDI entry in recent years, especially in developed countries.[20] Yet, even tiny Switzerland, with only one-eighteenth of Japan's population, attracted more M&A capital inflows in every single year from 1990 to 1998 than the world's second-largest economy. What is more, even when Japan experienced its recent FDI boom, all the other major economies – the United States, the United Kingdom, Germany, France – as well as Canada, the Netherlands, and Australia received more M&A investment than Japan.

The logical consequence of low levels of inward FDI is that the role of foreign companies in the Japanese economy remains limited. Figures by the OECD, for example, suggest that, in 2002, the share of manufacturing turnover generated by majority-owned foreign affiliates in Japan was less than 3 percent, while in the other OECD countries it ranged from 12 percent (Denmark) to almost 80 percent (Ireland). Similarly, in the service sector, the share of turnover generated by foreign-owned affiliates was less than 1 percent in Japan, compared with between 8 percent (United States) and 40 percent (Ireland) in other OECD countries.[21]

Figures for the employment share accounted for by foreign affiliates in the host economy confirm these patterns. OECD figures for the late 1990s (more recent data on employment for Japan are not available) indicate that majority-owned foreign affiliates accounted for only 0.8 percent of manufacturing employment in Japan, compared with 17 percent in Britain and 27 percent in France.[22] Figures by the United Nations Conference on Trade and Development (UNCTAD) also suggest that in 1998, the employment share

---

[19] All figures are obtained from or based on data from UNCTAD, *Key Data from WIR Tables,* online: <http://www.unctad.org/Templates/Page.asp?intItemID=3277&lang=1> (accessed January 15, 2007).

[20] See, e.g., UNCTAD (2003: 15).

[21] OECD (2005a), Figures C.1.1 and D.1.1.

[22] Source: OECD (2001: 108, 200, 349). Figures are for 1996 for Japan, 1997 for the United Kingdom, and 1998 for France.

accounted for by foreign affiliates in the manufacturing sector in Japan was much smaller than for other countries, but at 1.8 percent (compared with about 15–22 percent in the United States, Germany, the United Kingdom, and France) it was more than twice as high as in the OECD study.[23]

However, this divergence between the OECD and the UNCTAD figures highlights the importance of data issues in gauging the extent of FDI in Japan: the data on Japan in both cases are based on METI's annual survey on *Trends in Business Activities of Foreign Affiliates in Japan* which, as described in Chapter 1, suffers from severe reliability issues, and the discrepancy between the OECD and UNCTAD figures probably is simply due to differing definitions of foreign firms.[24] A more reliable dataset is provided by the *Establishment and Enterprise Census* (published by the Statistics Bureau, Ministry of Internal Affairs and Communications), which is compulsory, covers all firms in Japan, and includes information on foreign ownership. This dataset also has the advantage that it allows the calculation of employment shares using different definitions of foreign ownership. Doing so yields results suggesting that FDI penetration in Japan may not be quite as low as the preceding comparisons suggest (see Table 2.1). Using the 33.4 percent foreign ownership ratio (which corresponds to the definition of *Trends in Business Activities of Foreign Affiliates in Japan* and allows for multiple foreign owners, so that this definition may include cases of portfolio investment), the employment share by foreign affiliates certainly is very low: despite the increase in the late 1990s, it remains below 2 percent for the manufacturing sector and is barely above 1 percent for the economy as a whole.

However, the results change quite dramatically when the definition is changed somewhat, and we concentrate on those firms with only *one* foreign owner holding a stake of 20 percent or more. This is the definition allowed by the data that comes closest to the one used by the United States,[25] though it should be noted that it is, in fact, somewhat stricter than the U.S. definition, which uses only a 10 percent foreign-ownership ratio (one single owner). Based on this definition, the employment share by foreign affiliates in Japan overall is still quite low at 2.75 percent (2001), but this share is now almost half the level found in the United States in 1997. What is more, the value for the manufacturing sector now reaches 5.91 percent, considerably higher

---

[23] UNCTAD (2002), Table I.6.

[24] The OECD data only include firms that are majority foreign-owned, while the UNCTAD data are based on a much lower cut-off ratio (in general, 10 percent).

[25] Bureau of Economic Affairs, *Foreign Direct Investment in the United States: Establishment Data for 1997*, online: <http://www.bea.gov/bea/ai/iidguide.htm#FDIUS> (accessed January 15, 2007).

Table 2.1. *Employment in foreign affiliates as a share of total employment*
(in percent)

Code	Industry	JAFF (33.4%) 1996	JAFF (33.4%) 2001	JAFF (20%, single owner) 2001	USAFF (10%, single owner) 1997
	All sectors total	n.a.	**1.15**	**2.75**	**5.61**
	Manufacturing total	**1.36**	**1.94**	**5.91**	**10.78**
03	Food products	0.29	0.34	1.32	8.38
04	Textiles and apparel	0.15	0.17	0.93	5.83
05	Wood and paper products	0.06	0.16	0.83	4.95
06	Publishing and printing	0.13	0.22	0.38	7.83
07	Chemical products	3.61	3.27	13.50	21.80
08	Drugs and medicine	7.21	15.49	15.27	31.90
09	Petroleum and coal products	7.24	2.91	2.31	22.20
10	Plastic products	0.41	0.45	3.22	10.03
11	Rubber products	1.08	1.15	2.81	40.18
12	Ceramic, stone and clay	0.28	0.35	1.55	21.45
13	Iron and steel	0.01	0.13	0.27	19.35
14	Nonferrous metals	1.61	0.44	7.72	15.73
15	Metal products	0.31	0.20	0.72	7.52
16	General machinery	1.68	1.78	6.82	12.75
17	Electrical machinery	2.46	2.48	12.51	13.78
18	Motor vehicles and parts	4.72	10.79	18.32	15.60
19	Miscellaneous transport equipment	0.7	0.62	12.71	4.23
20	Precision instruments	0.41	0.90	5.04	11.16
21	Miscellaneous manufacturing	0.47	0.72	1.71	6.62
	Services total	**0.65**	**0.97**	**2.04**	**4.31**
22	Construction and civil engineering	0.05	0.05	0.30	1.72
23	Electricity, gas, steam, and water supply, etc.	0.00	0.00	0.04	1.96
24	Wholesale trade	2.31	2.57	4.24	7.89
25	Retail trade	0.29	0.49	0.77	4.50
26	Financial intermediary services	1.47	1.75	10.00	6.10
27	Insurance	1.67	6.69	12.57	6.40
28	Real estate	0.02	0.08	0.28	1.64
29	Transportation and postal service	0.50	0.27	3.52	4.82
30	Telecommunications and broadcasting	0.22	2.31	6.55	7.66

Code	Industry	JAFF (33.4%) 1996	JAFF (33.4%) 2001	JAFF (20%, single owner) 2001	USAFF (10%, single owner) 1997
31	Education and research institutes	0.34	0.97	1.76	6.39
32	Medical services, health and hygiene	0.02	0.04	0.16	1.99
33	Computer programming and information services	1.83	2.55	4.33	3.88
34	Goods and equipment rental and leasing	0.88	1.20	0.49	3.66
35	Other business services	0.52	1.71	2.10	4.77
36	Eating and drinking places	1.58	2.36	3.89	2.48
37	Other personal services	0.12	0.39	0.38	4.23
38	Other services	0.01	0.00	0.00	n.a.

Notes: JAFF (33.4%): Japanese Affiliates of Foreign Firms (33.4% or more foreign-owned, one or more foreign companies); JAFF (20%): Japanese Affiliates of Foreign Firms (20% or more foreign-owned by a single foreign company); USAFF: U.S. Affiliates of Foreign Firms (10% or more foreign-owned by a single foreign company).

Sources: Compiled from micro-data of METI's *Establishment and Enterprise Census* for 1996 and 2001 and Bureau of Economic Analysis, *Foreign Direct Investment in the United States: Establishment Data for 1997*, online: <http://www.bea.gov/bea/ai/iidguide.htm#FDIUS> (accessed February 16, 2007).

than in the estimates provided by METI, the OECD, and UNCTAD, and more than half the level found in the United States (1997). In contrast, the share in the service sector remains quite low at 2.04 percent, though this, too, is almost half the level registered in the United States (see Table 2.1).

Data that allow a similar definition for the 1996 survey in order to compare the trend in these shares unfortunately are unavailable. Using the definition employed by METI (33.4 percent ownership or more by one or more foreign owners), however, shows that foreign companies have made significant inroads in the intervening five-year period: both in the manufacturing and in the service sector, the employment share of foreign affiliates increased by more than 40 percent.

Japan is less unusual when it comes to the composition of inward FDI. In line with patterns in other developed countries, the majority of cumulative FDI flows into Japan over the past decade and a half have gone into the service sector. Moreover, and again in line with trends elsewhere, FDI has shifted further away from manufacturing and toward services in recent

Table 2.2. *Share of FDI in Japan by industry, 1989–2004*
(in percent)

	1989–1997	1998–2004	1989–2004
Food	1.0	0.7	0.8
Textile	0.2	0.1	0.2
Rubber and leather	1.4	0.1	0.4
Chemical	14.1	5.4	7.2
Metal	3.0	0.2	0.8
Machinery	19.9	12.5	14.0
Petroleum	1.6	2.2	2.0
Glass and ceramics	0.1	0.1	0.1
Other manufacturing	2.1	0.7	1.0
Manufacturing total	43.3	22.0	26.4
Telecommunication	0.9	15.1	12.2
Construction	0.1	0.1	0.1
Trading	21.9	9.5	12.0
Finance and insurance	12.0	42.0	35.8
Business services	14.9	8.2	9.5
Transportation	0.5	1.3	1.2
Real Estate	5.0	1.7	2.3
Other	1.4	0.1	0.4
Nonmanufacturing total	56.7	78.0	73.6
TOTAL	100.0	100.0	100.0

Note: More recent comparable data are unavailable as publication of the Ministry of Finance notification-basis FDI data was discontinued.
Source: Authors' calculations based on Ministry of Finance, online: <http://www.mof.go.jp/english/e1c008.htm> (accessed January 15, 2007).

years. Although manufacturing accounted for 43 percent of cumulative FDI inflows during 1989–1997, this share dropped to only 22 percent during 1998–2004. Conversely, the share of nonmanufacturing sectors (i.e., services, given the lack of any significant investment in the primary sector) in total FDI inflows increased from 57 to 78 percent (see Table 2.2).

However, an analysis of the composition of FDI inflows also reveals that these are heavily concentrated in a small number of industries: only two – the chemical and the machinery industry – account for the largest share by far of all foreign investment in the manufacturing sector. The same goes for the service sector, where finance and insurance, trading, telecommunications, and other business services make up the lion's share. Most other sectors have attracted hardly any foreign direct investment at all.

For a more detailed picture of the sectoral pattern of the presence of foreign companies in Japan, it is useful to return to Table 2.1. This confirms that the employment accounted for by foreign affiliates is heavily concentrated in the chemical industry (chemical products, drugs and medicine) and the machinery industries (general machinery, electrical machinery, motor vehicles and parts, miscellaneous transport equipment, and precision instruments). However, rather than indicating that the other manufacturing sectors are necessarily closed to FDI, this pattern suggests that foreign companies invest in knowledge-intensive industries where Japan's high costs of doing business are less relevant than in resource and/or labor-intensive industries.[26] Nevertheless, compared with the United States, where the share of employment accounted for by foreign affiliates is at least 4 percent in every single industry, and well in excess of 10 percent in many, the concentration in Japan is conspicuous. At the same time, though, this heavy concentration also means that, following the recent wave of foreign investment in the car industry, foreign affiliates' employment share in the motor vehicles and parts industry as well as the miscellaneous transport equipment industry may now be higher than in the United States.

Government regulations – of FDI and of market entry more generally – play a larger role in explaining patterns in the service sector. Much of the recent increase in service sector FDI has been concentrated in four industries: telecommunications, insurance, banking, and business services. These are the industries at the center of recent liberalization measures, and along with the jump in FDI in these industries, employment by foreign affiliates has increased rapidly. In fact, the employment shares by foreign affiliates in the finance and insurance industries and in computer programming and information services in Japan (using the single owner definition) in 2001 exceeded the level observed in the United States in 1997.

Yet, there are also a number of industries that have remained "sanctuaries," where foreign companies are virtually absent. If "sanctuaries" are defined as industries in which foreign affiliates account for less than

---

[26] Yet, it should be noted that although foreign investment is concentrated in knowledge-intensive industries, this does not necessarily mean that it is based on the asset-seeking motive. While this motive is likely to be important in industries where Japan is highly competitive, such as motor vehicles and parts and electrical machinery, this is not the case with regard to pharmaceuticals (drugs and medicine). Instead, as Chapter 6 shows, FDI in the pharmaceutical industry until the late 1990s was largely of the market-seeking variety, reflecting regulations that required firms wishing to sell drugs in Japan to have manufacturing facilities in the country. Conversely, the low FDI penetration in labor- and resource-intensive industries such as textiles and apparel, wood and paper products, and iron and steel may indicate not that barriers to FDI are high but that barriers to trade are relatively low, so that foreign firms tend to supply the Japanese market from abroad.

0.5 percent of employment, no matter which foreign-ownership definition is chosen, there are quite a number of such sectors, including construction and civil engineering, utilities (electricity, gas, water, etc.), real estate, medical services, health and hygiene, and other personal services. These are industries that do not always readily lend themselves to FDI; yet, the equivalent share in the United States in each of these sectors nevertheless ranges between 1 and 2 percent. The reason for the absence of FDI in these industries in Japan in most cases is not the existence of outright bans or restrictions on foreign companies – though some do remain – but rather the presence of regulations that restrict market access more generally.

Overall, FDI and the role foreign companies play in the economy remain much smaller in Japan than in other industrialized countries. The gap may not be quite as large as the most frequently cited measures, many of which are based on highly unsatisfactory data, suggest. And at least in some sectors – the motor vehicle industry, finance, and insurance being prime examples – FDI penetration these days in fact seems to be on par with that in the United States. Nevertheless, and despite recent increases, FDI in Japan remains limited both in its overall economic weight and in its breadth in terms of the number of industries it has reached.

Why Is FDI in Japan So Low?

The low level of FDI in Japan has been the subject of intense debate among businessmen, policy makers, and academics. Western observers have frequently claimed that, along with its "unfair" trade practices, Japan has failed to create a "level playing field" that would allow foreign companies to invest in the country. Even when most formal trade and investment barriers were removed in the 1970s and 1980s, other structural impediments remained.[27] The official Japanese reply to such allegations during that period often was that, rather than any barriers to trade and investment, the true reason for low investment and import levels was the lack of sufficient effort and commitment by foreign companies in a demanding and out-of-the-way market.[28]

Because Japan's low FDI penetration is often seen as the result of a more general "closedness" of the economy, it is useful to digress for a moment and consider Japan's international trade. This is relevant to FDI because companies that enter a foreign market often do so by first exporting to that

---

[27] For a survey of the literature on Japan's trade barriers during this period, see, e.g., Lawrence (1993).

[28] For a popular account of such mutual allegations, see, e.g., Wilkinson (1990: 200–22).

country; only when they have established a foothold allowing them to gain experience in the local market do they typically consider setting up local operations in order to better meet local customers' needs.[29] The lack of such a foothold – providing market recognition, an established customer base, access to the distribution system, and so forth – significantly increases the risk and initial costs that any direct investment would involve. It therefore matters that Japan's import penetration rate, that is, purchases of goods and services as a percentage of total final expenditure, at 13.1 percent, are the lowest among the 30 OECD countries.[30] Considering, moreover, that approximately one-fifth of Japanese merchandise imports consist of mineral fuels and that the country imports most of its other raw materials, a more relevant indicator may be the ratio of manufactured imports to GDP. In 2000, this ratio stood at only 6.3 percent, and although this represents an increase over the 4.5 to 5.3 percent during 1980–1995, it seems likely that much of this rise was the result of re-imports of Japanese firms engaged in production abroad.[31] On the other hand, what is easily overlooked is that Japan's export propensity at 14.3 percent is also extremely low.[32] Yet, nobody would argue that the country has pursued policies that explicitly discriminate against its own exports.

Japan's low export and import ratios suggest that there may be factors other than explicit barriers to trade and investment that account for the country's limited "openness." Comparing Japan with, for example, the countries of the European Union, the latter clearly enjoy various trade- and investment-promoting advantages: geographical proximity, shared cultural roots, and, of course, policies aimed at economic integration such as the creation of the Common Market and a common currency, the Euro. In addition, the populations and economies of European countries are smaller, many of them in fact much smaller, than Japan's – another factor accounting for the greater reliance on international trade and investment.

One way to take these differences into account is to estimate a "gravity model" which seeks to analyze trade and investment flows adjusted for aspects such as economic size, geographic distance, and factor endowments. The evidence of studies in this vein suggests that these aspects do indeed explain a large part of Japan's low level of manufactured imports, and once

---

[29] This argument obviously only applies to firms selling tradable goods.
[30] At current prices and exchange rates. The figure is for 2005. Source: OECD Statistics (online database).
[31] Figures from Ito and Fukao (2004).
[32] At current prices. The figure is for 2005 and is the second-lowest among the OECD countries after the United States (10.5 percent). Source: OECD Statistics (online database).

these factors are controlled for, Japan's trade is no longer so different after all.[33] Thus, what mainly seems to determine the country's low import ratio is its geographic isolation and economic structure, that is, its large manufacturing sector relative to the economy overall, rather than any discriminatory policies or implicit barriers to trade.[34]

In contrast with the findings on trade, gravity models do produce some evidence suggesting that FDI is unusually low. One such study for the period 1985–1990, for example, comes to the conclusion that Japan is more closed to American FDI than Western European countries.[35] A more detailed gravity model estimate of the regional distribution of overseas sales of U.S. firms' foreign affiliates for the more recent years of 1994, 1999, and 2000, finds that such sales are indeed significantly lower for affiliates in Japan in the manufacturing sector. Yet, no significant difference is found in the case of the service sector, suggesting that in this sector Japan is not more closed than other countries.[36]

On balance, the evidence suggests that the low degree of Japan's international trade integration is not unusual, once the various factors that determine a country's trade patterns are taken into account. In other words, at least in the past two decades, on which the evidence presented here concentrates, Japanese imports do not appear to have been hampered by any obstacles that would set the country apart from other nations – despite the repeated friction Japanese trade has caused. On the other hand, when it comes to FDI, gravity models do lend support to the conclusion that – at least in the case of the manufacturing sector – Japan is an outlier. One possible explanation is that, at least until recently, FDI in Japan has faced explicit as well as implicit barriers.

---

[33] See, e.g., Eaton and Tamura (1994) and Harrigan and Vanjani (2003). In fact, the latter suggest that, once country size, industry output, bilateral distance, and industry fixed effects are controlled for, Japan is actually more open to manufactured imports from the United States than vice versa.

[34] Harrigan and Vanjani (2003). Also see Saxonhouse (1993), who provides a broader overview of the evidence on Japan's trade, including intraindustry trade, international price differentials, and the *keiretsu*.

[35] Eaton and Tamura (1994).

[36] Fukao, Ito, and Kwon (2004). Interestingly, the language dummy (for countries in which English is not the dominant language) is statistically significant in most specifications, meaning that American firms tend to prefer investing in countries in which English is spoken, giving some justification to the claim that American firms have been failing to make the effort to overcome language (and, by extension, cultural) differences. On the other hand, geographic distance is found to be statistically insignificant in most specifications, implying that for firms from the United States, being located more or less half-way between the major markets of Europe and Asia, Japan is not more "out of the way" than other countries. In other words, the low level of FDI in Japan cannot be explained by the country's distance from the world's leading investor, the United States.

Another is that the lingering perception that Japan is a difficult market to enter – as evidenced by the large body of literature on the topic – has itself acted as a "mental" barrier. Both explanations are not mutually exclusive and point to the importance of understanding the history of FDI in Japan.

From the Origins to the End of the Tokugawa Shogunate
(Twelfth Century to 1867)

The dearth of FDI in Japan is not due to a lack of trying: throughout the centuries, foreign merchants have attempted to gain access to the Japanese market, but have often met with little success. Among the earliest foreign businessmen in Japan were Chinese traders living in the port town of Hakata (Fukuoka) on Kyushu Island in the twelfth century. Commercial exchange between Japan and China during this period, the Kamakura era (1192–1333) flourished and formal trade relationships were established in 1325. However, during the fourteenth and fifteenth centuries, official trade became more sporadic, though unofficial trade continued to thrive.

The first attempt by Westerners to establish commercial outposts in the archipelago followed soon after Portuguese seafarers first reached Japanese shores around 1543. These early endeavors, in fact, were not without success: visiting the ports of western Japan on a regular basis, Portuguese merchants and their exotic goods – especially their superior weapons technology – were initially well received, and some of the Kyushu daimyo were keen to attract trade with the "Southern Barbarians." The Tokugawa rulers that unified the country and, in 1603, founded the shogunate that was to last until 1868, were also eager for commerce with the outside world. The shogunate thus permitted the Dutch in 1609 and the English four years later to establish trading posts on the island of Hirado, marking the first recorded foreign investments by Westerners in Japan.[37]

Along with trade, however, the Portuguese also brought missionaries to Japan. Having converted several hundred thousand Japanese, including several Kyushu *daimyo*, to Christianity, the missionaries soon alienated Tokugawa leaders through their aggressiveness and intolerance. Following failed earlier attempts to curtail missionary activity, the country's leaders imposed increasingly stringent controls that also regulated foreign trade and by 1616 left only the two ports of Nagasaki and Hirado open to European ships. In 1635, all Japanese were prohibited, on pain of death, from going abroad.

---

[37] See Fairbank, Reischauer, and Craig (1973).

Failure to engage in profitable trade had led the British East India Company to close its office in Japan as early as 1623. When the Portuguese were expelled in 1639, the only remaining European trading mission was that of the Dutch, and this was moved to the tiny island of Deshima in Nagasaki harbor. With the exception of this isolated outpost, where traders were kept as virtual prisoners, as well as sporadic trade with Korea and China from outlying islands in the south and with Russia and China from Hokkaido in the north, Japan had cut off all contact with the outside world, launching the period of *sakoku* or national isolation.

This isolation lasted more or less undisturbed until the arrival of Commodore Matthew C. Perry and his "Black Ships," ushering in the forced opening of Japan in the 1850s that resulted in the "unequal treaty" negotiated by U.S. envoy Townsend Harris in 1858. This treaty and similar ones subsequently agreed with Britain, France, and other Western powers deprived Japan of autonomy over its tariffs, granted foreigners extraterritoriality rights, and provided for the opening of a limited number of Treaty ports for foreign business.

Foreign traders subsequently began to settle in the designated port areas and a group of American entrepreneurs established the first U.S. direct investment in the country. Yet, outside the so-called Treaty Settlements, foreign investments continued to be effectively banned.[38] Nevertheless, most Japanese regarded the growing number of Westerners with suspicion and hostility, and the indecisiveness of the Tokugawa rulers in their dealings with the foreign powers led a group of young samurai leaders to overthrow the shogunate and "restore" imperial rule.

The Meiji Era to the End of World War II (1868–1945)

A central motive of the Meiji Restoration had been to maintain Japan's economic and political independence in the face of the threat posed by Western powers. The early Meiji rulers therefore soon moved to restrict the entry of foreign capital and transferred existing foreign interests into Japanese hands. Areas where foreigners continued to be allowed to do business – trade and finance – were rarely worth the trouble: one contemporary described Japan as "the graveyard of the merchant's hopes."[39] At the same time, the knowledge and technology necessary to meet the central aims of the new government – "enriching the country, strengthening the military" through industrialization – were to be acquired by sending study missions

---

[38] See Mason (1992).
[39] Quoted in Weinstein (1996: 138).

overseas, bringing foreign scholars and experts to Japan, importing capital equipment, and copying foreign products.

This situation, however, changed in 1899, when Japan, in return for a revision of commerce treaties with Britain, the United States, and other nations, granted foreigners the right to invest in Japan. Incentives for foreign firms to invest in the country grew stronger when Japan regained tariff autonomy in 1911 and significantly increased import levies on industrial and other goods. Following the complete freeze of imports of manufactured goods during World War I, tariffs were further increased after the war and again after the 1923 Great Kanto Earthquake, providing ample inducement for "barrier hopping" FDI.[40]

With the exception of the most recent period, this era can be considered as the "golden age" of FDI in Japan and, as will be shown in greater detail further below, saw the establishment of a number of ventures that gave rise to some of Japan's most successful companies today. Yet, despite the relative openness of the Japanese economy during this period, the number of foreign companies operating in the country remained limited. According to a survey by the Ministry of Commerce and Industry in 1931, there were only 23 firms that were financed and managed exclusively or mainly by foreigners. Another 36 were owned by both foreigners and Japanese, but management was in the hand of the latter. In addition, there were 29 sales offices of foreign companies in Japan.[41]

This period of relative openness was brought to an end during the 1930s by rising nationalism and militarism in Japan and the international tension this created. The government gradually tightened controls over foreign investment until most companies – including Ford and General Motors – decided to withdraw. With the outbreak of war, U.S. assets in Japan were frozen in 1941, and American and other Allied investments were expropriated to be utilized in the war effort.

The High-Speed Growth Era (1945–1970)

Following Japan's defeat, the American occupation authorities that governed Japan until the country regained full and formal independence in 1952 continued to impose major restrictions based on the fear that FDI would introduce unneeded complications in the postwar reconstruction process and allow foreign companies an unfair advantage to take over weakened and

---

[40] Mason (1992: 20–3).
[41] Udagawa (1990: 3).

vulnerable Japanese companies.[42] However, foreign firms that had operated in Japan before the war were allowed limited investments, and expropriated capital was returned, but because of the state of the war-devastated economy, many companies – including Ford and General Motors – decided not to seek reentry.[43] Measures introduced by the occupation authorities were the 1949 Foreign Exchange Control Law and the 1950 Foreign Investment Law. While intended to be only temporary, these two laws in fact served as the major instruments by which the Japanese government subsequently screened investment proposals and, more often than not, effectively shut them out for the following two decades.

Japan certainly soon offered a highly attractive market in which to invest. Following the devastation of the war, the economy recovered rapidly and entered a period of sustained high-speed growth: between 1956 and 1970, real GDP expanded at an average annual rate of close to 10 percent. Moreover, given the government's policy of import substitution, which relied on substantial tariff and nontariff barriers, foreign companies that wanted to participate in this rapidly growing market faced considerable incentives to invest in the country. However, Article 1 of the Foreign Investment Law stated that foreign investment was permitted only if it "contributed (1) to the attainment of self-sufficiency and the sound development of the Japanese economy and (2) to the improvement of Japan's balance of payments."[44] In practice, the government applied these provisions in a highly restrictive, case-by-case manner that aimed to discourage most FDI but to encourage the inflow of foreign technology. Foreign companies that applied to invest in Japan therefore were typically urged to license their technologies to Japanese firms instead.[45]

From the 1960s onward, though, pressures mounted to liberalize FDI. The government therefore relaxed the screening criteria from admitting only those investments that positively contributed to the Japanese economy to prohibiting those deemed "harmful." That this was hardly an improvement is revealed by the criteria on which proposals were judged, providing officials with ample leeway for interpretation: foreign investment was admitted "as long as it did not (1) unduly oppress small-size enterprises, (2) seriously disturb industrial order, and (3) seriously impede the domestic development of industrial techniques."[46]

[42] Mason (1992: 105–7).
[43] Mason (1992: 146–7).
[44] Yoshino (1970: 349).
[45] Mason (1992).
[46] Yoshino (1970: 349).

Pressure continued to build as Japan joined the OECD and accepted Article 8 of the International Monetary Fund (IMF) in 1964, respectively obliging the country to deregulate foreign capital and foreign exchange controls. Liberalization proceeded, but with important exceptions. For example, extensive restrictions remained in those sectors where Japanese firms were deemed to still lack international competitiveness – primarily in the high-tech industries.[47] These sectors, in fact, were not fully liberalized until the mid-1970s, by which time strong domestic competitors and high labor costs had significantly reduced the attractiveness of investing in these industries. Various barriers to imports also remained in place, preventing foreign companies from pursuing a forward strategy for investment to follow exports. Finally, a limit was set on the ratio of shares a foreign company could acquire in a Japanese firm, making hostile takeovers all but impossible. Given the severe restrictions on FDI during this period, direct investment in the manufacturing sector by U.S. firms between 1951 and 1970 never exceeded US$67 million in any single year and the total value for the period amounted to less than US$320 million.[48]

The 1970s to the Mid-1990s

The gradualist approach adopted by the Japanese government toward FDI deregulation continued throughout the 1970s, reflecting officials' grudging acknowledgment that the country could no longer ignore the international clamor. Thus, foreign investment in the automobile industry was deregulated in 1971. Further measures in 1973 in principle completely liberalized foreign investment in all areas, with the exception of twenty-two designated industries. Restrictions on FDI in seventeen of these industries were gradually lifted between 1974 and 1976. Investments in retail trade were liberalized in 1975, and in 1980, the Foreign Investment Law was finally abolished altogether: foreigners now only had to notify the authorities rather than to seek their approval prior to a specific investment. Procedures were further simplified in 1992 with the change from prior notification to ex post facto reporting. An overview of this process of FDI liberalization in Japan is provided in Table 2.3.

From a historical perspective, FDI deregulation in the 1970s meant that official policy toward FDI became the most liberal it had been since the first

---

[47] Examples are the manufacture of computers, integrated circuits, pharmaceutics and precision electronic machines (Mason 1992: 204).
[48] Figures from Mason (1992: 197).

Table 2.3. *The process of FDI liberalization in Japan*

	For newly established firms Number of industries			For existing firms in all industries Foreign ownership	
	Up to 50% foreign ownership permitted	Up to 100% foreign ownership permitted	Total	By one foreign "person"[a]	By all foreign "persons"[a]
Japan joins OECD, accepts IMF's Article 8 (1964)					
Phase I (July 1967)	33	17	50	Up to 7%	Up to 20%
Phase II (March 1969)	160	44	204	Up to 7%	Up to 20%
Phase III (Sept. 1970)	447	77	524	Up to 7%	Less than 25%
Automobile industry liberalization (June 1971)	Automobile and 5 related industries (automatic approval for up to 50% foreign ownership)				
Phase IV (August 1971)	All industries other than those 100% liberalized (next column) and 7 industries subject to individual screening[b]	228	–	Less than 10%	Less than 25%
Phase V (May 1973)	In principle, "complete liberalization," with the exception of 22 industries (17 of which subject to delayed liberalization)[c]			100% foreign ownership allowed (excluding 22 specified industries), but only with consent of target firm	
Liberalization of the 17 industries subject to delayed liberalization (December 1974 to May 1976)	December 1974: Integrated circuits. May 1975: Meat products, tomato processed products, prepared feed for animals, pharmaceuticals and agricultural chemicals, ferroalloy, music records, real estate, electronic precision machinery, packing machinery, oil pressure instruments, apparel (including wholesale trade of apparel), prepared food products for food service industry. December 1975: Manufacture of computers, sale and leasing of computers. April 1976: Information services.				

	For newly established firms Number of industries			For existing firms in all industries Foreign ownership	
	Up to 50% foreign ownership permitted	Up to 100% foreign ownership permitted	Total	By one foreign "person"[a]	By all foreign "persons"[a]
Retail trade liberalization (June 1975)					
Amendment to the Foreign Exchange Law (December 1980)	Change from prior permission of FDI to prior notification to the Ministry of Finance and other ministries in charge of the industry concerned to determine whether an inquiry was necessary. Takeover by foreigner(s) no longer requires consent of acquired firm.				
Abolition of the "System of Restricting Foreign Participation in Designated Companies" (*Shitei Kaisha Seido*) (July 1984)	Under this system, foreign investments in the following 11 companies were subject to government assessment for national security reasons: Hitachi, Fuji Electric, Katakura Industries, Tokyo Keiki, Tokimec, Arabian Oil, General Sekiyu (now: TonenGeneral Sekiyu), Showa Sekiyu (now: Showa Shell Sekiyu), Mitsubishi Sekiyu (now: Mitsubishi Shoji Sekiyu, Koa Oil (now: Nippon Oil).				
Amendments to the Foreign Exchange Law (January 1992)	Change to ex post facto reporting of FDI; only in certain cases, prior notification to the Ministry of Finance and other ministries in charge of the industry concerned required to determine whether an inquiry is necessary.				
Amendments to the Foreign Exchange Law (April 1998)	FDI in telecommunications and broadcasting was changed from prior notification to ex post facto reporting.				

Notes:

[a] The term "person" refers to any natural person, any government or its representatives, or any juridical person or association.

[b] The seven industries subject to screening were: 1. Agriculture, fishery, and forestry; 2. Petroleum refinery and sales of refined petroleum; 3. Production of leather products; 4. Production, sales and leasing of computers; 5. Information processing; 6. Retail activity with more than eleven shops; and 7. Real estate.

[c] The remaining five of the 22 exceptions were: 1. Agriculture, fishery, and forestry; 2. Oil; 3. Mining; 4. Leather and leather product manufacturing; and 5. Retail trade.

Source: Compiled by authors based on Nakamura, Fukao, and Shibuya (1997), Sangyo Kenkyusho (1983), MITI, Tsusho Sangyo Seisakushi Hensan Iinkai Hen (1991), and APEC (1999).

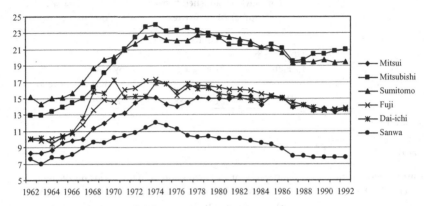

Figure 2.2. Intra-*keiretsu* shareholding ratio (percent)
Source: Keizai Chosa Kai (various years), *Keiretsu no Kenkyu.*

three decades of the twentieth century. Yet, by the time direct controls were removed, other, indirect barriers had been put in place. To limit the actual effect of capital liberalization, the government took "countermeasures" that included a stricter application of the Anti-Monopoly Law to curb the transfer from foreign companies to their local subsidiaries of technologies not available to Japanese competitors.[49] More importantly, the private sector erected barriers of its own. Anticipating the inevitable advance of capital liberalization, Japan's firms increased their cross-shareholdings to protect themselves and their business partners from unwanted foreign takeovers (Figure 2.2). The strategy was not only condoned but in fact supported by the government through the revision of the Commercial Code in 1966, which made it easier for Japanese corporations to issue new shares to third parties of their choice.[50]

In the manufacturing sector, companies in the automobile and electrical machinery industries, for example, strengthened their relationships with suppliers and associated firms by swapping shares, giving rise to the so-called vertical production *keiretsu.* The mutual shareholdings not only meant that it became virtually impossible for foreigners to acquire companies in these production *keiretsu* but, by cementing existing business relationships on a long-term basis, also precluded foreign companies from acting as suppliers

---

[49] Mason (1992: 205).
[50] The link between the fear of foreign takeovers, the change in the Commercial Code, and the rise in cross-shareholdings has been questioned by Weinstein (1997). However, most analysts, both foreign and Japanese, clearly see these issues as closely connected (Mason, 1992: 205–7; Miyajima, Haramura, and Enami, 2003; Tachibanaki and Nagakubo, 1997).

to the likes of Toyota, Mitsubishi, or Hitachi. Similar strategies were pursued by the bank-centered horizontal *keiretsu*. Cross-shareholdings among the members of the six leading *keiretsu* increased significantly following the liberalization of foreign exchange and capital controls that began in 1964 and 1967, respectively. How pervasive the role of such bank-centered *keiretsu* came to be is shown by the fact that, in 1988, 89 percent of all firms listed on the Tokyo Stock Exchange were members of bank groups.[51]

As a result, by the time that foreigners were allowed to acquire Japanese companies – albeit only with the consent of the target company – following the "complete" liberalization of 1973, cross-shareholdings effectively prevented them from doing so. The abolition of the Foreign Investment Law in 1980, which removed the need for consent of the target company, had little meaning in practice as cross-shareholding ratios remained high throughout the following decade. Multinational companies' preferred mode of entry into developed economies the world over – mergers and acquisitions – thus remained practically unavailable in Japan even after the dismantling of most official barriers to FDI.

This, however, was not the only obstacle. The removal of government regulations exposed a number of other, structural characteristics that served to discourage potential foreign investors. The extent to which these structural features – individually and collectively – represented actual barriers is a matter of debate. What is clear, however, is that they kept alive the perception, shaped by decades of official obstructions to FDI, that Japan is a very difficult market for foreign companies to enter. Features of the Japanese economy that have frequently been cited as structural impediments are the presence of *keiretsu* ties, the distribution system, and labor issues.[52] The *keiretsu*, in addition to preventing takeovers, have often been seen as making it difficult to break into the Japanese market because members prefer to deal with firms belonging to the same group rather than with outsiders.[53] The distribution system is relevant because of its multitiered structure, consisting of a large

---

[51] Weinstein (1996: 151).

[52] For a more detailed discussion of these issue, see, for example, Weinstein (1996).

[53] Encarnation (1992: 7), for example, suggests that "Japanese oligopolists have moved to replace government regulations with private restrictions on business relationships [. . . . which] deny foreigners access to the Japanese market long after all formal government controls are abolished." Weinstein (1996), in contrast, in the edited volume by Yoshitomi and Graham (1996), argues that there is no conclusive evidence to support such assertions. However, in the same volume, Jordan (1996), the president of the American Chamber of Commerce in Japan (ACCJ) at the time, complains that while "[. . .] companies within a *keiretsu* grouping cooperate well with each other [. . .] they will not allow a new company to join them, especially a newly arrived American company."

number of very small wholesalers and retailers, many of which are organized into distributional groups that pass goods down from manufacturers
through various layers of wholesalers and finally to retailers. The scarcity
of large, independent distributors, which are more likely to stock imported
goods and goods manufactured by foreign entrants, has meant that foreign
firms either had to invest substantial sums in setting up their own distribution network, or they had to negotiate access to distribution channels
of established manufacturers.[54] The specific features of the Japanese labor
market have presented a further hurdle to foreign entrants. Much of the
job training that in other countries would occur in colleges and universities
takes place in the company; job training is often highly company-specific and
wages are low initially but rise above a worker's marginal productivity when
he (it is rarely a she) approaches retirement, thus rewarding employees that
stay with one company throughout their career. This "lifetime employment
system" has not only discouraged job-hopping but also favored firms with
a well-established market position and a reputation for not firing workers,
making it difficult for new entrants to hire competent mid-career employees
and to attract promising graduates. Japan's unions, which are company-
based rather than industry-wide as in the West, and their strong opposition to layoffs have further contributed to the absence of a mid-career
labor market. Foreign entrants have therefore not only found it difficult to
locate and hire qualified personnel, but have also had to pay substantially
higher wages to do so.[55] Whether these obstacles can be termed "barriers"
depends on how one chooses to define them, since many of the structural
features do not actively discriminate against foreign companies per se but
new market entrants more generally. But if the term "barrier" is defined
as any feature of the Japanese economy that has impeded market access
and therefore lowered FDI, then these characteristics may be considered as
barriers.

A range of other factors has often been cited, especially by foreign executives, to explain why FDI in Japan is so low. Top of the list typically is
the high cost of doing business in Japan, which is partly the result of the
country's economic success. Especially during and immediately after the

[54] Belderbos (1998). Again, Weinstein (1996) in the edited volume by Yoshitomi and Graham
(1996) argues that the distribution system has had little impact on FDI in Japan, whereas
Jordan (1996) in the same volume cites difficulties in penetrating the controlled distribution
systems as one important area that adds to the cost of doing business in Japan. The
distribution system also featured prominently as an impediment to investment in survey
after survey carried out by the ACCJ among its members (Bergsten, Ito, and Noland, 2001).
[55] See Weinstein (1996), Jordan (1996), and Bergsten, Ito, and Noland (2001).

bubble period, high costs – including land prices, office rents, wages, and social security costs – featured prominently. Other aspects include very progressive individual taxes that make it expensive for foreign companies to dispatch personnel to Japan; the general complexity of doing business in the presence of myriads of regulations; and a lack of transparency when dealing with the government.[56] Even if domestic companies face the same problems and many foreign firms have managed to penetrate the Japanese market nevertheless, the continuing perception alone that Japan is a difficult or even closed market acts as a barrier in itself.

Actual FDI into Japan from 1970 to 1995 reflects the gradual liberalization process. Annual inflows did increase from less than US$200 million during the first half of the 1970s to US$500 million at the end of the decade.[57] They jumped further during the bubble period, reaching a peak of US$4.3 billion in 1991. However, to put these figures into perspective, Japanese FDI outflows during this period were more than ten times as large as inflows.[58] The growth in FDI inflows during this period therefore seems substantial only because it started from such a low base.

The Mid-1990s to the Present

Following the collapse of the stock market and real estate bubble of the 1980s, Japan's economy entered a phase of stagnation from which it has only recently begun to recover. The prolonged malaise exposed deep-rooted structural problems that provided the impetus for further deregulation of both FDI and domestic business more generally. Attitudes toward inward FDI changed quite dramatically, to the extent that MITI/METI – which during the 1960s and 1970s played the role of gatekeeper, tightly controlling foreign firms' entry into Japan – has transformed itself into one of the most ardent proponents of foreign investment in Japan. Thus, beginning in the early 1990s, not only were FDI procedures simplified; the government

---

[56] Jordan (1996: 197), for example, asserts that "Japanese companies can post up to four or five Japanese executives in the United States for the same amount that it costs an American company to transfer only one American executive to Japan." The general complexity of doing business in Japan ranks prominently in the surveys cited by Bergsten, Ito, and Noland (2001), while Jordan (1996) claims that Japan has the most highly regulated economy among the G7 nations with more than 11,000 regulations.

[57] Based on MOF data on a notification basis.

[58] These figures are Ministry of Finance data and on a notification basis. UNCTAC figures, which are on a balance-of-payments basis, show that there were actually significant negative FDI inflows, i.e., withdrawals, in 1988 and 1989. If the UNCTAD figures are used to calculate the ratio between outflows and inflows during the 1987–1992 period, then the former outstripped the latter by a factor of 35 even during this period of "booming" FDI inflows.

also started introducing measures aimed at actively seeking FDI, such as the provision of some tax incentives and support services for foreign companies wishing to invest in Japan. The weight attached to attracting FDI received a further boost with the establishment, in 1995, of the Japan Investment Council, chaired by the prime minister. Finally, in 1998, the government liberalized foreign investment in two important service sectors: telecommunications and broadcasting. Though limits on foreign ownership in these and a range of other sectors – agriculture, mining, air and maritime transportation – remain (see Table 2.4), these restrictions are, by and large, no longer qualitatively different from similar barriers to FDI, often for national security reasons, in other advanced economies. In fact, according to one study, by the year 2000, restrictions such as limits on foreign ownership and screening requirements in Japan were no more severe than in most other OECD countries.[59]

More significant than the removal of remaining barriers to FDI, however, were measures to deregulate the economy more generally. As the recession dragged on, it became increasingly clear that overregulation and the presence of public corporations served as a drag on the economy by restricting market access, not only to foreign, but to domestic companies as well. To make the economy more flexible and enhance competition, measures were taken to make it easier for companies to spin off subsidiaries and to facilitate M&As, and a range of service sectors were deregulated, including such important areas as retail, finance and insurance, and telecommunications.

Details of these measures, as well as their effect on FDI, are discussed in the next chapter. Suffice it to say that, coupled with other developments in the economy – such as falling land and share prices, a weak yen, declining cross-shareholdings, a looming crisis in the financial sector, and a growing number of financially distressed companies – the measures set the stage for a surge in inward FDI, most of which took the form of M&As. Following

---

[59] See OECD (2003: 170), where Figure VIII.2 shows that Japan scores rather well in terms of these two indicators. The country's poor result overall – it is singled out as one of the countries with the highest levels of overall restrictions (ibid.: 169) – is due to "restrictions on foreign personnel and operational freedom." However, in this area, too, Japan is moving ahead. Working visas are now typically granted for three years rather than just one year and the government is taking steps to further improve the employment and living environment for foreigners through social security agreements with other nations to avoid dual coverage, the recognition of foreign qualifications, and the granting of visa extensions to foreign students who have studied in Japan (see "Follow-Up Program for the Promotion of Foreign Direct Investment in Japan," Cabinet Office; online: <http://www.investment-japan.go.jp/statements/files/20060401-1.pdf>; accessed January 16, 2007).

Table 2.4. *Exceptions to national treatment*
*FDI in Japan is subject to the Foreign Exchange and Foreign Trade Law. In addition
to general stipulations, the Law contains the following exceptions to national
treatment for the purpose of foreign investment.*

Sector	Restriction
Air transport	A license to operate a domestic air transport business shall only be granted to a juridical person or association with less than a third of voting rights controlled by foreigners.
Maritime transport	Transport of goods and passengers between Japanese ports is reserved to Japanese ships. Foreign ownership of Japanese ships can be obtained only through an enterprise incorporated in Japan in accordance with Ship Law.
Telecommunications	Foreign capital participation in Nippon Telegraph and Telephone Corporation (NTT) is restricted to less than one-third.
Broadcasting	Foreigners or foreign-controlled enterprises (where any of the executive officers is a foreigner, or one-fifth or more of voting rights in aggregate are owned by foreigners) are not granted licenses for broadcasting stations or approvals for program-supplying broadcast business.Foreigners or foreign-controlled enterprises (where any of the corporate representatives is a foreigner, or one third or more of voting rights in aggregate are owned by foreigners) are not granted licenses for broadcasting stations of facility-supplying broadcasting or licenses for broadcasting stations used for relay broadcasting for preventing reception disturbance.
Mining	No one other than Japanese citizens or Japanese juridical persons shall become mining right owners.
Banking	The deposit insurance system only covers financial institutions which have their head office in Japan. Branches of foreign banks in Japan are not covered by the Deposit Insurance Law, mainly because jurisdictional problems might hinder Japanese authorities in taking prompt and appropriate action against them at the time of resolution of failed financial institutions.

Source: Adapted from APEC, *Guide to the Investment Regimes of the APEC Member Economies,* Fifth Edition, 2003; online:<http://www.apec.org/apec/publications/free_downloads/2003.html> (accessed February 17, 2007).

initial concerns among politicians and in the media about the "fire sale" of Japanese companies as well as fears that foreign managers would initiate mass lay-offs and fail to respect Japanese business practices, public and official attitudes today seem more favorably disposed toward FDI than at any time in the past.

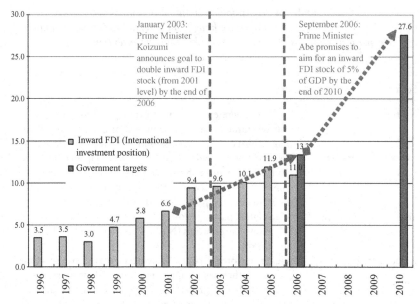

Figure 2.3. Government targets for inward FDI (¥ trillion)
Source: International investment position figures from Ministry of Finance, online:
<http://www.mof.go.jp/bpoffice/e1c018.htm#bm1> (accessed February 2, 2007).
Notes: (1) The value for 2006 is the preliminary estimate for the end of September.
(2) The value for 2010 is the authors' estimate. Japan's GDP in 2006 was ¥510 trillion.
Assuming annual nominal GDP growth of 2.0%, Japan's GDP in 2010 will be ¥552
trillion. 5% of this is ¥27.6 trillion.

The change in attitude is also reflected in ambitious goals for inward
FDI set by the government. In January 2003, then-Prime Minister Koizumi
announced that the government was seeking to double the amount of the
inward FDI stock in the space of five years, from ¥6.6 trillion in 2001 to ¥13.2
trillion by the end of 2006. And even before that goal was achieved, Koizumi
in March 2006 set the new aim of reaching an inward FDI stock equivalent
to 5 percent of GDP by the end of 2011. His successor, Shinzo Abe, maybe
to prove his reformist credentials, subsequently in one of his first policy
speeches in September 2006 promised to aim for the early achievement
of this goal by 2010. Although it seems that Koizumi's first goal will have
been missed (see Figure 2.3) because of substantial disinvestments in 2005
and 2006,[60] and, moreover, such goals have little meaning without any new

---

[60] Major disinvestments include General Motors' reduction of its stake in Suzuki worth ¥0.23
trillion and Vodafone's sale of its mobile phone business in Japan to Softbank worth ¥1.7
trillion.

substantial policy initiatives, they do demonstrate that Japan's leaders today, at least in principle, recognize the contribution foreign firms can make to the Japanese economy.

Foreign Firms' Role in the Japanese Economy Before the 1990s

Finally, since one of the principal aims of this study is to examine the impact of the recent surge in FDI in Japan, it is useful to have brief look at the role of foreign firms in the Japanese economy before the 1990s. Doing so reveals two things: first, foreign firms played an instrumental role in Japan's early industrialization process during the first three decades of the twentieth century; and second, there was a clear break regarding the impact of foreign investment after World War II, reflecting the strict controls on FDI exercised during much of the period. It is not until the most recent period in the late 1990s/early 2000s, that foreign firms again play a clearly discernable role in the Japanese economy.

As seen earlier, the period from 1899 to the early 1930s can be considered a "golden age" of FDI in Japan. Not only were foreign firms relatively free to invest; the government even sent missions abroad to draw their attention to the Japanese market, such as in the case of Western Electric, which, together with Japanese investors, established Nippon Electric Company (NEC) in 1899, with 54 percent of the equity stake held by the American company.[61] Further examples of early foreign investments are International Oil (with a 100 percent foreign-ownership rate, established in 1900), and Osaka Gas (54 percent, 1902). They were followed by a number of joint ventures between foreign and domestic investors from a range of industries, including Yokohama Rubber (established by Goodrich with a 50 percent stake held by the American company), Japan-U.S. Glass (Libby Owens Sheet Glass, 34.6 percent), and Toyo Otis Elevator (Otis Elevator, 60 percent).[62] In addition, foreign enterprises from the United States and Europe were active in trading, banking, and shipping.[63]

But it is in the electric machinery and equipment and motor vehicle industries that most foreign investment was concentrated and where it had the greatest impact on Japan's industrial development. In the former, General Electric established with Shibaura Electric the Tokyo Electric Company in 1905 (55 percent owned by G.E.) and in 1910 took a 24 percent stake

---

[61] Mason (1992: 28–32).
[62] Yamamura (1986: 68–9).
[63] See, e.g., Mason (1987, 1992), Yuzawa and Udagawa (1990).

in Shibaura Machine Works.[64] Tokyo Electric and Shibaura Electric subsequently merged in 1939 to form Toshiba, one of Japan's giants in the electronics industry today. Other important foreign investments in the sector include Westinghouse's stake in Mitsubishi Electric (1924, 50 percent) and the establishment of Fuji Electric in 1935 as a joint venture between Germany's Siemens, which held 30 percent, and the Furukawa group. In contrast, in the automobile sector, foreign firms preferred to set up wholly owned operations, with Ford entering the country in 1925, followed by General Motors in 1927.

It is difficult to exaggerate the impact that these investments have had on the course of Japan's industrial development. Not only were foreign firms directly involved in the establishment of some of Japan's most successful companies in the electrical machinery/electronics industry, such as NEC, Toshiba, Mitsubishi Electric, and Fuji Electric, which subsequently gave birth to Fujitsu as an offshoot of the communications division, they also provided the patents, experience, skill, and knowledge in general that enabled these firms to play the role they did in helping Japanese industry to close the substantial technological gap vis-à-vis Western firms that still existed during this period. The Japan Industrial Bank in a report published in 1948, for example, noted that General Electric's contributions were "the prime reason for Shibaura's becoming the leading producer of heavy electric machinery in Japan."[65]

Moreover, the production technology that foreign firms introduced in the electrical machinery industry, as well as the motor vehicle industry, laid the foundation for Japan's machine tool industry, another leading export sector during the postwar period. Describing the substantial technological gap at this time, Kozo Yamamura, a leading Japanese scholar, observes: "In 1921, the judges at a machine tool exhibition, held under the auspices of the Ministry of Agriculture and Commerce, found that 'in all categories of machine tools, the quality of Japanese products was no more than an inferior imitation of imported machine tools.'"[66] He continues: "During the 1920s and early 1930s, technological improvements in this industry were due mainly to either the transfer of machine technology as a by-product of joint ventures with Western firms in industries other than the machine tool industry or by continued imitation."[67]

[64] Yamamura (1986: 68).
[65] Quoted in Yamamura (1986: 76).
[66] Yamamura (1986: 79).
[67] Yamamura (1986: 80).

The contribution of foreign firms was equally significant in the car industry. In 1900, there was no Japanese car industry and even by the end of the 1920s, government support for the sector had yielded only modest results.[68] The Japanese car market was dominated by major foreign automakers, first through imports of completely built-up units (CBU) and then, following the investments by Ford and GM, imported knock-down kits (KD) assembled in Japan. In 1928, for example, CBU and KD imports taken together accounted for 99 percent of the supply of motor vehicles in Japan. Because Ford's and GM's were wholly owned subsidiaries, the two companies were not directly involved in the establishment of Japanese car manufacturers. However, they provided precious training to managers and workers, some of whom subsequently moved to Toyota and Nissan.[69] Moreover, their entry was followed by rapid technology transfer and active encouragement of local suppliers, one of which was Nissan, which in its early development efforts received critical support owing to its supply relationship with Ford.[70] These local companies soon came to produce a wide range of parts and components,[71] and when the two American companies were forced to leave Japan toward the end of the 1930s as a result of rising nationalism and militarism, they provided Nissan and Toyota with an invaluable infrastructure to develop their own motor vehicle manufacturing capabilities and meet domestic demand.[72]

But it can be argued that the impact of FDI in this period goes far beyond playing a role in the establishment of the three industries – electrical machinery, machine tools, and motor vehicles – that came to define Japan's postwar economic success. Machine tools, for example, are instrumental in industrial development more generally because they are indispensable in the manufacture of everything from firearms to sewing machines and bicycles.[73] Similarly, the increased technological and productive capabilities of the electrical machinery industry enabled Japan to generate more electricity at lower cost, leading Yamamura to suggest that "[. . .] virtually all Japanese industries were changed as the result of the transfer of Western technology from a

---

[68] Mason (1992: 60–1).
[69] Mason (1992: 81–7).
[70] Mason (1992: 62–81). Yamamura (1986: 88) observes in this context: "It is, therefore, hardly accurate to say that Japan could or would have produced automobiles in the twenties had it not been for the domination of the market by Ford and General Motors."
[71] By the mid-1930s, Japanese companies produced, for example, tires, batteries, other electrical goods, tools chassis components, body material, springs, etc. See Mason (1992: 81–5) for more details.
[72] Mason (1992: 81).
[73] See Yamamura (1986: 86).

handful of Western firms to a small number of Japanese firms."[74] Added
to this may be the increased transportation capacity provided by the production of motor vehicles which, in turn, aided market integration and the
division of labor. Yamamura therefore concludes that "Japan industrialized
rapidly because it was able to borrow and imitate the heart of the necessary
technology, quickly and effectively, by taking maximum advantage of the
willing and wide-ranging assistance provided by the most technologically
advanced Western firms."[75]

The absorption of Western technology was also at the center of Japan's
catch-up industrialization during the 1950s, 1960s, and 1970s, although
FDI played a negligible part in this, if any. Government policy in this period
was uniquely designed to unbundle the FDI package of capital, management, control, and technology by restricting investment and encouraging
license and patent arrangements instead.[76] Consequently, direct participation by foreign-owned firms in the Japanese economy during this period
was extremely limited. In the 1960s, for example, their share in the sales
and assets of all firms in Japan was only between 1 and 2 percent, and in
the manufacturing sector, their share in sales did not exceed 3 percent.[77]
However, these totals conceal some variations. In the petroleum industry,
for instance, foreign firms had gained exemption from the investment controls imposed by the American occupation authorities due to the desperate
need for supplies immediately after the end of the war.[78] As a result, this
industry accounted for the largest share of FDI during this period.[79] Operating typically on a 50-50 basis (i.e., 50 percent was foreign- and 50 percent
was Japanese-owned) due to government restrictions, these firms accounted
for approximately 60 percent of industry sales in Japan during the 1960s.[80]
Another sector with a relatively high sales share of foreign firms was the
chemical industry with a little less than 20 percent.[81] However, these two
industries are the exception that confirm the rule. Moreover, although some
technology transfer took place – in the latter, for example, joint ventures with
Japanese firms were typically set up in order to produce certain chemicals

[74] Yamamura (1986: 87).
[75] Yamamura (1986: 93).
[76] Hugh Patrick in his comment on Komiya (1972). Mason (1992: 151) makes a similar point.
[77] Komiya (1972: 140–1).
[78] Samuels (1987: 188–9).
[79] Mason (1992: 144–5).
[80] Komiya (1972: 140–1).
[81] Komiya (1972: 141).

using patents and know-how owned by the foreign firm[82] – there is little evidence of a wider impact on the course of industrial development.[83]

The same is true of individual cases that have been documented. Throughout the postwar period, there are examples of firms that managed to overcome the various investment hurdles. These include Coca-Cola, which, after years of trying, was allowed to enter Japan in 1956 and introduced an "innovative" marketing model by circumventing the traditional complex retail and wholesale system by using its own delivery fleet to directly distribute to retailers and other outlets.[84] Another example is IBM which, according to one account, between 1957 and 1964 held a share of 40 percent in Japan's computer industry on the basis of purchasers' expenditure. Yet, when allowed to invest in Japan in 1960, the government used various discriminatory measures – such as subsidies for leases of Japanese-made computers and controls on private-sector purchases of IBM and other foreign-made machines – that hampered its market penetration.[85] In the 1970s, GM and Ford reentered Japan by taking minority stakes in Isuzu and Toyo Kogyo (today's Mazda), respectively. In both cases, the Japanese car makers were in financial trouble and in need of cash, technology, and access to overseas distribution channels, while their American counterparts were looking to gain a foothold in the Japanese market.[86] In the financial sector, foreign banks had been allowed to open branches in 1969 and a number of them achieved moderate success by concentrating on niche markets such as arranging foreign currency loans – a business that largely evaporated when changes in the Foreign Exchange and Banking Laws in 1980 and 1981 allowed Japanese banks to raise funds overseas.[87] Reflecting increasing FDI liberalization, foreign investment banks entered in the early 1980s, offering services that were not high on the agenda of Japanese banks such as M&A advisory services.[88]

---

[82] Komiya (1972: 142).

[83] Although foreign oil multinationals' affiliates in Japan played a role in supplying Japan's rising energy needs during the postwar boom, their presence had little impact on the structure or competitiveness of Japan's oil industry, which remained truncated and weak throughout this period (see Samuels 1987). In the 2006 Fortune Global 500, petroleum refining companies took five of the top ten places among the biggest corporations in the world. Yet, the biggest Japanese firm in the industry, Nippon Oil, came only in 118th place overall, or nineteenth among petroleum-refining firms.

[84] Komiya (1972: 146–7). A detailed description of the efforts required by Coca-Cola to enter Japan can be found in Mason (1992).

[85] Mason (1992: 191).

[86] Mason (1992: 236–40).

[87] Rapp (1999: 108).

[88] Rapp (1999: 106).

Their number rose quickly throughout the decade, but having entered during the frenzy of the bubble economy, many of them were forced to leave when it burst.

Although anecdotal, the nature and circumstances of these cases suggest that if foreign firms were allowed to invest in Japan, FDI restrictions, other government policies, industry structures, and business practices typically prevented them from establishing majority-owned affiliates, obstructed market penetration, and/or confined them to niche markets. To be sure, some of these firms, such as Coca-Cola or IBM, managed to firmly establish themselves in the Japanese marketplace. But it is difficult to discern any significant wider ramifications: despite Coke's "innovative" marketing, Japan's multilayered distribution system remained firmly in place at least until the 1990s; GM's and Ford's tie-ups with Isuzu and Mazda may have helped to keep the Japanese firms afloat, but otherwise left the industry unchanged; and in the financials sector, foreign firms were confined to niche markets and have come to play a more prominent role only when demand for their services increased with wider changes in the economy over the past decade or so (see Chapter 6).

A final element that explains the minimal impact of FDI in this period is that even once inside, foreign firms' room to maneuver and their ability to "rock the boat" were limited. One reason is that much of economic policy during the postwar period – MITI's industrial policies, the Ministry of Finance's "convoy system" for the financial sector – was designed to maintain "industrial order" and prevent "excessive competition." A prime example is the insurance sector, where a number of foreign firms have operated in Japan for decades. Allowed to invest in the country if they introduced a novel product, they were then however barred from entering rival business areas but also protected in their own field from competition (see Chapter 6). They thus became part of the established order. Another reason – quite apart from government policies – is the combination of minority ownership, of which most foreign investments consisted, and prevailing attitudes and industrial structures. For instance, GM's proposed investment in Isuzu was greeted with words such as "encirclement," "landing," and "invasion" in Japanese newspaper headlines and to calm Japanese fears, GM's chairman found it necessary to state that the company would never take control of Isuzu.[89] In addition, Isuzu organized an exclusively Japanese "blocking party of stabilized shareholder," and when GM did acquire a stake in Isuzu, the accord between the two companies stipulated that Isuzu officers would hold the

[89] Mason (1992: 237–8).

positions of Chairman of the Board and President, GM's officers would only have limited proxy power, and the company would have to obtain prior consent from Isuzu before investing in Isuzu subsidiaries, suppliers, or dealers.[90] Under such circumstances, GM's influence on the direction of the company, and the Japanese car industry more generally, could only be marginal.

Conclusion

The past few decades have seen an unprecedented rise in worldwide FDI activity. Japanese companies have actively participated in this trend and count among them some of most recognized names in the world. Yet, the presence of foreign companies in Japan is much smaller than in other advanced countries around the world. Although the gap may not be quite as large as some of the most frequently cited statistics suggest, Japan nevertheless appears to be an outlier.

Part of the reason is that the country is also an "outlier" in geographical and cultural terms. More important, however, are government policies that actively restricted foreign direct investment for much of the past four centuries. And when official barriers began to be gradually removed from the 1960s onward, structural features of the Japanese economy continued to impede FDI. Only during the past decade and a half or so have many of these structural impediments also begun to disappear – a consequence of both the government's reform program and changes in business practices resulting from the prolonged recession.

Yet, even though inward FDI was restricted in most periods, Japan's own experience shows what an influential role it can play: during the first three decades of the twentieth century, foreign firms were instrumental not only in the establishment of the country's most important export industries today; the technologies they introduced also provided some of the key elements in Japan's rapid industrialization that followed. By contrast, as a result of restrictions on FDI, foreign firms' role in the Japanese economy during most of the postwar period has been severely limited. However, over the past decade, this has begun to change and it is to the surge in inward FDI around the turn of the millennium that the discussion now turns.

[90] Mason (1992: 238–9).

THREE

The Surge in Inward Foreign Direct Investment

Given the various formal and informal entry barriers, foreign direct investment (FDI) flows into Japan were little more than a trickle during most of the postwar period. However, toward the end of the 1990s, the trickle turned into what by the country's own standard can only be described as a deluge, and during the space of only two years, 1999 to 2000, Japan attracted more such inflows than in the entire preceding three decades.[1] Foreign investments at this time were headline-grabbing news, including such prominent deals as Renault's acquisition of a controlling stake in Japan's second-largest motor vehicle manufacturer, Nissan, and the sale of venerable Long-Term Credit Bank to an American private equity fund, Ripplewood Holdings. Both the sums involved and the nature of many of the investments during this period – the acquisition of struggling or failed Japanese firms – represent a watershed in the history of FDI in Japan.

The aim of this chapter is to examine this surge in inward FDI and the underlying reasons in detail. It will be argued that a host of interrelated developments during the 1990s significantly improved the investment climate for foreign companies wishing to do business in Japan: the deteriorating economic situation during the "lost decade" eroded many of the real or perceived informal obstacles to FDI, such as high prices and cross-shareholdings, spurred the government to deregulate, produced distressed companies that became potential takeover targets, and led to a general shift in attitudes toward foreign companies in Japan. Taken together, these developments for the first time made it possible for foreign firms to enter Japan through the acquisition of local firms.

But it is also important to note that the surge in foreign investment in Japan coincided with a global boom in FDI and cross-border mergers and

---

[1] On a balance-of-payments basis (net inflows), inward FDI reached US$21.1 billion in the two years together versus US$16.6 billion for 1970–1998.

acquisitions (M&As). A comparison of FDI trends in Japan and worldwide around the turn of the millennium shows that the former closely followed the latter, suggesting that although reforms and structural change in Japan created the necessary conditions, the magnitude of the surge in Japan at least partly owes to the global boom. Thus, it could be said that in addition to the "pull" exerted by greater investment opportunities in Japan, there was also the "push" of the worldwide M&A boom.

Nevertheless, it appears that FDI inflows into Japan have developed a momentum of their own. Following the initial surge around the turn of the millennium, *gross* investment flows have remained strong, indicating that the developments of the 1990s have resulted in a lasting transformation of the investment climate in Japan. At the same time, though, withdrawals have also been on the rise, so that *net* inward investment actually turned negative in 2006 – a development that should be of considerable concern to the government and makes it doubtful that the ambitious target to increase the stock of inward FDI to 5 percent of gross domestic product (GDP) by 2010 can be reached. The prospects for future FDI in Japan will be discussed in detail in Chapter 7. First, however, it is necessary to address how the surge in inward FDI came about.

The Boom in Inward FDI

The trend in Japanese inward FDI over the past four decades closely reflects the gradual opening up of the Japanese economy. Step-by-step liberalization during the 1970s resulted in a slow but steady increase in such inflows from little more than US$100 million at the beginning of the decade to about US$300 million in 1980. Thanks to further liberalization as well as the lure of the bubble economy, further increases were registered during the second half of the 1980s and the early 1990s, when they reached between US$2 billion and US$4 billion annually on a notification basis, although on a balance of payments (BOP) basis, they were actually negative in some years – indicating net withdrawals – and peaked at US$2.8 billion in 1992. Yet, despite the gradual increase, the figure amounts to little more than a trickle, considering that during the same period, Sony's acquisition of the film and television production company Columbia Pictures in 1989 alone was worth US$3.4 billion.[2]

---

[2] Japan's total *outward* FDI flows on a balance-of-payments basis reached US$44 billion in 1989 and climbed further to US$48 billion in 1990, although it should be noted that outflows during this period were also bubble-induced and subsequently contracted substantially.

58   *Foreign Direct Investment in Japan*

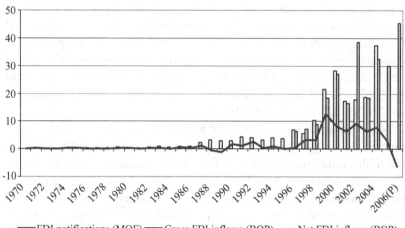

☐FDI notifications (MOF) ▭ Gross FDI inflows (BOP) ——Net FDI inflows (BOP)

Figure 3.1. FDI in Japan (US$ billion)
Sources: Net FDI inflows (BOP): United Nations Conference on Trade and Development (UNCTAD), "Key Data from WIR Annex Tables," online: <http://www.unctad. org/Templates/Page.asp?intItemID=3277&lang=1>. FDI notifications (MOF): for 1970– 2001, JETRO, *2002 White Paper on International Trade and Investment,* Table I-9; for 2002–2004, figures are from the Ministry of Finance (MOF) website (<http://www. mof.go.jp/english/fdi/reference06.xls>) and, following the JETRO example, converted to US$ using the interbank average exchange rate for the fiscal year; average exchange rates are calculated from Bank of Japan, online: <http://www2.boj.or.jp/en/dlong/stat/data/ cdab0780.csv>. Gross FDI inflows: Ministry of Finance balance of payments statistics on inward direct investment, online: <http://www.mof.go.jp/bpoffice/bpdata/fdi/ efdi2bop.htm>; converted to US$ at the interbank average exchange rate for the calendar year.
Note: FDI notifications (MOF) are for financial years, while the BOP data are for calendar years.

Compared with the levels recorded up until the mid-1990s, it is therefore appropriate to describe what followed as a veritable torrent of inward FDI. On a BOP basis, annual *net* inflows increased to US$3.2 billion in 1997 and 1998 and further jumped to U$12.7 in 1999, while *gross* inflows, representing new (and follow-up) investments, soared to US$27 billion in 2000 and, according to preliminary figures, may have reached US$45 billion in 2006 (see Figure 3.1). However, at least as notable as these figures is the way in which this surge came about. For the first time, M&As have played a significant role in FDI in Japan. In a string of high-profile deals, foreigners bought controlling shares in some of the country's largest and best-known companies. The value of so-called "out-in M&As," where a foreign company acquires a stake in a domestic firm, jumped from an annual average of only US$320 million during 1990–1995 to more than US$15 billion during 1999–2001. M&As traditionally are the most important form of FDI in developed economies and, as will be shown below, the rise in inward FDI is not only closely linked with, but essentially the result of, increased out–in M&A activity.

As mentioned in Chapter 2, FDI in Japan historically has been heavily clustered in a small number of industries. This is also true for the recent FDI boom, which saw a further shift toward the service sector, largely as a result of large investments in the telecommunications industry (see Table 2.2). This industry also represents the only "new" sector to attract substantial foreign investment, registering a jump from 0.9 percent as a share of total FDI in 1989–1997 to 15.1 percent in 1998–2004. Taken together, the telecommunications industry and the finance and insurance sector account for a full two-thirds of the increase in inward FDI in 1998–2004 when compared with the earlier period. Add retail and wholesale trade, (business) services, and the machinery industry (led by the automotive sector), and these five sectors were responsible for more than four-fifth of all FDI inflows. At the same time, a considerable number of sectors continued to see hardly any FDI at all, including the food, textiles, rubber and leather, and glass and ceramics industries in the manufacturing sector and construction, transportation, and real estate in the nonmanufacturing sector. The overall pattern thus is very much in line with the impression given by headline-grabbing deals such as the acquisition of Japan Telecom, first by British Telecom (BT) and AT&T and then Vodafone; the purchase of controlling stakes in Nissan and Mitsubishi Motors by Renault and DaimlerChrysler; and the dozens of deals in the financial sector, where companies from the United States and Europe bought more than a dozen ailing Japanese insurance and other financial firms.

International Factors Behind the Surge in Inward FDI

In order to examine the reasons behind the surge in FDI flows into Japan it is useful to distinguish between international and domestic factors. Although domestic changes, to be addressed shortly, were important in removing barriers to FDI, inflows into Japan would not have increased to the extent they did without the FDI global boom. This global boom saw annual FDI outflows worldwide rise sevenfold from around US$200 billion in 1990 to a peak of US$1,400 billion in 2000 (see Figure 3.2).

A number of political, economic, and technological factors contributed to this trend. Throughout the 1990s, countries around the world were

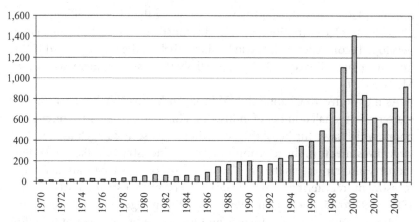

Figure 3.2. Global inward FDI flows (US$ billion)
Source: UNCTAD, "Key Data from WIR Annex Tables," online: <http://www.unctad.org/Templates/Page.asp?intItemID=3277&lang=1>.

liberalizing trade and investment regimes and, in many cases, competed to attract export-oriented FDI. At the same time, technical progress in areas such as transportation, logistics, and especially communication greatly facilitated the coordination of globally dispersed activities. In addition, economic liberalization and technical progress interacted to create fiercely competitive global markets, forcing multinational corporations (MNCs) to invest in new markets and seek low-cost factors of production. Finally, the United States, home to the largest MNCs and the most important source of FDI, registered extraordinarily rapid economic growth throughout the decade, providing companies with the necessary financial resources to invest overseas.

A prime example of the interplay of deregulation, technological change, and intensifying global competition is provided by the telecommunications sector. Still dominated by state monopolies at the beginning of the 1990s, the sector turned into the growth industry par excellence – as a result of (partial) privatization, liberalization, and the rapid spread of mobile telephony. By the end of the decade, a handful of companies were vying for global dominance and seeking to establish a presence in each of the major markets. The quickest route to do so was to acquire a local incumbent, offering instant market access. These dynamics resulted in a rise in the value of annual cross-border M&As in the telecommunications sector from about US$3–4 billion in the early 1990s to a peak of US$366 billion in 2000, and the share of the sector in total cross-border M&As jumped from less than 5 percent to almost a third.[3]

---

[3] Strictly speaking, these figures are for "Transport, storage, and communications." *Source:* UNCTAD online database.

Other sectors where global cross-border M&A activity accelerated considerably during the second half of the 1990s were finance and trade in the service sector and the chemical, electrical machinery, and motor vehicle industries in the manufacturing sector. Economic deregulation, technological progress, and the ensuing increase in competition played a central role in most of these sectors as well. Financial services, for example, formed part of the World Trade Organization (WTO) agenda to liberalize international trade in services and saw rapid increases in productivity thanks to the widespread introduction of information technology. These trends have combined to turn financial services into an increasingly global business. Cross-border M&As in the sector rose from about US$12–14 billion annually in the early 1990s to a peak of US$184 billion in 2000.[4] This growth was more or less in line with overall trends: the sector's share in total cross-border M&As hovered at about 16–17 percent throughout most of the period.

Finally, to take a prominent example from the manufacturing sector: driven by economies of scale, the car industry has been consolidating almost since it was born, and in the 1990s, this consolidation reached a global level. Worldwide excess capacity had been rising throughout the decade and eroded the profitability of the weakest makers. M&A activity in the sector culminated in a number of megamergers, including the ones between Daimler-Benz (Germany) and Chrysler (United States) as well as Renault (France) and Nissan (Japan). While cross-border M&As in this industry had been below US$5 billion a year for most of the decade, they jumped to US$51 billion in 1998 and, at US$19 billion and US$25 billion in the following two years, remained substantially above earlier levels.

These global trends, overall and in the different sectors, are important because inward FDI flows and out–in M&As in Japan form an almost perfect mirror image. At first impression, this is not a particularly deep insight; after all, the country is part of the world economy and any global trend would also affect Japan. However, in attempting to assess the reasons for the recent upsurge in FDI in Japan, it is essential to keep this global background in mind.

Domestic Factors

While the global FDI/M&A boom meant that huge sums of money were sloshing around the world economy, it is doubtful that much of this would have found its way to Japan were it not for wide-ranging domestic changes that made it much easier for foreign companies to invest in the country. These

---

[4] Figures from UNCTAD online database.

changes are the result of a mixture of different, intertwined developments. To some extent, the opening of the Japanese economy to foreign business simply represents a continuation of the gradual liberalization of foreign investment that was begun in the 1960s and broadened in the 1970s and 1980s. In addition, the decade-long recession since the early 1990s triggered a number of reform measures aimed at making the economy more flexible. And finally, the ongoing malaise itself served as a catalyst for structural change. Although economic policy and structural change in Japan have often been described as progressing at a snail's pace, cumulatively, these developments have led to a substantial transformation of the economy. The following policy measures or economic trends were particularly important for FDI activity in Japan.

Deregulation in the Service Sector
Deregulation in the service sector facilitated FDI in two ways: first, by lifting some of the remaining formal barriers to FDI; second, and more importantly, by removing informal barriers that restricted market access more generally. A combination of the two can be found in the telecommunications industry. First steps toward the liberalization of the market occurred following the (partial) privatization of Nippon Telegraph & Telecom (NTT), the government monopoly, in 1985. In 1994, the Telecommunications Business Law was introduced, relating, among other things, to mobile phones, which until then had been illegal in Japan. Next, all restrictions on foreign investment in Type I carriers, except for KDD (Kokusai Denshin Denwa Ltd.) and NTT, were lifted in 1998.[5] Foreign telecommunications companies moved almost immediately to take advantage of these changes: in June 1999, Cable & Wireless acquired International Digital Communications (IDC) in the first successful hostile takeover bid by a foreign company in Japan, while only a few months later, British Telecom and AT&T jointly bought a 30 percent stake in Japan Telecom.

Sectors that benefited from deregulation more generally are retail and finance. In the retail sector, FDI had been hampered by the Large Retail Store Law, which was designed to protect smaller shops by restricting the activities of retail giants and forcing the latter to go through a time-consuming consultation and adjustment process. The law was revised in 1992 and again

---

[5] Type I telecommunications carriers under the Japanese Telecommunications Business Law are those carriers that use their own infrastructure. In addition to the liberalization of FDI in the telecommunications sector, all barriers to foreign ownership in the cable TV business were abolished in 1999.

in 2000, when it was replaced by the Large Retail Store Location Law. While during the 1980s only a handful of foreign companies, mainly luxury goods makers, established retail outlets in Japan, both the number and range of retailers expanded substantially during the 1990s.

Finally, FDI received a significant boost by deregulation in the finance sector. Though few independent observers would really call it a "Big Bang" as Japanese officials are wont to do, the Financial System Reform Law enacted in 1998 removed regulatory obstacles separating different categories of financial institutions and made it possible to sell new types of financial product in Japan. Stock brokerage commissions were liberalized the following year. On their own these steps probably would not have been sufficient to attract the amount of foreign investment in the sector actually observed. But in combination with the presence of a large number of ailing Japanese banks and insurance companies that were easy takeover targets, these measures provided the basis on which foreign firms could bring their products and business models to Japan.

Although many of the regulations that were lifted in the 1990s did not explicitly discriminate against foreigners, they stifled competition and market entry more generally, no matter what the nationality of potential competitors. The removal of such regulations and the introduction of greater competition in these service sectors thus allowed foreign investors to participate in the Japanese market for the first time. However, this still would have been very difficult had it not been for the gradual weakening of informal barriers that had compounded the problem of official regulation.

Unwinding of Cross-Shareholdings

Another barrier to FDI in Japan in the past was the presence of the *keiretsu*. While it remains a moot point whether the corporate groups restricted foreign market access through oligopolistic business practices, what seems beyond dispute is that the substantial cross-shareholdings that *keiretsu* members engaged in severely restricted the supply of acquirable assets.[6] However, beginning in the mid-1990s, these cross-shareholdings, as well as one-way long-term shareholdings, started to unwind – and did so with increasing speed. Quite stable at 17–18 percent and 45 percent, respectively, until the mid-1990s, they have since dropped markedly (see Figure 3.3). In the case of cross-shareholdings, the ratio fell by more than half,

---

[6] For conflicting views on whether the *keiretsu* restricted FDI in Japan, see, e.g., Lawrence (1993) and Weinstein (1996). Both authors agree, however, that the presence of the *keiretsu* restricted the supply of acquirable assets.

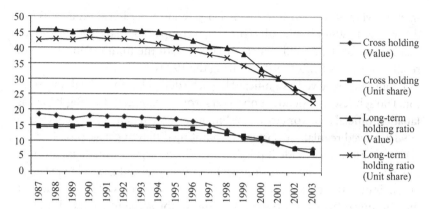

Figure 3.3. Cross- and long-term shareholding ratio (percent)
Source: NLI Research Institute (2004).

reaching 7.6 percent in 2003, while in the case of long-term shareholdings, it declined by more than a third to 24.3 percent.[7] In fact, these are the latest figures available, since the research institute compiling these figures has stopped doing so, explaining that the ratio had become so low that cross-shareholdings were either difficult to discern in the data or had disappeared altogether.[8]

Most of this unwinding of cross-shareholdings has been undertaken by financial institutions.[9] Four main factors are responsible.[10] The first is the profitability of such cross-shareholdings: already low to begin with, their profitability deteriorated further during the 1990s amid the deepening recession. In addition, the recession added further incentives to take capital gains to compensate for depressed cash flows and, in the case of banks, to obtain funds to write off nonperforming loans. The second factor is increased risk consciousness among banks: the decline in share prices during the 1990s

---

[7] It should be noted that not all of the decline in the cross-shareholding and long-term shareholding ratios is due to the unwinding of such relationships. Another factor is the changing composition of the stock market as new companies with no existing shareholding relationships emerged, reducing the weight of banks and other established companies with long-term shareholding relationships (NLI Research Institute 2003).

[8] NLI Research Institute (2004). However, it should also be noted that although cross-shareholdings remain much lower than before, they appear to be on the rise again as a defensive measure against potential takeovers. See Chapter 7 for details.

[9] In contrast, the cross-shareholdings of other businesses have declined only marginally (see Okabe 2001; NLI Research Institute 2002, 2003).

[10] See Okabe (2001); NLI Research Institute (2002, 2003); _The Economist_, "Japan restructures, grudgingly," February 4, 1999; "Brace yourselves," November 25, 1999; "Out for the count," October 11, 2001.

eroded their capital base and thus threatened their capital adequacy ratios as required by the Bank for International Settlements. The third factor is the overhaul of Japanese accounting rules implemented during 1999–2001 to bring them into line with international standards. Increased transparency showed that most Japanese corporations were even less profitable than previously assumed, forcing financial institutions to reassess their shareholdings in terms of both their valuations and their inherent risk. Moreover, mark-to-market rules meant that financial institutions were no longer able to disguise poor performance – both their own, by using unrealistic book values, and of their shareholdings. The fourth factor, finally, was the introduction of emergency measures in 2001, triggered by impending financial crisis, that limit banks' shareholdings and thus compelled them to further reduce their shareholdings.

However, underlying all these factors is a more fundamental change in institutional arrangements. The *keiretsu* system, of which the long-term and cross-shareholdings were a key feature, was underpinned by a cosseted banking system in which competition was stifled under the government's "convoy system," designed to ensure stability by avoiding bank failures at almost all costs. Yet, these arrangements began to unravel as measures to deregulate the financial sector were enacted, the crisis in the financial sector threatened to spiral out of control, and the government began to get serious about tackling the problems in the banking sector. Several banks, including two of the three long-term lending banks as well as several second-tier banks, went bankrupt and were either closed or sold, including to foreign investors.[11] Others had to be propped up with funds from the government, which used the influence it thus gained to orchestrate large-scale bank mergers across *keiretsu* lines. Thus, the government no longer could nor would uphold the "convoy system" and cross-shareholdings no longer served their purpose.

The implications are obvious: if cross-shareholdings had restricted the supply of acquirable assets in the past, then their unwinding increased this supply. While this trend did not exactly open the gates to unsolicited takeovers, which are still a rarity in Japan, the unwinding of cross-shareholdings and long-term holdings has increased the proportion of shares held by foreign portfolio investors and Japanese institutional investors that put much greater emphasis on the returns of their investments.[12] The

---

[11] Similar developments also occurred in the insurance sector, which, together with the banks, was at the center of long-term and cross-shareholding arrangements. Also see Chapter 6.

[12] See, e.g., Okabe (2001).

growing influence of these groups of investors has not only begun to change the way in which Japanese companies are run but has also lowered one of the barriers to M&As and hence FDI in Japan.

Changes in Accounting Rules and Measures to Facilitate Mergers and Corporate Restructuring

Japanese accounting rules were substantially revised in 1999–2001 to bring them into line with international standards. The two most important of these changes concern the consolidation of subsidiaries' finances and the valuation of securities holdings. Whereas in the past, firms had been able to hide financial losses by moving these off-balance sheet, the new bookkeeping rules aim to prevent such practices by requiring the finances of partly owned subsidiaries to be consolidated with those of the parent. Moreover, companies must now value their securities holdings at market price rather than at book value, making it more difficult to gloss over poor results by selling or revaluing shareholdings.[13]

The improved transparency of Japanese corporate accounts has facilitated M&As in at least three important ways. First, it has contributed to the unwinding of cross-shareholdings, as seen earlier. Second, greater transparency has reduced the risk for foreign companies of finding hidden liabilities when acquiring a Japanese firm. And third, the accounting changes have forced Japanese companies to reexamine their operations and, in many cases, have led them to sell unprofitable divisions or subsidiaries.[14]

Such sales, moreover, have been simplified by several pieces of legislation passed between 1997 and 2000 aimed at streamlining merger procedures and facilitating corporate restructuring more generally.[15] For example, the way was cleared for stock swaps which are frequently used to finance M&A deals.[16] Other measures include the lifting of the ban on holding companies and revisions of the tax code to remove tax disincentives to corporate spin-offs. Legal procedures regarding spin-offs were also revised. For example, firms now are no longer required to notify and gain approval from all

---

[13] *The Economist*, "Brace yourselves," November 25, 1999.
[14] See Japan Research Institute (2000). In addition, the urgency of reassessing the profitability of individual operations has increased with the growing share ownership of foreign and domestic institutional investors and their emphasis on investment returns, demonstrating how the different developments are closely interlinked and often reinforce each other.
[15] For an overview of M&A-related legal changes, see the RECOF website: <http://www.recof.co.jp/english/ma.html> (accessed February 9, 2007).
[16] However, the use of stock swaps for M&As remained limited to domestic companies until the lifting of the ban on "triangular mergers" in May 2007. See Chapter 7 for more details.

creditors individually in advance of a merger or spin-off but only need to put a notice in a daily newspaper. Also abolished were provisions that required the assessment of a company's asset value by a court-appointed lawyer prior to a planned spin-off, a process that usually took six months to a year, during which time the part to be spun off had to stop its operations.[17]

Taken together, these reforms of Japan's accounting practices and regulations relating to mergers, spin-offs, and holding companies greatly increased the transparency and flexibility of the market for corporate acquisitions. As a result, the number of M&As conducted in Japan has risen dramatically: in–in M&As increased from less than 300 cases during the mid-1990s to 2,175 in 2006, while out–in M&As jumped from about 30 per year to a peak of 206 in 2004, before dropping to 171 in 2006.[18] Of course, the number and value of annual M&A deals in Japan still lags considerably behind those in the United States (even after accounting for the difference in the size of the two economies): for 2006, Thomson Financial recorded 1,428 completed M&A deals worth US$108 billion in Japan vis-à-vis 8,086 deals worth US$1,308 billion in the United States.[19] However, as a result of the increase in M&A activity in Japan over the past decade or so, the gap between Japan and the United States and other advanced economies has narrowed substantially. In fact, in recent years, the value of M&A activity in Japan has been on a par with or exceeded that in Germany or France, though it continues to trail behind that in the United States and Britain.[20]

Falling Costs and Weak Companies

Another constraint on FDI in the past was that Japan simply was an expensive place in which to do business. Among other things, foreign businessmen frequently complained about the high wages, land costs, and office rents in Japan.[21] What is more, even if companies had been available for acquisition, the high price of Japanese shares and high price-earnings ratios acted as a

---

[17] Muramatsu (2001); Poe, Shimizu, and Simpson (2002).

[18] The data are courtesy of RECOF.

[19] Thomson Financial, "Mergers & Acquisitions Review" (Fourth Quarter 2006), online: <http://www.thomson.com/pdf/financial/league_table/ma/150587/4Q06_MA_Global_Finl_Advisory> (accessed February 9, 2007).

[20] Of course, for a proper comparison these figures would need to be put in relation to the size of the economy of each country. Nevertheless, the catch-up is quite impressive. Figures can be found at: Thomson Financial, "Mergers & Acquisitions Review" (Fourth Quarter 2006), online: <http://www.thomson.com/pdf/financial/league_table/ma/150587/4Q06_MA_Global_Finl_Advisory> (accessed February 9, 2007).

[21] See Jordan (1996) for a typical example of foreign businesses' complaints about high costs in Japan.

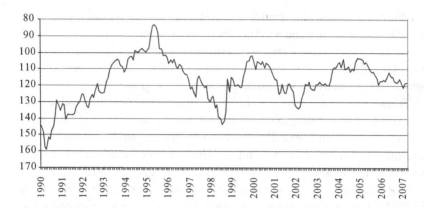

Figure 3.4. Yen/US$ exchange rate (inverted scale)
Source: Bank of Japan, online: <http://www.boj.or.jp/en/type/stat/dlong/fin_stat/rate/cdab0780.csv>.

constraint. Following the collapse of the bubble economy, asset prices, wages, and even the consumer price level fell dramatically: having reached almost 39,000 points at the end of 1989, the Nikkei 225 index rapidly shed more than 50 percent of its value and at one point, in 2002, was four-fifths below its all-time high. Similarly, average urban land prices have dropped by 55 percent since peaking in 1991, while commercial property prices have fallen even more – by 70 percent.[22] Meanwhile, the yen, which had strengthened vis-à-vis the U.S. dollar during the first half of the 1990s, declined during 1996–1998, although it has since fluctuated within a relatively limited range between 100 and 130 yen/US$ (Figure 3.4). Nominal and real wages started falling in 1998 and consumer prices followed in 1999; both only began to marginally rise again in 2005/2006. The cumulative result of these trends is that the cost of doing business in Japan has declined and buying a Japanese company has become much more affordable.

In fact, the prolonged recession considerably weakened Japan's corporate sector. The number of bankruptcies rose throughout the 1990s, while the associated liabilities reached record levels, climbing from less than ¥5 trillion during 1965–1990 to a peak of ¥24 trillion in 2000 (see Figure 3.5).[23] As a result, a number of Japanese companies had to be bailed out – sometimes

[22] Based on figures from the *Japan Statistical Yearbook*, online: <http://www.stat.go.jp/english/data/nenkan/ 1431-17.htm> (accessed February 9, 2007).

[23] Data for the period before 1994 were read off a chart on the Teikoku Databank website (<http://www.tdb.co.jp>) that no longer appears to be available. The relevant page was originally accessed on January 20, 2005.

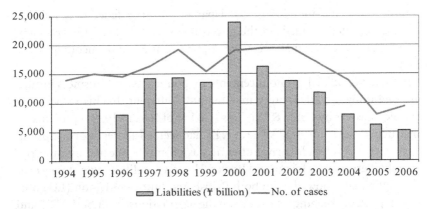

Figure 3.5. Bankruptcies
Source: Teikoku Databank.

by foreigners, as in the case of the Long-Term Credit Bank and Kyoei Life Insurance. In other cases, financial difficulties forced firms – among them some of the country's largest and most famous, such as Nissan and Mitsubishi Motors – to accept foreign capital participation to ensure long-term survival.

Changing Attitudes Toward Foreign Companies

The continuing deterioration of the Japanese economy, culminating in a growing sense of gloom in the years 1998–2002 as the recession deepened and the country again seemed on the brink of financial crisis, has led to a widespread change in attitudes toward foreign direct investment among policy makers, businessmen, and the public. Official resistance, for example, has given way to efforts to attract foreign capital. A council headed by the prime minister to promote FDI was set up as early as 1994. Government-backed bodies such as the Japan External Trade Organization (JETRO) and the Development Bank of Japan (DBJ) began providing information and consulting services, and since the early 1990s, various incentives have been offered to foreign firms investing in designated industries and special Foreign Access Zones.[24]

The attitude of Japanese business to FDI also changed considerably. Whereas in earlier decades, Japanese companies often colluded with the bureaucracy to block the entry of foreign competitors, in the 1990s, foreign firms were increasingly seen as important allies in pressing for structural

[24] Muramatsu (2001); JETRO website.

reform. Since the mid-1990s, the Japanese business federation Keidan-ren has repeatedly called on the government to deregulate the economy to increase international access to Japan's market and encourage new FDI.[25]

Of course, official pronouncements by politicians and business groups are one thing, but the reality may be quite different. In this respect, the hostile takeover by Cable & Wireless (C&W) of IDC in 1999 represents an instructive case study. IDC's sale to NTT had seemed a foregone conclusion, and when C&W made a rival offer, it was promptly rejected by minority shareholders such as Toyota and Itochu. However, politics hung closely over the battle that followed, with both British and European Union (EU) offi-cials reportedly keeping a close eye on the negotiations. After both NTT and C&W had raised their offers, minority shareholders, led by Toyota, finally agreed to the sale to C&W. Toyota's maneuvering during the episode shows how the company was torn between traditional Japanese values, such as seek-ing to guarantee workers' job security, and the need to avoid international repercussions, both for Japan and its own business. Similarly, the govern-ment was generally perceived as taking a neutral stance, though the Ministry of Posts and Telecommunications said afterward that it would monitor the takeover to ensure that IDC maintains "Japanese style-employment prac-tices."[26] The case suggests that, although their natural reflexes may still be different, both government officials and business leaders in the end stuck by their professed commitment to allowing foreign companies equal access to the Japanese market.

What is more, one might even suspect that in their comments regarding job security and employment practices, Toyota spokesmen and Ministry offi-cials were, to some extent, simply going through the motions they thought the public expected of them. Yet, it seems that even the public no longer is overly concerned about the growing role of foreign business in general and the takeover of Japanese companies in particular. Probably no single person contributed more to this change of perception than Carlos Ghosn, the CEO installed at Nissan after the takeover by Renault. The first moves of

---

[25] See, e.g., the address of Keidanren Chairman Toyoda to the Keidanren general assembly in 1995 (online: <http://www.keidanren.or.jp/english/speech/spe005.html>; accessed Febru-ary 16, 2007) and Keidanren proposals for an improvement of the Japanese investment envi-ronment (online: <http://www.keidanren.or.jp/ english/policy/2002/042/proposal.html>; accessed February 16, 2007).

[26] *The Economist*, "Shareholder power," November 25, 1999; *The Japan Times*, "Cable and Wireless connects," June 11, 1999.

"le cost-cutter," as he was known, included the closure of five factories and the cutting of 21,000 jobs worldwide, confirming Japanese concerns about hard-nosed Western management practices. Yet, the spectacular turnaround from record losses to successive record profits in the space of only two years turned Ghosn into a business icon in Japan. As a result, foreign takeovers – at least of the "friendly" variety – have hardly raised an eyebrow in recent years.

Labor Market Changes

One of the areas where the changes in attitudes are most easily discernable, and have the greatest impact on the operations of foreign companies in Japan, is the labor market. The difficulties faced by foreign companies in hiring qualified personnel, and the resulting high wage costs, used to be among foreign executives' most frequent complaints. The reluctance of the Japanese to work for foreign companies – and the weakening of that reluctance – is closely bound up with traditional employment practices and their gradual erosion as a result of the prolonged recession.

Central to this issue is the so-called lifetime employment system. While far from universal,[27] lifetime employment has been most widespread among Japan's professional elite and is closely intertwined with the country's education system, which has generally provided young people with excellent training through high school but has lagged behind other Western countries in producing PhDs and other highly trained professionals such as lawyers or engineers. This gap has traditionally been filled by Japanese companies, who have provided their employees with world-renowned on-the-job training. However, to prevent workers from leaving once their expensive training was complete, firms typically paid employees little at the beginning of their careers but raised their salaries rapidly toward the end, thus rewarding lifelong dedication to the company and discouraging mid-career changes. The second and complimentary cornerstone in this arrangement has been firms' commitment to their employees. To be able to attract employees, firms needed to be well established in the market and to have a reputation for not laying off workers at the first sign of trouble, that is, before employees reaped the rewards for accepting low starting salaries. This explains why Japanese firms historically have been reluctant to lay off workers even in difficult times. The upshot of this lifetime employment system is that Japan's

---

[27] Lifetime employment is generally confined to full-time employees at the big companies, i.e., about one-third of all workers.

labor market has been extremely rigid compared with the countries of the West, forcing foreign firms – unwilling or, as newcomers, unable to credibly guarantee lifetime employment – to pay considerably higher salaries than their Japanese competitors to attract qualified personnel.[28]

However, this pillar of Japanese-style capitalism too eroded during the deepening recession as Japanese companies were no longer able to stick to their side of the bargain. Their initial response to the worsening economic conditions had been to stop hiring new graduates, leading not only to a jump in unemployment among the young, but also doing little to lower wage bills as the average age of employees rose. Yet, with no upturn in sight, firms were increasingly compelled to undertake across-the-board job cuts, culminating in a spate of mass lay-offs during 1999–2001. In early 1999, even before Ghosn's radical restructuring plan for Nissan involving the loss of 21,000 jobs, Sony announced it would cut its global workforce by 17,000, while at NEC some 15,000 jobs were to go. A second wave followed in the autumn of 2001, when, amid the global downturn in the information technology (IT) sector, the four electronics makers Fujitsu, Toshiba, Hitachi, and Matsushita alone announced job cuts totaling more than 60,000. These headline figures relate to the global operations of the companies concerned, but whereas in the past jobs cuts were mainly confined to overseas operations, for the first time Japanese firms were also laying off workers at home.

News such as these as well as the inexorable rise in the unemployment rate from 2.0 percent in 1990 to a peak of 5.5 percent in 2002 seriously undermined the faith in the lifetime employment system and contributed to an increased willingness to work for a foreign company. What is more, the new job insecurity dealt a serious blow to the image of the *sarariman*, hitherto respected as the "corporate warrior" that rebuilt Japan, but now often portrayed as a sad, middle-aged man who dedicated his life to the company for little reward. It therefore comes as no surprise that a recent survey by a job agency found that only 31 percent of university graduates were planning to work for the same company until retirement age, while 41 percent indicated they wanted to hop jobs to develop their careers.[29] The change in attitudes is also reflected in the growing attractiveness of foreign companies: in an annual survey among university graduates asking them

---

[28] The lifetime employment system is also one important reason – apart from government regulations – why most foreign investments in earlier decades consisted of joint ventures with local firms: necessary staff could be temporarily transferred from the Japanese company, allowing employees to remain within the *nenko joretsu* system providing seniority-based pay and promotions (Komiya 1972: 147–148).

[29] *Mainichi Daily News*, "New graduates balk at lifetime employment," January 11, 2004.

to name the most desirable companies to work for, foreign firms have been steadily moving up the ladder.[30]

Push or Pull?

The regulatory and structural changes that began in the 1990s have done away with many of the formal and informal barriers that in the past hampered foreign business activity in Japan, paving the way for the surge in inward FDI flows. But does this mean that the country all of a sudden has become a magnet for global investment? Or did Japan simply benefit from the worldwide boom in FDI? Put differently, is it mainly push or pull factors that explain the jump in FDI flows into Japan? While it is analytically difficult to separate these factors, a closer inspection of aggregate FDI flows, their sectoral composition, and the relationship between investment trends in particular industries and changes in the business environment provides some clues. They suggest that a considerable part of the surge between 1998 and 2002 was driven by global trends. Yet, obscured partly by the global boom as well as substantial disinvestments in recent years, inflows do seem to have developed a momentum of their own. Unfortunately, however, detailed examination of inward FDI trends is hampered by the fact that consistent industry-level data are not available.[31] For this reason, the analysis here concentrates mainly on the period of the initial surge around the turn of the millennium and then looks at more recent developments separately.

Aggregate FDI Flows
For a first, intuitive indication that the initial surge in FDI may have been primarily driven by global developments, all that is needed is a brief glance at both trends (see Figure 3.6): both the timing and the magnitude of FDI in Japan are highly correlated with global flows. Both in Japan and worldwide, FDI inflows soared around 1997–1999/2000 and contracted again in 2001. Similarly, both global inward FDI and *net* inward FDI flows to Japan at

---

[30] JETRO, *New Business Practices and Opportunities in the Japanese Economy*, online: <http://www.jetro.org.au/sydney/publi/econ_practices.pdf> (accessed April 6, 2004).

[31] The industry-level data of the MOF statistics, which go up to 2004, do not include disinvestments, whereas industry-level data of the balance of payments provide an industry breakdown only from 2005. Moreover, as seen in Chapter 1, the aggregate data during the period where the two sets of statistics overlap show substantial discrepancies in some years. Thus, even if it were possible to obtain *gross* inflow data by industry, the two datasets would not be comparable.

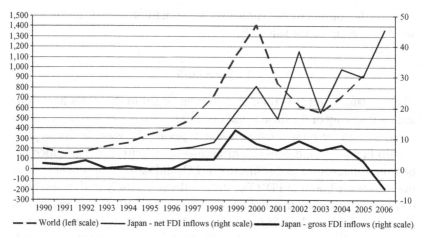

Figure 3.6. Inward FDI flows: World and Japan (US$ billion)
Sources: Gross FDI inflows for Japan are from Ministry of Finance balance of payments statistics on inward direct investment, online: <http://www.mof.go.jp/bpoffice/bpdata/fdi/efdi2bop.htm>; converted to US$ using the interbank average exchange rate; average exchange rates are calculated from Bank of Japan, online: <http://www2.boj.or.jp/en/dlong/stat/data/cdab0780.csv>. Net inflows for Japan and world inflows (also on a net basis) are from UNCTAD, "Key Data from WIR Annex Tables," online: <http://www.unctad.org/Templates/Page.asp?intItemID=3277&lang=1>. Net inflows for Japan for 2006 are taken from the same source as gross FDI inflows and are converted to US$ in the same manner. The data for 2006, both for gross and for net inflows, are preliminary.

the end of the decade (1997–2000) exceeded those at the beginning (1991–1994) by a factor of between four to five. This means that Japan's share of global inward FDI during this period virtually stagnated or at best saw a very modest increase, depending on what indicator and periods are chosen for comparison (see Table 3.1). For example, at about 1.0 percent, Japan's share in global FDI stock has actually been *lower* in recent years than in 1995, when it was 1.2 percent. Similarly, even during the boom in the second half of the 1990s, Japan's share in global inward FDI flows at 0.7 percent was only marginally higher than during the first half, when it was 0.5 percent, and virtually unchanged from the 0.6 percent registered in 1981–1985. Only in 2001–2005 did this share rise somewhat, to 0.9 percent.

Compare these figures with those for the United States or China, which in contrast to Japan acted as genuine magnets for global investment flows during the 1990s. Following its opening up at the beginning of the decade, China attracted vast amounts of direct investment by companies from around the world lured by the promises of a rapidly expanding market of a billion consumers and a seemingly inexhaustible supply of cheap labor. As a

Table 3.1. *Comparison of FDI in Japan, the United States, and China*

	Japan	United States	China
Share in global inward FDI flows			
1970–1980	0.5	16.4	0.0
1981–1985	0.6	32.6	1.7
1986–1990	0.2	34.5	1.9
1991–1995	0.5	17.2	10.0
1996–2000	0.7	23.4	5.2
2001–2005	0.9	14.0	7.9
Share in global inward FDI stock			
1980	0.6	14.8	0.2
1985	0.6	22.9	0.7
1990	0.6	22.1	1.2
1995	1.2	19.4	3.7
2000	0.9	21.7	3.3
2005	1.0	16.0	3.1

Source: Authors' calculations based on UNCTAD, "Key Data from WIR Annex Tables," online: <http://www.unctad.org/Templates/Page.asp?intItemID=3277&lang=1> (accessed February 16, 2007).

result, the country's share in global FDI inflows jumped from 1.9 percent in 1986–1990 to 10.0 percent in 1991–1995. Though this figure dropped again during the second half of the decade, China's share in global FDI stocks at 3.1 percent in 2005 was three times larger than Japan's (Table 3.1). Similarly, while the share of the United States in global FDI inflows halved during 1991–1995 compared with the preceding decade, it then grew again by more than six percentage points to 23.7 percent in the second half of the decade. Foreign investors were attracted to America by the opportunities offered by the longest expansion in postwar history. Juxtaposed with these increases by several percentage points, the rise in Japan's share in global FDI flows by just a few tenths of a percentage point is little more than a blip. The comparison with the other two countries also points to a likely explanation why Japan's share in global FDI did not expand in a similar fashion: the country offers neither low production costs (like China) nor a rapidly expanding market (like China and the United States) that multinationals cannot afford to ignore.

Sectoral Trends
Although Japan's share in global inward FDI did not increase substantially at an aggregate level, it could still be the case that deregulation and structural

change exerted a pull on investment in certain sectors of the economy. Yet, here again, a closer look reveals that Japanese trends were primarily shaped by global ones: in four of the six most important sectors, FDI into Japan closely followed worldwide patterns.

Globally, only four sectors accounted for the lion's share of the surge in M&A activity during 1998–2000: telecommunications, finance, machinery, and business services.[32] Together, these accounted for 62.1 percent of the value of all M&As in that period and for a full 72.4 percent of the increase when compared with the preceding three-year period. In Japan, the concentration of inward FDI in these sectors was even more pronounced: they accounted for 77.0 percent of total inflows during 1998–2000 and for 85.4 percent of the increase compared with 1995–1997 (see Figure 3.7). What is more, as Figure 3.8 illustrates, the sectoral trends of global M&As and FDI inflows into Japan are highly correlated in the telecommunications, finance, and machinery industries, though less so in the business service sector.

Two other sectors in which Japan has received substantial FDI inflows in the past, but whose role has been somewhat eclipsed by the surge in the four industries just mentioned, are trade and chemicals. These two sectors accounted for a third of Japanese FDI inflows during 1995–1997, but this share halved during 1998–2000. Nevertheless, both sectors also experienced considerable increases, and in the case of the trade sector, too, the pattern again mirrors global trends with the exception of 2002–2004 (Figure 3.8). Thus, the only sector of importance in which inward FDI did not closely follow worldwide flows is the chemical industry.[33] In sum, looking at the six industries that accounted more than 90 percent of FDI into Japan during the surge in 1998–2000 confirms the view that sectoral trends, like aggregate flows, largely followed the pattern of the global boom in M&A activity during this period.

Investment Dynamics and the Business Environment

Finally, for a more differentiated view, it is useful to consider the sectoral trends by looking at some of the individual M&A cases and to relate these to the deregulatory measures and structural changes that have transformed the business environment in Japan. Three sectors in particular will be examined:

---

[32] A global breakdown of FDI by sector is not available, so that figures on M&As are used.

[33] A more detailed breakdown unfortunately is not available. However, it seems likely that FDI inflows in the chemical industry largely reflect those in the pharmaceutical sector, where regulatory changes have played an important role in attracting FDI. See Chapter 6 for details.

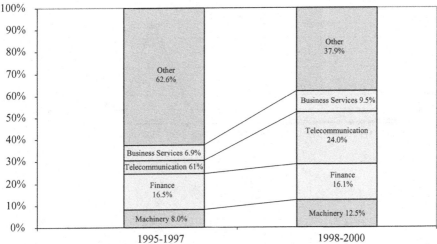

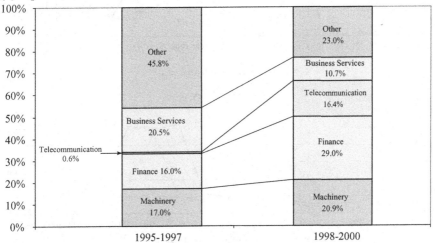

Figure 3.7. Global M&As and Japanese inward FDI by sector, 1995–1997 and 1998–2000
(a) Global M&As
Source: UNCTAD, "Key Data from WIR Annex Tables," online: <http://www.unctad.org/Templates/Page.asp?intItemID=3277&lang=1>.
(b) Japanese inward FDI
Source: Ministry of Finance, online: <http://www.mof.go.jp/english/e1c008.htm>.

Foreign Direct Investment in Japan

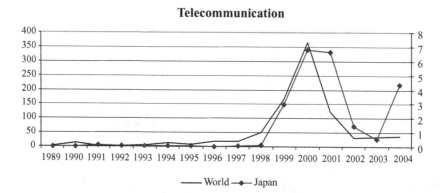

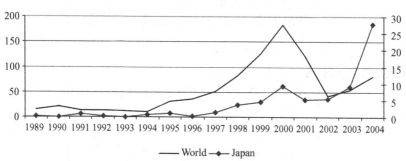

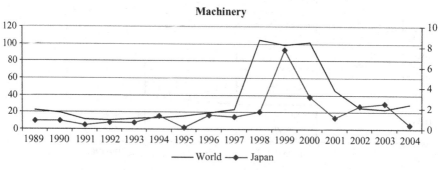

Figure 3.8. Comparison of global M&As (left scale) and Japanese inward FDI flows (right scale) by industry (US$ billion)

Sources: UNCTAD, "Key Data from WIR Annex Tables," online: <http://www.unctad.org/Templates/Page.asp?intItemID=3277&lang=1>. Ministry of Finance, online: <http://www.mof.go.jp/english/e1c008.htm>.

Note: MOF data are on a notification basis. Sectoral flows were converted into US$ using the average annual interbank exchange rate.

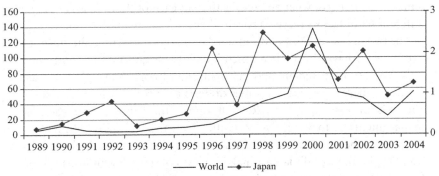

Business services

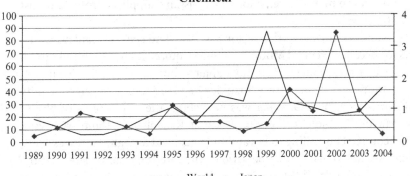

Chemical

Trade

Figure 3.8 (*continued*)

automobiles, telecommunications, and finance. Though the overall picture remains unchanged, what emerges is that, in each of these sectors, quite a different set of factors played a role in shaping investment dynamics.

The two major M&As that dominated foreign investment in the automotive industry have already been mentioned: the acquisition of controlling stakes in Nissan by Renault and in Mitsubishi Motors by DaimlerChrysler. However, there were also a number of deals on a somewhat smaller scale: after Nissan was acquired by Renault, one of the first moves of the new management was to merge two of its affiliated parts suppliers, Calsonic and Kansei, and then to sell a stake in the newly created Calsonic Kansei to America's Delphi, the world's largest maker of auto parts. A few months earlier, German parts maker Bosch had already increased its capital participation in injection pump maker Zexel, another of Nissan's suppliers, from 32 to just over 50 percent.

Foreign investments in this sector have faced no specific regulatory barriers for decades. General Motors not only acquired an equity stake in Isuzu as early as 1971, as mentioned in Chapter 2, but subsequently also in Fuji Heavy Industries (Subaru) and Suzuki, while Ford took a 25 percent equity stake in Mazda in 1979. What was new about the acquisitions of Nissan and Mitsubishi Motors, though, was that Renault and DaimlerChrysler both acquired controlling stakes and then installed foreign executives. This, of course, was possible only because of the dire financial situation of the Japanese companies.[34] Yet, the international context was also important: at the time, it was predicted that, in the future, probably only a handful of car makers would remain independent and European companies were seeking to strengthen their position in Asia. The acquisitions were therefore part of a global consolidation in the car industry.

In contrast with the automotive sector, deregulation played an important role in the telecommunications and the finance industry. The lifting of foreign investment restrictions for Type I carriers in the telecommunications sector in 1998 paved the way for acquisitions in this field. Again, two cases take center stage. The first is the already mentioned hostile takeover of IDC by Cable & Wireless for US$699 million. The second is Japan Telecom: in September 1999, British Telecom and AT&T bought stakes in the company worth US$1.83 billion, and Vodafone acquired a 15 percent share worth US$2.2 billion in December 2000. After purchasing British Telecom's and AT&T's stake for a combined US$6.7 billion in the spring of 2001, Vodafone

---

[34] In early 1998, Nissan and Mitsubishi Motors each had debts amounting to about ¥2 trillion (about US$16 billion at the prevailing exchange rate).

subsequently raised its investment by another US$2.64 billion in October of the same year for a controlling interest of 69.7 percent. Adding up these sums, the takeover of Japan Telecom involved the tidy amount of US$13.4 billion. Comparing this figure with the total inward FDI in the sector for the three-year period 1999–2001 of US$16.4 billion (on a notification basis), it becomes clear that the surge was due almost exclusively to the takeover of one single company.[35] This certainly would not have been possible without the liberalization of foreign ownership in the industry. However, had it not been for the global M&A boom in the sector during that period, it is doubtful that investment in Japan would have reached anything near the level it did.

Probably the most convincing case that deregulation and structural change have acted as an enticement to foreign investment in Japan can be made for the financial sector. Banks and insurance companies used to form the core of the *keiretsu* and played a central role in the unwinding of cross-shareholdings, which hitherto had limited the availability of acquirable assets; nonperforming loans and the slump in the stock market pushed a large number of banks and insurance companies to, and in quite a few cases over, the verge of bankruptcy; and the Financial System Reform Law passed in 1998 sufficiently liberalized the sector to introduce competition into the market and allow foreign firms to take advantage of their superior management methods and products.

Whereas foreign investment in the automobile and the telecommunications sector revolved largely around megadeals involving less than a handful of targeted companies, this was not the case in the financial sector. To be sure, the sector also saw a number of deals breaking through the billion dollar barrier, topped by the US$6.6 billion acquisition of Japan Leasing Corporation by GE Capital. But the surge in foreign investment is much

---

[35] Admittedly, this calculation is rather rough-and-ready, relying on figures published in various press reports without any detail on how the deals were financed. It is therefore possible that part of the US$13.4 billion involved in the purchase of Japan Telecom was raised in Japan and therefore does not represent capital inflows. MOF data, however, suggest that most of this sum did come from abroad. Vodafone channeled its investment in Japan Telecom through a subsidiary in the Netherlands, and MOF data show a huge jump in FDI in the telecommunications sector from the Netherlands worth US$6.7 billion in 2001 alone.

Another problem with the figures is that they double-count the investment by BT and AT&T that was subsequently sold on to Vodafone. Because this applies to both the headline figures and MOF notification data, this presents no problems in terms of the preceding calculation. However, on a BOP basis, the resale of BT's and AT&T's stake would show up as a negative inflow, i.e., the MOF data overstate the extent of foreign investment. Unfortunately, FDI data on a BOP basis, broken down by industry for the period in question, are unavailable.

more distributed across a larger number target companies, ranging from banks via equipment financing to insurance. In fact, foreigners have bought a collapsed bank (the Long-Term Credit Bank of Japan) and more than half a dozen failed insurance companies. What is more, though FDI into Japan in this sector closely followed the global pattern, rising steeply until 2000 and contracting the following year, on a notification basis it jumped to a new record level in 2004 – in contrast with M&As worldwide, which recovered only at a much slower pace.

Most Recent Trends
Although there are striking parallels between global FDI/M&A and inward FDI in Japan around the turn of the millennium, the trends in aggregate flows seem to diverge thereafter. Referring again to Figure 3.6, global FDI flows contracted not only in 2001, but also in 2002 and 2003, and recovered only slowly in the following two years. In contrast, *gross* FDI flows into Japan continued their upward trend, setting new records in 2002 and 2006. Yet, at the same time, *net* inflows stagnated between 2001 and 2004, contracted in 2005, and even turned negative in 2006.

This divergence between gross and net inflows represents one of the most conspicuous developments in inward FDI in recent years. On the one hand, Japan continues to attract growing amounts of fresh investment, with recent examples including Wal-Mart's increased stake in Seiyu, the incorporation of Deutsche Securities, and Cerberus' investment in the financial restructuring of Kokusai Kogyo, a company providing transportation and leisure-related services. On the other hand, however, there have also been substantial disinvestments. To some extent, these reflect the improved business conditions in Japan and the success of foreign investors, such as in the case of withdrawals of investment capital by corporate revival funds. These include the listing of Tokyo Star Bank on the Tokyo Stock Exchange following successful restructuring by Lone Star, a private equity group; the sale of First Credit Corporation, another Lone Star acquisition, to Sumitomo Trust and Banking; the sale of Asahi Securities by The Carlyle Group, another private equity firm; and Goldman Sachs' sale of a string of hotels. In all these cases, the aim of the acquisition was not to operate these businesses on a long-term basis, but to turn them around and, once this had been achieved, sell them at a profit.

Other prominent withdrawals include the sale of General Motors' stakes in Fuji Heavy Industries, Suzuki, and Isuzu Motors as part of a wider asset restructuring that is more a reflection of the American firm's financial difficulties at home than any problems with the partners in Japan. However, the list also includes cases such as Vodafone and the French retailer Carrefour, both of which had entered Japan during the investment boom around the turn of the millennium but failed to succeed. What remains to be seen is whether these latter cases remain the exception, reflecting strategic miscalculations at individual companies, or whether their withdrawals signal the beginning of a wider trend.

Conclusion

Without question, the recent surge of FDI into Japan is an important development in a country that so far has seen relatively little of it. Domestic regulatory, structural, and other changes have played a crucial role in making the country more receptive to foreign participation in the economy, and higher levels of inward FDI, along with greater M&A activity, look like they are here to stay. Yet, as the detailed analysis has shown, it is unlikely that, by themselves, domestic changes would have triggered a rise in FDI of the scale actually observed had it not been for the FDI boom sweeping the globe during 1998–2000.

More recent data indicate that, at least on the basis of *gross* inflows, FDI into Japan seems to have developed a momentum of its own. This suggests that foreigners' perception of Japan as place in which it is very difficult to do business may have begun to change. On the other hand, any "Japan enthusiasm" could also be easily dampened. Although the Renault–Nissan alliance in the car industry has proved to be an impressive success, that between DaimlerChrysler and Mitsubishi Motors has turned out to be an equally impressive failure and, in April 2004, the German company decided to abandon its Japanese partner to its fate. This and other prominent failures in Japan serve as a reminder that notwithstanding the improved investment environment, foreign companies may still find it easier to make money in other, more vibrant parts of Asia. Given that, despite the recent recovery, the Japanese economy still faces serious long-term problems, this would be a loss not only for foreign firms, but also for Japan.

FOUR

Japan's Economic Growth and Foreign Direct Investment

By any measure, Japan's economic performance over the past century and a half has been a huge success. Forced to open up to the outside world in 1859, the country embarked on wide-ranging institutional and economic reforms that set it on a path of rapid industrialization. Defeat in World War II was followed by even more spectacular progress, with the country registering sustained rates of economic growth unprecedented anywhere in the world. The acquisition of foreign technology played a central role in Japan's rapid development; yet, in contrast with more recent Asian success stories such as Malaysia, Thailand, or China, foreign direct investment (FDI) played no part in Japan's postwar economic rise.[1] This quite naturally raises the question: if the country's economy fared so well without inward direct investment until only quite recently, why should the low levels matter now?

The reason, of course, is the dismal performance of the Japanese economy during the 1990s and early 2000s and the deep-seated structural problems that the prolonged recession exposed. Following the era of high-speed growth from 1955 to 1973, during which the economy expanded at an average annual rate of 9.3 percent, and a still respectable average annual growth rate of 3.8 percent during 1974–91, the economy almost came to a standstill, with average annual growth reaching barely 1 percent from 1992 to 2002 (see Figure 4.1).[2] What caused the Japanese economy to stagnate for more

---

[1] As discussed in Chapter 2, Japan was relatively open to foreign investment during the early part of the twentieth century and foreign firms played a critical part in the early development of key industries such as the automobile, electrical machinery, and machine tool industries. However, following this brief episode, FDI in these sectors was severely restricted and had little influence on their further development.

[2] Technically, a recession is typically defined as two subsequent quarters of negative growth. Using this definition, Japan suffered three periods of recession between 1994 and 2006, in 1997, in 1998, and in 2001 (year-on-year change, constant 2000 prices, seasonally adjusted,

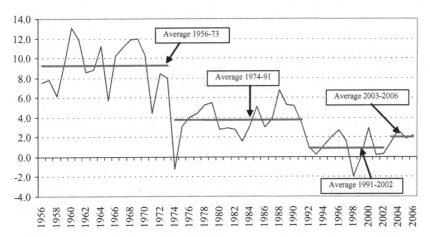

Figure 4.1. Japan's real GDP growth, 1956–2006
Source: Economic and Social Research Institute (ESRI), Cabinet Office, online. For 1956–1980: <http://www.esri.cao.go.jp/en/sna/qe011-68/gdemenue68.html>; for 1981–1994: <http://www.esri.cao.go.jp/en/sna/qe052-2/gdemenuebr.html>; for 1995–2005: <http://www.esri.cao.go.jp/en/sna/qe064-2/gdemenuea.html> (all accessed April 2, 2007).
Note: Consistent data for the entire period from 1956 to the present are not available. The growth rates for 1956–1980 are based on 68SNA, while those thereafter are based on 93SNA. Growth rates from 1981 to 1994 use 1995 as the base year. Growth rates thereafter use 2000 as the base year and reflect various other changes in the compilation of GDP figures. See the ESRI, Cabinet Office, website for details.

than a decade remains a hotly debated issue. Several competing explanations have emerged, putting the blame either on macroeconomic factors such as a "classical liquidity trap" or on mistaken monetary and fiscal policies, or on a host of microeconomic factors ranging from depressed investment following the excesses of the bubble period via problems with financial intermediation to a decline in productivity growth.[3] Each of these

based on the 93SNA series). However, another definition views as a recession any period in which a country's actual growth falls short of its long-run potential. Though economists disagree about what Japan's long-term potential growth rate is, few would deny that actual growth since the early 1990s has fallen below this rate, so that the term "recession" is applied to the entire period.

[3] For a brief overview of Japan's economic crisis and the role played by different factors, see IMF (1998a), chapter IV. A prominent proponent of the "insufficient and mistaken macroeconomic policy response" school of thought is Posen (1998), while the liquidity-trap argument is most closely associated with Krugman (e.g., Krugman 1998). More numerous than the advocates of macroeconomic explanations, however, are those putting forward microeconomic accounts. Underlying the prolonged slump is a large decline in private investment, and much of the debate centers on whether this is a cyclical response to the overinvestment during the bubble period or the result of a "credit crunch." Bayoumi

explanations receives considerable support, suggesting that it is a combination of some or all of these factors that are responsible for the prolonged slump.[4] In fact, much of the debate is about what weight should be attached to the individual factors rather than the validity of competing explanations.

Although Japan has recently managed to pull out of the recession, serious structural challenges remain, and it is with respect to these that FDI can potentially make a significant difference. To see why and how this should be the case, two separate aspects need to be considered: first, the nature of the structural problems that have been plaguing the Japanese economy and how they came about; and, second, the way in which foreign companies can potentially contribute to overcoming these structural problems. This chapter is primarily concerned with the first aspect, that is, the structural problems, while Chapters 5 and 6 deal with the (potential) contribution of FDI. The analysis in this chapter focuses on three related structural issues that have shaped economic developments in Japan: (1) trends in labor input and human capital accumulation, (2) consumer demand and private investment, and (3) trends in the growth rate of total factor productivity (TFP). Each of these three has contributed to the slowdown in economic growth in the 1990s: the working-age population and working hours have declined; private investment has dropped, and TFP growth has stalled. Moreover, looking at the prospects for each of the major components driving economic growth – labor input, capital input, and technological progress (i.e., TFP) – it becomes clear that if the Japanese economy is to achieve sustained growth in the coming decades, this will largely have to be based on improvements in TFP. Consequently, if foreign firms investing in Japan are more productive than domestic firms, then they can make an important contribution to economic growth. That foreign firms indeed tend to be more productive than domestic firms, and that FDI can therefore help to lift Japan's economic growth, is shown in Chapter 5.

(2001), for example, claims that the disruption of financial intermediation is the major explanation for Japan's poor economic performance during the 1990s. Most analysts, however, dismiss this explanation, arguing that only for 1997–1998 is there any evidence of a link between the availability of bank credit (or lack thereof) and investment (e.g., Motonishi and Yoshikawa 1999; Krugman 1998; Hayashi and Prescott 2002). According to Motonishi and Yoshikawa (1999), the main cause for the decline in investment, therefore, simply has been the lack of profit opportunities following the bust of the bubble economy. Finally, prominent champions of the view that Japan's economic slowdown is primarily due to a decline in productivity growth (plus a reduction in the workweek length) are Hayashi and Prescott (2002).

[4] Given the extraordinary length and severity of the recession, it would be surprising to find that one single factor alone was responsible. Rather, cyclical and structural, financial and real factors have been reinforcing each other, explaining also why it has proven so difficult to find an adequate policy response.

Before that, however, it is useful to look at the origin of Japan's economic travails in recent years. The analysis falls into three parts. The first deals in greater detail with the three major structural issues mentioned above, looking not only at the 1990s, but also at earlier decades. Such a long-term view shows that many of Japan's present economic problems are in fact deep-rooted, presenting, in some respects, a hangover not only from the bubble period but also from the high-speed growth era that ended in the early 1970s. In particular, it will be suggested that Japan's structural excess savings problem goes a long way in explaining much of the country's recent economic developments and, moreover, that the impressive growth recorded during the immediate postwar era relied heavily on increases in factor inputs and therefore quite naturally had to run out of steam. That this indeed was the case, and that TFP growth has failed to make up for the slack – in fact, TFP declined during the 1990s – will be shown in the second section, which provides growth accounting for the Japanese economy during the period 1980–2004. The analysis of the country's growth record will show why the performance of TFP growth is such a crucial issue.

The third section, finally, looks at TFP trends in different sectors and industries, showing that TFP stagnated in the manufacturing sector, fell in other production activities, and grew only minimally in market services. While this helps to explain Japan's disappointing growth record in recent years, it also suggests that there is considerable potential for improving growth performance in the future. To illustrate this point, this section also introduces a few examples of sectors where Japan's productivity lags behind that of other countries and briefly discusses why this is so.

Structural Problems

What caused Japan's economy to grind to a halt in the 1990s? One way to address this question is to use a basic accounting identity that states that economic growth must derive either from an increase in the factors of production – labor and capital – or an increase in the efficiency with which these are used. The analysis that follows looks at each of these potential sources of growth and the structural issues related to them.

Labor Input and Human Capital Accumulation
Growth in labor input played a central role in underpinning Japan's economic growth until the early 1990s, although the nature of this growth in labor input changed over the years. Initially, most of the increase was propelled by population growth, thanks to the baby boom during the early postwar period: during the 1950s and 1960s, Japan's working-age population

expanded at annual rates of about 2 percent. This growth rate fell to about 1 percent during the 1970s and 1980s, but the slowdown was partly compensated by increases in the hours worked. Nevertheless, the growth in man-hour input overall gradually decelerated and the quantity of labor input peaked in 1991.

A number of factors contributed to this reversal. The first is the long-term demographic trend: in the early 1970s, Japan experienced a second, though smaller, baby boom, and although the working-age population continued to increase until the mid-1990s, it did so at diminishing rates. Since then, the working-age population has actually been shrinking due to low birthrates. The second factor contributing to the decline in labor input is cyclical: the collapse of the bubble economy in 1990/91 and the ensuing economic downturn, which led to a sharp rise in unemployment (the unemployment rate climbed from 2.1 percent in 1990 to 5.4 percent in 2002) and a reduction in overtime work for those who remained in employment. The third factor was government policy: between 1988 and 1992, the government reduced the statutory workweek from 48 to 40 hours, that is, from six workdays to five, and introduced three new national holidays. A further revision of the labor law added another day of paid vacation in 1998. Due to these changes and the cyclical reduction in overtime, the average monthly number of hours worked by regular employees fell from 171.0 hours in 1990 to a low of 153.1 hours in 2002.[5] Taken together, the three factors have meant that the actual labor input in terms of man-hours has been shrinking since 1991.

Another important factor contributing to economic growth apart from the sheer quantity of labor input is human capital accumulation, that is, increases in the *quality* of labor through education and the acquisition of skills. The most commonly used, because it is the most easily quantifiable, measure of human capital accumulation is the average years of schooling. Here, too, Japan made rapid advances during the high-speed growth era, raising average schooling from 7.6 years per person in 1950 to 9.8 years in 1970 – an annual increase of 1.3 percent. Average schooling grew further to 11.5 years per person in 1990, which, however, represents a slowdown in the rate of increase to 0.8 percent.[6] Of course, such a slowdown in the rate of human capital accumulation was only natural as primary and secondary education became universal and tertiary education widespread. Yet, what is remarkable is that although average tertiary schooling in Japan continued

---

[5] Figures from Statistics Bureau, *Japan Statistical Yearbook*, online: <http://www.stat.go.jp/data/nenkan/ zuhyou/y1638000.xls> (January 17, 2007).

[6] Figures from Godo and Hayami (2002).

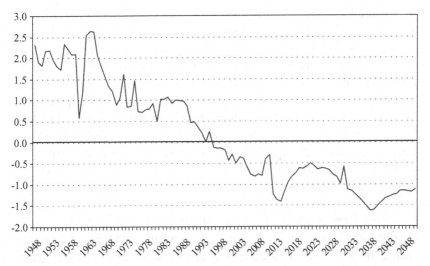

Figure 4.2. Annual change in Japan's working-age population, 1948–2050
Sources: Authors' calculation based on the following sources. For 1948–2000: Statistics Bureau, "Population Estimates of Japan 1920–2000," online: <http://www.stat.go.jp/english/data/jinsui/wagakuni/index.htm>; for 2001–2004: Statistics Bureau, "Current Population Estimates," online: <http://www.stat.go.jp/english/data/jinsui/2.htm>; for 2005–2050: National Institute of Population and Social Security Research, "Population Projections for Japan: 2001–2050," online: <http://www.ipss.go.jp/pp-newest/e/ppfj02/ppfj02.pdf> (all accessed January 17, 2007).
Note: The working-age population is defined as those aged between 15 and 64 years.

to increase through to the 1990s, the gap relative to the United States actually widened.[7] One possible explanation for the latter trend is that the wage premium for college graduates declined as economic growth decelerated in the 1980s and the supply of college graduates grew faster than the number of suitable management positions.[8] Thus, following the rapid catch-up during the high-speed growth era, human capital accumulation also slowed in subsequent decades.

While the gap in tertiary education vis-à-vis the United States suggests that there remains further room for human capital upgrading, there is little prospect that the decline in labor input will be reversed in the future. On the contrary, although there is some scope for a cyclical upturn in labor input, long-term demographic trends mean that Japan's working-age population will continue to shrink, probably at an accelerating rate (see Figure 4.2).

[7] In contrast, average schooling in primary and secondary education in Japan has continued to catch up with the United States. See Godo (2001).
[8] See Genda (1998).

In fact, the rapid aging and incipient decline of the population probably represent the most serious challenge facing the country at present, both in economic and in social terms. The implications are wide-ranging: for example, rapid population aging places growing strains on Japan's pension system and hence public finances; a population with a large share of pensioners is likely to be much less dynamic in terms of innovative and entrepreneurial energy; and the decline in the proportion of young people is bound to slow the rate at which human capital is accumulated. Thus, current population trends put a brake on Japan's potential growth rate through a variety of mechanisms, meaning that the economy as a whole is going to be much less vigorous than in the past.

Private Investment and the Excess Savings Problem

Rapid capital accumulation provided the second pillar of high-speed growth: during the period from 1956 to 1973, private investment expanded at an average annual rate of about 16 percent and in 1970, for example, accounted for 31 percent of gross domestic product (GDP). Such frenzied investment was brought to a sudden halt by the first oil shock in 1973, which was followed by a second one in 1979, and investment never regained the kind of momentum it had displayed in earlier decades. A brief exception was the bubble era during the second half of the 1980s, when private investment accelerated again, with growth rates reaching about 10 percent per year and its share in GDP leaping to 27 percent (see Figure 4.3). But by this time, of course, such heady investment rates were no longer sustainable and the economic stagnation of the 1990s to a large extent represents the necessary adjustment to the excesses of the bubble era. On average, private investment between 1992 and 2000 shrank by 0.3 percent per year, so that, by 2003, it had fallen to 19 percent of GDP.

In many respects, the contraction of investment over the past decade or so represents a belated reaction to the end of the high-speed growth era rather than simply an adjustment to the excesses of the bubble period. One way to understand the problems that have plagued the Japanese economy over the past 20 years or so is to look at the national savings–investment balance. Although Japan enjoyed an unusually high savings rate during the high-speed growth era which provided the basis for high investment rates, domestic savings nevertheless still fell short of the voracious demand for capital. The shortfall manifested itself in a chronic current account *deficit*, which turned into the chronic surplus we are accustomed to today only after the two oil shocks in the 1970s brought an end to the investment drive.

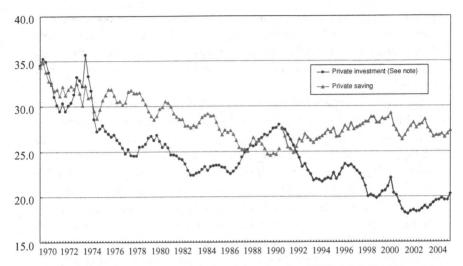

Figure 4.3. Private investment and saving as a percentage of GDP, 1970–2006Q1
Sources: "Major Economic and Financial Statistics CD-ROM, 2003 Data Published by the Bank of Japan," Tokiwa General Service, 2004; Department of National Accounts, Economic and Social Research Institute, *Annual Report on National Account 2006*; and ESRI website: <http://www.esri.cao.go.jp/en/sna/menu.html>.
Note: Private investment (including public corporations) = fixed capital formation + changes in inventories (excluding general government). Private savings = private investment + private surplus, where private surplus = net exports of goods and services + general government deficit. General government deficit and private savings in 1998 exclude the capital transfer from the general government to the nonfinancial sector, which is generated by taking over the debt from the Special Account for National Forest Service (about ¥24,163 billion), and the Japan National Railways Settlement (about ¥2,842 billion) to General Accounts. For reference, the nominal GDP for fiscal 1998 was ¥513.2 trillion (93SNA basis). Data until 91/1Q = 68SNA basis, data from 91/2Q = 93SNA basis.

The oil shocks, however, provided only the immediate trigger. Underlying the cyclical trends were long-term structural changes that were responsible for permanently lowering investment growth rates: as already seen, the 1970s were also the decade when the growth in Japan's working population started to slow, increasing labor costs and dragging down the returns on new investment. Similarly, returns on investment were lowered by the exhaustion of productivity gains ensuing from the technological catch-up with the West. As a result, Japan was beginning to reach the limits of growth based on simple capital deepening, that is, additional units of capital per worker were no longer producing commensurate increases in productivity and hence output. The cumulative effect of these trends was to significantly lower the returns on capital: whereas until the 1970s, Japan had enjoyed considerably higher returns than other Organisation for Economic Co-operation and Development (OECD) countries, the gap rapidly narrowed during this decade and by the 1980s had virtually disappeared.[9] Lower returns meant that capital accumulation in Japan was bound to slow, even without the two oil shocks.

Yet, while investment in relation to GDP fell sharply during the 1970s and early 1980s, the level of savings declined much more slowly and to a lesser extent, leading to the excess savings problem that runs like a thread through recent economic developments in Japan. The reverse side of excess savings is depressed effective demand, which in turn has contributed to the country's growing trade surplus, especially with the United States, leading to trade friction and eventually, in 1985, the Plaza Agreement, which triggered the rapid appreciation of the yen. This prompted Japan's authorities to embark on a policy of loose money that gave rise to the asset bubble and an investment boom that channeled funds into projects yielding only low returns. Once the asset bubble collapsed, many of the loans extended for asset speculation and/or for fixed capital investment turned sour, saddling banks with a mountain of nonperforming loans, which eventually led to the credit squeeze that further dampened private investment.[10] Finally, excess savings as a result of declining private investment have also been held responsible for the deflation and zero-interest liquidity trap that have been plaguing the Japanese economy since the mid-1990s.[11]

From an accounting perspective, there are basically three outlets for private savings: they can be used for private investment, lent to the government, or lent/invested abroad. As already seen, private investment contracted during the 1990s, leaving only two possible outlets for increased private savings. Of these, lending abroad also provided little room for expansion: although the U.S. current account deficit ballooned during the 1990s, a number of factors – such as the fear of renewed trade friction with the United States, yen appreciation, the relocation of production to the rest of Asia, competition from emerging Asia, and so on – put a cap on this use of Japan's excess savings.

The only remaining outlet thus consisted of lending to the government, and the government did indeed make efforts to use the excess savings to stimulate domestic demand. Unfortunately, though, the way this was done

---

[9] Pyo and Nam (1999).

[10] While talk of a credit squeeze emerged much earlier, most economists think that problems in the banking sector began to have an effect on the real economy, i.e., private investment, only in 1997–1998 (e.g., Krugman 1998; Motonishi and Yoshikawa 1999; Hayashi and Prescott 2002).

[11] See, e.g., McKinnon and Schnabl (2003) and Krugman (1998).

did little to solve the basic problem and in many respects exacerbated it. Rather than using excess savings to spur private consumption – for example, via lowering taxes or raising welfare payments – the government instead chose to increase spending on public works projects, many of which were of questionable value, such as "roads and bridges to nowhere" or local airports in thinly populated rural areas. Not only were such projects ineffective in spurring lasting demand, they also did little to raise the overall efficiency of the economy.[12]

For Japan to achieve sustainable growth, it is therefore necessary to overcome the problem of excess savings. This can be achieved by a lowering of the savings rate through a rise in consumption, by an increase in private investment, or by a combination of the two. Contrary to popular perceptions, households have indeed lowered their savings.[13] At the same time, however, savings by the corporate sector have increased, presumably because investment opportunities have been limited and firms face little pressure to pay out unused funds to shareholders. As a result, total private savings (i.e., household and corporate savings together) remained more or less unchanged during the 1990s, hovering around 10–11 percent of GDP. This suggests

[12] Of course, the extent to which alternative policies would have stimulated private consumption remains a matter of debate. Assuming that consumers anticipate that lower taxes (or higher welfare payments) now imply higher taxes (or lower welfare payments) in the future, the impact of such policies on current consumption might have been minimal. On the other hand, though, if consumers do adopt such forward-looking behavior, then the increases in government debt incurred as a result of expenditures on public construction projects would similarly lead them to curtail consumption. (Indeed, it could be argued that the weakness of private consumption during much of the past decade has at least partly been induced by the growing level of government debt.) There seems to be no reason to assume that the reaction of a forward-looking consumer to mounting government debt should differ depending on whether that debt is accumulated through public construction expenditure or lower taxes/higher welfare payments. The differences in the effects of the policies thus would depend on what the added public liabilities are spent on: construction projects chosen by the government in one case, or goods and services chosen by consumers in the other. While the former cemented existing economic structures, the latter would have contributed to structural changes already taking place.

[13] The most likely explanation for this development is demographic trends. According to the life-cycle hypothesis, people accumulate savings during their working years and draw down their savings as they retire. Thus, as the population ages and the ratio of retired to working people increases, so the household savings rate declines. This also suggests that the household savings rate is bound to decline further over the coming decade as the generation of baby boomers reaches retirement age. However, what the effect on overall savings is going to be is less clear as this also depends on future trends in the government balance. Ito and Tsuri (2003), for example, argue that although the impact of population aging on household savings is important, this will be more than offset by smaller government deficits; Japan's current accounts will thus "remain positive in the indefinite future" (Ito and Tsuri 2003: 23).

that as the economy recovers and firms invest again, Japan's savings surplus should diminish. However, any increase in investment that could fuel sustained long-run growth – and avoid the excess investment and low returns observed in the past – would have be based on an acceleration of TFP growth.

TFP and Its Importance for Future Growth

TFP is that part of economic growth that is not explained by an increase in factor inputs but rather is the result of gains in the efficiency with which these factors are used. This "residual" is typically referred to as the growth contribution made by technological progress in the broadest sense, including not only advances in technology but also changes in work organization, the accumulation of intangible assets such as management and marketing know-how, and many other factors – for example, the degree of competition in the economy – that affect the efficiency with which factors of production are employed.[14]

Looking at Japan's historical experience, it seems clear that TFP grew rapidly and made a substantial contribution to overall economic growth during the 1950s and 1960s.[15] The underlying reason, of course, is the impressive technological catch-up achieved during this period, when Japan imported technologies from abroad, primarily through license agreements with American and European companies. However, most economists would agree that the process of technological catch-up was largely exhausted by the early 1970s.[16] This was the time when Japan was emerging as an industrial powerhouse in fields such as automobiles, electronics, and precision instruments (e.g., cameras and watches), suggesting that in these sectors the technology gap had indeed largely been closed.

As a result, Japan's TFP growth performance during the following decades was less impressive – judged both against its own record and in international comparison – as the next section will show. However, the exhaustion

---

[14] In the dominant neoclassical approach, this technological progress is considered to be exogenous. New growth models attempt to open this "black box" by endogenizing technical change, i.e., explaining it within the model. While neoclassical analysis is useful in examining *what* happened to productivity growth, new growth theory can help to explain *why* it happened. See Steindel and Stiroh (2001) for an excellent introduction to the issues surrounding the productivity debate and Stiroh (2001) on the differences between neoclassical and new growth theories.

[15] See, e.g., Christensen, Cummings, and Jorgenson (1995).

[16] Note, however, that TFP trends tend to be procyclical as a result of changes in capacity utilization rates and labor hoarding. Because the drop in the TFP growth rate observed in the early 1970s coincides with the first oil shock and the subsequent recession, it is likely that estimates overstate the extent of the slowdown in TFP growth rates. On the other hand, estimates by Christensen, Cummings, and Jorgenson (1995) suggest that the slowdown had already begun in 1971, i.e., before the impact of the oil shock.

of technological catch-up opportunities represents only part of the story. Another important reason for the poor TFP performance seems to be rigidities in the economy such as regulations and other factors that have inhibited competition and the establishment of new firms that help to accelerate the adoption and spread of new technologies, business models, and products. As will be shown, TFP performance differs considerably across industries, and it is only by looking at these differences and the wider economic context that the overall weakness in Japan's TFP growth can be explained.

Before addressing these issues, however, it is useful to briefly consider why the drop in TFP growth is a serious problem for Japan. Growth in TFP yields a number of closely related benefits. First, it is an important component of overall productivity and hence economic growth. Second, while economic growth based on the accumulation of physical or human capital is subject to diminishing returns, so that increases in these inputs sooner or later will cease to yield commensurate output gains, increases in TFP raise the return to physical and human capital, thereby leading to economic growth that is sustainable in the long run. TFP growth also plays an important role in raising companies' profits, since TFP by definition is the residual that remains after the contributions of physical assets (capital costs) and labor inputs (labor costs) are subtracted from total output. And finally, TFP growth raises wages and the demand for higher educated and technologically skilled workers. This, in turn, boosts the incentive for workers to upgrade their skills. Improvements in the quality of labor spur further economic growth, thus creating a "virtuous cycle." Consequently, TPF represents the single most important engine of growth for advanced economies and is of particular significance in Japan's current circumstances, where neither labor (due to population trends) nor capital (due to low returns) can make a decisive impact on future growth.

Accounting for Japan's Growth

While the ideas underlying growth accounting and productivity measurements are straightforward, the actual measurement of the various components, and especially of TFP, are fraught with both conceptual and practical difficulties.[17] As a result, actual estimates of TFP growth often arrive at

---

[17] On a conceptual level, neoclassical growth accounting typically assumes, for example, that returns to scale are constant, while new growth theories question this assumption and allow for increasing returns to scale. Consequently, part of the TFP growth considered to be the result of technical change in neoclassical models could in fact be the result of increasing returns to scale, thus diminishing the growth contribution of technology. On a practical level, the choice of price deflators for capital inputs can have a considerable

Table 4.1. *Japan's growth performance, 1980–2004 (market sector; average annual rate of change in percent)*

	1980–1991	1991–2000	2000–2004
Output growth	4.82	1.05	0.71
Growth in total hours worked	0.47	−0.57	−0.60
Labor productivity	4.35	1.62	1.32
Contribution of labor quality	0.28	0.34	0.32
Contribution of capital deepening	2.03	1.36	0.42
Contribution of TFP	2.04	−0.08	0.58

Note: Calculated on a value-added basis.
Source: Authors' calculations based on EU KLEMS Database, online: <www.euklems.net>.

differing results, and cross-country comparisons based on a unified methodology and similar time spans used to be difficult to come by. The situation has greatly improved with the publication, in March 2007, of the EU KLEMS Database, which makes it possible to dissect Japan's growth performance between 1980 and 2004 and compare it with that of other major economies.

Looking first at the factors explaining Japan's growth performance, it is useful to divide the two-and-a-half decades for which data are available into three periods that coincide with distinct episodes in economic developments in Japan. The first period, spanning the years 1980–1991, represents an era of relatively rapid growth that includes the bubble economy during the second half of the 1990s. The second period, from 1991 to 2000, is Japan's "lost decade" with minimal growth in the wake of the collapse of the bubble economy. Although growth did not pick up until 2003, it is useful to distinguish a third period, from 2000 to 2004, to examine whether growth patterns have changed following the economic reforms of the 1990s.

Showing developments in the market sector of the economy (i.e., excluding nonmarket services, such as public administration, defense, and education), Table 4.1 shows that average annual output growth dropped sharply from 4.8 percent during 1980–1991 to 1.1 percent in 1991–2000 and then decelerated further to 0.7 percent during 2000–2004. About one percentage point of the decline in growth during the 1990s is due to the reversal in total hours worked: still rising at about half a percent a year during the 1980s,

impact on the size of the residual that is considered to represent TFP growth. Thus, there is no consensus on the "correct" measurement of TFP growth and hence the exact magnitude of its contribution to overall growth.

hours worked actually declined during the 1990s and continued to drop during the early 2000s.

However, even more important than hours worked was the slowdown in labor productivity growth: from about 4.4 percent in the 1980s, the average annual rate of increase dropped by almost three percentage points during the 1990s and registered another, albeit smaller decline during the early 2000s. Looking at the different components contributing to labor productivity growth, the contribution of increases in labor quality – that is, the upgrading of knowledge and skills – remained more or less unchanged throughout the three subperiods. However, large variations can be seen in the contributions of capital deepening and TFP.

The contribution of capital deepening slowed from about 2.0 percentage points in the 1980s to 1.4 percentage points in the 1990s and then dropped further to 0.4 percentage points in the early 2000s. This trend is very much in line with overall trends in capital investment shown in Figure 4.3, with the large increase during the bubble period and steady decline thereafter. Most interesting in the context of the present discussion, however, is the trend in the contribution of TFP, which during the 1980s, together with capital deepening, made the greatest contribution to overall growth, but then dropped substantially, from about 2.0 percentage points to become even slightly negative during the 1990s. It recovered somewhat during the early 2000s to reach 0.6 percentage points.

It should be noted that these TFP figures should be interpreted with some care because, as the "residual," TFP picks up everything that is not explicitly included in the other categories and therefore may reflect factors other than technological change in its broadest sense. An example is labor hoarding, that is, the fact that during a recession firms retain workers who work regular hours, even though they have little to do; the resulting decline in labor productivity would show up in the residual. Nevertheless, the overall trend suggested by the figures in the table seems clear: Japan's disappointing growth performance during the "lost decade" is the result of a combination of falling labor input, a deceleration in capital deepening, and a substantial decline in TFP growth. On a slightly more positive note, TFP growth appears to have picked up somewhat in the early 2000s, which could be an indication that economic reforms introduced during the preceding decade are having some effect.

Japan's economic performance in the 1990s is especially disappointing when seen against the growth achieved by other major economies, in particular, the United States and Britain (Table 4.2). Although Germany and France – economies that, similar to Japan, experienced severe structural

Table 4.2. *Japan's TFP performance in international comparison,*
1980–2004 (market sector; average annual rate of change in percent)

	Japan	USA	Germany	France	UK
Output growth					
1980–1991	4.8	2.7	2.5	2.1	2.3
1991–2000	1.0	3.9	1.6	1.9	2.7
2000–2004	0.7	2.7	1.0	2.1	3.0
Contribution of TFP growth					
1980–1991	2.0	0.6	1.4	1.3	1.4
1991–2000	−0.1	1.0	0.7	0.6	1.2
2000–2004	0.6	2.0	0.5	0.6	1.2

Note: Calculated on a value-added basis.
Source: Authors' calculations based on EU KLEMS Database, online: <www.euklems.net>.

problems and increasingly came to be seen as "sclerotic" – also registered a slowdown in economic growth, this slowdown was nowhere as severe as in Japan. All three countries also saw a substantial drop in TFP growth during this period, although again it was much more pronounced in Japan than in the two continental European countries. This experience contrasts starkly with the growth record posted by Britain and the United States: throughout the 1990s and early 2000s, overall growth was high and/or accelerated in both countries. And in contrast with Japan, TFP growth remained steady or even accelerated in both countries, providing the underpinning for long-term sustained GDP growth.

Explaining Japan's TFP Performance

Why did TFP growth in Japan stall during the 1990s? TFP is primarily a microeconomic issue that depends on factors such as the adoption and spread of technologies and best practice that in turn depend on industry structures, the degree of competition, research and development (R&D) efforts, innovative capabilities, and so on. To get to the bottom of Japan's disappointing performance, it is helpful to have a closer look at individual sectors and the factors that have inhibited TFP growth. The analysis shows that TFP performance has been quite uneven across industries and a key factor in holding back growth is the lack of competition found in a range of sectors across the economy. Yet, every cloud has a silver lining, and the good news is that if appropriate policies are put in place, Japan could embark on a catch-up in the lagging sectors that could support sustained growth for years to come.

Sectoral TFP Performance

The first aspect that stands out when examining sectoral TFP performance is that, perhaps somewhat surprisingly, the slowdown during the 1990s was more severe in manufacturing than in services. In the manufacturing sector (excluding electrical and optical equipment), TFP growth went from an annual average of 1.8 percent in the 1980s to −0.9 percent in the decade that followed, although it recovered somewhat during the early 2000s to 0.7 percent (see Figure 4.4(a)). The only two sectors in which TFP did not stagnate or decline during the 1990s were the transportation machinery industry, which saw a small increase, and the electrical and optical equipment industry, which continued to register rapid TFP growth. This pattern is very much in line with the notion that Japan has a "dual economy," consisting of a highly competitive export sector (cars, electronics, and optical equipment) and a lagging domestic sector (comprising, e.g., food processing, textiles, and paper, printing and publishing). Unfortunately for Japan, the highly competitive and productive export industries make up only a small part of the economy overall: the transportation machinery and electrical and optical equipment industries together account for only 4.5 percent of total employment, which is smaller than the share of the food and beverages, textiles, and pulp, paper, printing and publishing industries combined.

Japan's TFP performance during the 1990s was even worse in other production activities, consisting primarily of construction and agriculture. Taken together, these industries, in which one in seven Japanese are employed, experienced a contraction in TFP at an average annual rate of 2.5 percent. Again, both are very much "domestic" industries that have been sheltered from competition and, moreover, have enjoyed various forms of direct or indirect government subsidies.

Turning next to the service sector (Figure 4.4(b)), this is divided into market services and nonmarket services (e.g., public administration, defense, and education). Like the manufacturing sector, market services (excluding post and telecommunications) experienced a substantial slowdown in TFP growth during the 1990s, although it did not turn negative. Again, industries enjoying respectable TFP growth rates during this period stand side by side with industries that saw a significant deceleration. It is no surprise to find the telecommunications industry in the former group, not only because of the ongoing revolution in information and telecommunication technology (ICT), but also because of deregulation in this sector, while the TFP growth

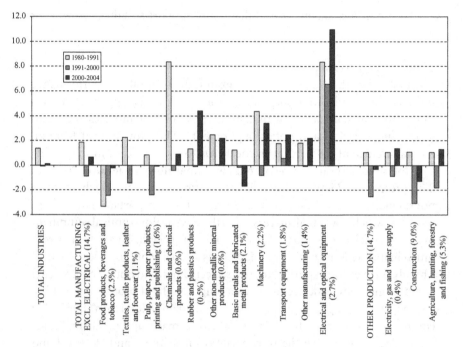

Figure 4.4(a). Average annual TFP growth by industry (total industries, manufacturing, other production)
Source: Authors' calculations based on EU KLEMS Database, online: <www.euklems. net>.
Note: Calculated on a value-added basis. Figures in parentheses show the industry's share in total employment.

in the wholesale sector may be the result of ongoing consolidation in the industry. On the other hand, TFP more or less stagnated or even declined in industries such as retail trade, transportation and storage, hotels and restaurants, and community, social, and personal services. And again, the number of persons employed in industries with stagnating or shrinking TFP is far larger than that in industries with rapid TFP growth. Finally, the financial industry saw a deceleration in the 1990s but was at the forefront of service sector TFP growth during the early 2000s, which may be a reflection of the structural change, deregulation, and inward FDI the industry experienced over the past decade or so.

What explains the diverging patterns of TFP growth? As already hinted at, an important determinant appears to be the degree to which firms in each industry are exposed to domestic and international competition. Both historically and most recently, the industries with the highest TFP growth rates in the manufacturing sector generally have also been the most

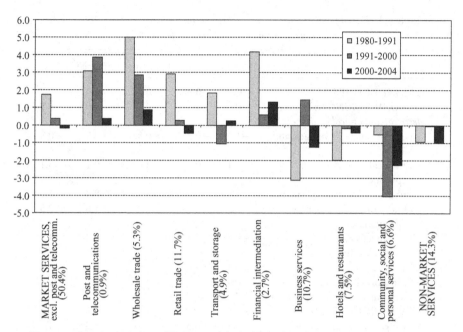

Figure 4.4(b). Average annual TFP growth by industry (market and nonmarket services)
Source: Authors' calculations based on EU KLEMS Database, online: <www.euklems.net>.
Note: Calculated on a value-added basis. Figures in parentheses show the industry's share in total employment.

export-oriented ones (such as electrical and optical equipment, transportation machinery, and, with the exception of the 1990s, other machinery). In the service sector, the industries that experienced continued TFP growth throughout the past two-and-a half decades – telecommunications, finance, and wholesale – have been at the center of deregulation efforts, have seen considerable industry consolidation, and have been increasingly exposed to competition, partly as a result of inward FDI.[18] In contrast, industries with the worst TFP performance, such as food processing, textiles, paper, printing and publishing, construction, and community, social and personal services, are those that serve primarily the domestic market, are often heavily regulated, and have seen little FDI.

Finally, it is instructive to compare sectoral TFP growth rates across the five major advanced economies (Table 4.3). To begin with, looking at TFP growth for the economy overall (i.e., this time including nonmarket services) during

---

[18] Details of liberalization measures and industry dynamics can be found in Chapters 3 and 6.

Foreign Direct Investment in Japan

Table 4.3. *International comparison of TFP performance by sector, 1991–2004*
(average annual rate of change in percent)

	Japan	USA	Germany	France	UK
TOTAL INDUSTRIES	**0.0**	**0.8**	**0.7**	**0.4**	**0.7**
MANUFACTURING (excluding electrical and optical equipment)	*−0.6*	*1.0*	*1.2*	*1.9*	*0.9*
Food products, beverages, and tobacco	−1.7	−0.2	−0.8	−0.5	−0.3
Chemicals and chemical products	0.3	0.9	4.6	0.1	3.1
Rubber and plastics products	0.6	3.0	1.2	8.8	1.0
Other nonmetallic mineral products	0.5	1.5	2.2	1.6	2.5
Basic metals and fabricated metal products	−1.2	2.6	1.5	0.4	1.3
Machinery	0.4	2.0	0.9	4.1	1.1
Transport equipment	0.9	2.4	1.1	1.8	2.1
Electrical and optical equipment	*7.4*	*10.5*	*3.2*	*6.1*	*3.7*
OTHER PRODUCTION	*−1.9*	*−0.2*	*0.3*	*0.4*	*1.8*
Electricity, gas, and water supply	−0.2	0.3	2.1	3.3	1.5
Construction	−2.5	−3.3	−0.7	−1.0	1.5
Agriculture, hunting, forestry, and fishing	−1.2	3.8	5.6	3.0	2.2
MARKET SERVICES (excluding post and telecommunications)	*0.3*	*1.0*	*−0.5*	*−0.5*	*0.7*
Wholesale trade	2.4	1.9	2.0	2.6	1.4
Retail trade	0.2	2.7	1.4	0.3	1.0
Transport and storage	−0.7	1.1	3.0	0.3	1.6
Financial intermediation	0.9	2.5	−0.3	−0.3	1.8
Business services	0.6	−0.8	−3.2	−2.2	0.1
Hotels and restaurants	−0.2	0.1	−0.6	−1.5	−0.7
Other community, social and personal services	−3.5	−0.4	−0.9	0.7	−0.9
Post and telecommunications	*3.1*	*0.4*	*5.5*	*5.3*	*5.6*
NONMARKET SERVICES	*−0.3*	*−0.2*	*1.1*	*0.3*	*−0.7*

Note: Calculated on a value-added basis.
Source: Authors' calculations based on EU KLEMS Database, online: <www.euklems.net>.

the period 1991–2004 confirms Japan's disappointing TFP performance. The greatest differences with the other countries emerge in terms of Japan's TFP growth in the manufacturing sector (excluding electrical and optical equipment), where Japan generally lagged behind the Western countries in all industries, and other production activities (utilities, construction, and agriculture). In contrast, in market services, Germany's and France's performance was even worse than Japan's, which nevertheless trailed that of the United States and Britain. Areas in which Japan's TFP performance especially lagged behind that of the two Anglo-Saxon economies are retail trade, transport and storage, and financial intermediation. On the other hand, Japan led these two countries or was on par with them in TFP growth in wholesale trade and post and telecommunications.

The upshot of the low TFP growth overall is that Japan's labor productivity – that is, the amount of output generated by a unit of labor input – has fallen considerably behind that of comparable countries. Although Japan does boast a number of highly competitive export industries, where, according to one estimate, labor productivity is about 20 percent higher than the average productivity level in the United States, these account for only 10 percent of Japanese employment.[19] The remaining 90 percent of the workforce, in contrast, are employed in domestic manufacturing and services, where productivity is only 63 percent of the level recorded in the United States. As a result of this "dual structure," where highly competitive export industries operate alongside uncompetitive domestic manufacturing and service industries, overall labor productivity in the Japanese economy is only 69 percent of the U.S. level.[20]

Explaining Low Productivity

The dual structure of the Japanese economy is not a particularly new phenomenon. In fact, it has existed throughout the postwar period; but while the Japanese economy was still performing strongly, the low productivity of the domestic sector did not seem to matter much as long as the prowess of the export industries was raising living standards overall. However, since the economy stalled in the early 1990s, raising productivity in the domestic sectors has become a key factor in restoring sustainable growth in Japan, especially because even showcase export-oriented industries succumbed to faltering growth rates and/or moved production overseas.

Reasons for the low productivity in many of the domestic industries are not difficult to find. First, by definition, domestic industries have been sheltered to varying degrees from international competition. In the food-processing industry, for example, few Japanese firms export overseas,

---

[19] McKinsey Global Institute (2000).
[20] Also see Fukao and Miyagawa (2007) for an international comparison of productivity levels.

imports are frequently stifled by tariff barriers, and exposure to global best practice is limited as food giants such as Nestlé have been confined to niche markets.[21] Exposure to international competition and best practice is also limited or nonexistent in the service sector. For example, in the construction and civil engineering, the retail, and the wholesale sectors, combined purchases from abroad and from foreign firms operating in Japan accounted for only 0.5 to 4.9 percent of overall sales in these sectors. In contrast, the corresponding figures for the United States range from 3.0 to 17.8 percent.[22]

The second reason for the low productivity of the domestic sectors is the low degree of competition more generally, of which the lack of foreign competition is only one manifestation. In many of these sectors, few companies enter or exit the market, and the market shares of the leading companies remain comparatively stable over the years. Regulatory policies typically play a large role in blunting competition, leading to subscale operators and weak product offerings. A widely cited example is that of the retail sector, where the Large Scale Retail (Location) Law has limited the entry of large-scale retailers and protected traditional family-owned stores with only two or three employees.[23] As a result, the latter still account for 55 percent of retail employment, compared with 19 percent in the United States and 26 percent in France. The fragmentation of the retail sector, in turn, has been blamed as one of the factors holding back the food-processing industry, which, in the absence of national markets for many of its products, has seen little pressure to consolidate and increase the scale of operations. As a result, labor productivity in these two sectors, which together account for approximately 10 percent of GDP and 14 percent of the workforce in Japan, is dismal: in the retail sector, it is estimated to be only half of the U.S. level, and in the food-processing industry it is little more than a third.[24]

Further examples abound of sectors where government regulations either directly inhibit competition or fail to provide the necessary framework to stimulate it. While health care is a domestic sector in all countries, most other advanced economies allow at least some degree of competition in the markets for health insurance (i.e., between consumers and payers) and health

[21] McKinsey Global Institute (2000).
[22] Fukao and Ito (2003).
[23] McKinsey Global Institute (2000); Høj and Wise (2004). However, it should be noted that not all observers are disparaging of Japan's high retail density. Flath (2003), for example, offers several good economic reasons for the proliferation of retail outlets, although he, too, stresses the distorting effects of regulations limiting large-scale retail stores.
[24] McKinsey Global Institute (2000).

care provision (between payers and providers and between consumers and providers). In Japan, competition is banned by law with the exception of the market between consumers and providers (i.e., clinics and hospitals), which, however, is distorted by government subsidies.[25] Government policies have also thwarted competition in the energy sector. In the electricity market, for example, at present no direct competition between utilities exists, though deregulation measures are now under way.[26] The list of sectors in which government policies have been blamed for either stunting or failing to foster competition continues, including residential construction, professional services, energy, and transportation, demonstrating the pervasiveness of the problem.[27]

What is more, the output of many of these sectors serves as an input for other sectors, meaning that low-productivity industries hold back the competitive parts of the economy. Thus, while labor costs certainly are one major factor why Japanese manufacturing firms have transferred production capacity overseas, the high overhead costs in Japan are another. These range from high transportation costs – important especially in the assembly industries which rely on just-in-time delivery – to high energy prices.[28] To provide one last example: in 2002 (the latest year for which comparable international figures are available), electricity prices for industrial users in Japan were twice the OECD average.[29]

---

[25] McKinsey Global Institute (2000).
[26] First steps toward liberalization in the sector have already been taken, allowing, for example, manufacturers to generate electricity on-site. However, as the industry continues to be dominated by vertically integrated utilities controlling generation, transmission, distribution, and retail supply and enjoying near monopolies in their respective regions, no genuine competition between different suppliers in the various segments has so far arisen. See Høj and Wise (2004).
[27] McKinsey Global Institute (2000); Høj and Wise (2004).
[28] According to Ministry of Economy, Trade and Industry (METI) (2000: 18), Japanese overseas affiliates' labor costs in relation to sales in Europe were less than 70 per cent of those in Japan, and in Asia only 40 per cent. But what is more, in all major areas (i.e., North America, Asia, and Europe) transportation costs and R&D costs to sales were half of those in Japan or less.
[29] International Energy Agency, *Energy Prices & Taxes*, 3rd Quarter 2006. Whereas industrial users in Japan paid 11.5 US cents/kWh, the OECD average was 6.0 cents. Electricity prices in major competitor countries were even lower at 4.8 cents in the United States (excluding taxes, however), 4.9 cents in Germany, 3.7 cents in France, and 5.2 cents in the United Kingdom (all figures for 2002). Of course, there are other factors, apart from industry efficiency, that determine electricity price levels. Such factors may include the mix of energy sources (nuclear, coal, oil, etc.), import duties on fuels, and other government policies. However, it seems unlikely that these factors alone account for the substantially higher electricity prices in Japan.

The third major reason for Japan's disappointing productivity performance is the low "metabolism" of the economy. This may be defined as the
pace with which successful companies enjoying high productivity growth
expand their market share, new firms enter the market, and uncompetitive
existing firms exit. The dynamics driving productivity growth in a particular
industry (or the economy as a whole) can be separated into five mechanisms
or "effects":

(1) the *within effect,* which occurs when increases in productivity within
    individual companies raise the productivity of the sector as a whole;
(2) the *between effect,* which results when companies with above-average
    productivity levels increase their market share, thus raising the overall
    level of that industry's productivity;
(3) the *covariance effect,* which occurs when companies with increasing
    productivity at the same time also raise their market share;
(4) the *entry effect,* which occurs when firms with a productivity level
    that is higher than the industry average enter the market; and
(5) the *exit effect,* which refers to the rise in the average productivity level
    of an industry resulting from the exit of firms with below-average
    productivity.

One indication of the low "metabolism" is that the market shares of leading
companies in many Japanese sectors have remained relatively unchanged
over the years. Looking, for example, at the retail market, little change
occurred in the ranking of the top ten competitors in Japan over the fifteen-
year period from 1983 to 1998 (Table 4.4). Four of the top five retailers were
the same in 1998 as in 1983, and only one company that was among the top
ten in 1998 had not already been so in 1983. Compare this with the United
States, where in the shorter period 1983–1993, the ranking changed quite
dramatically. The top spot in 1993 was taken by a company (Wal-Mart) that
had ranked only seventeenth ten years before, and two of the top ten had not
been ranked at all in 1983. One possible interpretation of the stable market
shares in Japan is that productivity growth must have been quite uniform
across competitors. A more plausible explanation, however, is that more
productive firms have found it difficult to expand market share and/or less
productive ones have been able to hold on to theirs. In either case, the likely
reason is a lack of competition as a result of regulatory or structural features
of the economy.

Stable market shares, moreover, are an indication of another, related
problem: the low start-up rate of new businesses. Defined as the number of

Table 4.4. *Ranking of top retailers in Japan and the United States*

Japan			United States		
1983	1998		1983	1993	
1	1	Daiei	17	1	Wal-Mart Stores
2	2	Ito-Yokado	1	2	Sears Roebuck
4	3	Jusco	2	3	K-Mart
5	4	Mycal	12	4	Dayton Hudson
7	5	Takashimaya	5	5	J. C. Penney
3	6	Seiyu	–	6	Home Depot
10	7	Uni	4	7	Kroger
6	8	Mitsukoshi	3	8	Safeway
9	9	Seibu	–	9	Costco
13	10	Marui	9	10	American Stores

Source: McKinsey Global Institute (2000).

new establishments divided by the number of existing ones, Japan's start-up rate has experienced a steady decline since the early postwar period,[30] so that by the early 1990s, at about 4 percent, it was less than half of the roughly 10 percent registered not only in the United States, but also in the European Union.[31] The gap between Japan and the United States widened even further during the 1990s, while the gap in exit rates (similarly defined as the number of closed establishments divided by the number of existing ones) was about equally as great (Figure 4.5). The low rate of entry and exit of companies matters because it determines the speed with which healthy, successful businesses are separated from ailing ones, and hence the overall competitiveness and productivity of an industry and of the economy overall.

The problem of low and falling start-up rates is most pronounced in the manufacturing sector, where from previously 6 percent they gradually declined to 3 percent during the 1970s and 1980s and then dropped further to less than 2 percent during the 1990s. This decline provides one important reason why TFP growth in this sector stalled during the 1990s. Empirical examination of TFP growth in the Japanese manufacturing sector using plant-level data for the period 1981–2003 in terms of the five mechanisms

---

[30] Japan Small Business Research Institute (2003: 87, Figure 2–2–6).
[31] Executive summary of the 4th Report of the European Observatory for SMEs (Figure 3), online: <http://europa.eu.int/comm/enterprise/enterprise_policy/analysis/doc/eurob4en.pdf> (accessed January 22, 2007).

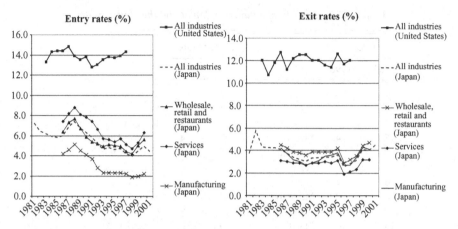

Figure 4.5. Entry and exit rates in the United States and Japan
Source: Fukao, Inui, Kawai and Miyagawa (2004).

outlined above shows that although the entry effect on TFP growth was indeed positive, its overall impact was in fact very small because the rate of new entries was so low.[32] What is more, the exit effect – which normally raises average productivity because of the exit of nonproductive firms or plants – was actually negative, suggesting that nonproductive firms/plants were staying in the market, while those with higher productivity were exiting – a trend possibly explained by the relocation of production overseas. However, the most important factor was the decline in the within effect, that is, the slow-down in TFP growth within firms, almost certainly as a result of the low start-up rate during the 1990s.

Though this is unlikely to be only the reason, one important factor contributing to the declining start-up rate and the negative exit effect seems to have been the problems in the banking sector. Saddled with huge amounts of nonperforming loans, banks have been reluctant to extend loans to new start-ups, while at the same time keeping uncompetitive firms afloat. Given the lack of alternative sources of finance, such as American-style venture capital firms, potential entrepreneurs in Japan thus faced large difficulties in obtaining the funding necessary to set up new businesses.

In sum, it seems that productivity growth in Japan has been impeded by three major factors: the low or nonexistent exposure to international competition in many sectors of the economy; insufficient domestic competition, often in the same "sheltered" sectors; and the low start-up rate of new

---

[32] The examination of the different effects can be found in Fukao, Kim, and Kwon (2006).

businesses. As a result, productivity growth has considerably lagged behind that in other countries, especially the United States. But this productivity gap also holds a promise: if Japan were able to unleash competitive forces in the lagging sectors, it could embark on a second catch-up, this time in the domestic sectors of the economy, that could be the source of a sustained growth spurt for years to come.

Raising Japan's Long-Term Rate of Growth

Having outlined the reasons for Japan's disappointing growth performance in recent years, it is now possible to address what role FDI can play in raising the country's long-term rate of growth. It was suggested that, given current population trends and low returns on capital, growth prospects crucially hinge on the ability to raise TFP growth. Moreover, it was argued that what is holding back TFP growth is a lack of competition and exposure to global best practice. The obvious way to raise TFP growth thus is to deregulate and to encourage more domestic and international competition. This, in fact, is what the Japanese government has started to do, for example, by liberalizing the financial and telecommunications sectors and by encouraging FDI. Although many observers think that Japan's deregulation record is mixed at best, the sectoral TFP estimates reported earlier suggest that, where the government did deregulate, the results were clearly discernible.[33]

The gains that could be achieved if Japan embarked on comprehensive deregulation are large. Studies trying to quantify the potential gain arrive at GDP increases of between 2.3 and 18.7 percent, with the OECD, Ministry of International Trade and Industry (MITI), and the Economic Planning Agency (EPA) all putting the figure at about 6 percent.[34] And McKinsey Global Institute (2000) estimates that if barriers to competition are removed, productivity can grow by 4.7 percent a year and per capita GDP by 4.0 percent a year for a period of ten years. The EPA (1998) study is particularly revealing, because it shows how half of the productivity increase in telecoms and aviation during the period 1987–1995 resulted from increased competition following the entry of a single new competitor in each industry.

FDI could contribute to an acceleration of growth in broadly two ways. The first is simply by creating or increasing competition in sectors that

---

[33] For a brief assessment of Japan's deregulation program, see, e.g., Bergsten, Ito, and Noland (2001).

[34] The studies are reported in IMF (1998b: 161).

so far have seen little of it. In this context, the relative productivity level of foreign competitors would be of secondary importance – what matters is the erosion of monopoly rents. The second way in which foreign firms could contribute is through higher productivity. If foreign firms indeed enjoy higher TFP levels and growth than their Japanese counterparts, then the entry of foreign firms would contribute to a rise in overall productivity in Japan. Whether this is the case is the subject of Chapter 5.

FIVE

The Performance of Foreign Firms and
the Macroeconomic Impact of Foreign
Direct Investment

Firms wishing to do business in another country face a variety of challenges they need to overcome if they are to be successful. Operating away from home means having to contend with a foreign legal and political framework, adjusting to a different culture, building new business networks, and so on. All of these factors put foreign firms at a disadvantage vis-à-vis established domestic rivals. Thus, in order to flourish, multinational corporations need to possess firm-specific advantages that more than compensate for the disadvantages of operating in a foreign environment. Economic theory therefore considers foreign direct investment (FDI) as a form of long-term capital movement that is accompanied by investors' intangible assets. Examples of such intangible assets include firms' managerial capabilities, technological knowledge accumulated through research and development (R&D), and marketing know-how based on past advertising activity. Moreover, because of these intangible assets, affiliates owned by foreign firms are expected to enjoy higher total factor productivity (TFP) and profit rates than the average firm in the host country. If this is indeed the case, then FDI should help to lift productivity in the economy overall and contribute to economic welfare through higher growth and wages.

The aim of this chapter is to explore the impact of FDI on the Japanese economy by examining these issues in greater detail. In particular, the analysis looks at whether the affiliates of foreign firms in Japan are indeed more productive than their domestic counterparts and, because the evidence suggests that they are, the extent to which this higher productivity represents the result of TFP-enhancing transfers of intangible assets. Because the majority of FDI cases consists of mergers and acquisitions (M&As), the analysis concentrates on the performance of Japanese firms acquired by foreigners. It will be suggested that such firms indeed enjoy considerably higher TFP levels than their domestic counterparts and slightly higher TFP growth. However,

111

at least in part, this result can be explained by the fact that foreigners tend to acquire Japanese firms that are already more productive than the average firm to begin with. Nevertheless, the empirical evidence suggests that acquisition by a foreign firm does help to lift the TFP growth of the acquisition target.

The second task of this chapter is to consider the macroeconomic impact of FDI in Japan. This is obviously not an easy task given that FDI impinges on the host economy in many different ways, most of which are difficult to quantify. The focus here, therefore, is on the most immediate effect of FDI, namely the effect on the productivity growth of acquired firms and the macroeconomic ramifications. Specifically, based on a standard general equilibrium model of the economy, various scenarios taking into account the empirical evidence on TFP growth induced by inward FDI and government goals for FDI are considered. However, rather than aiming to provide accurate estimates of the macroeconomic impact of FDI, the purpose of these calculations is to gain an overall impression of the magnitude of the effects under various assumptions. The calculations suggest that the growth contribution of FDI ranges from small, though not negligible, under a conservative scenario, to quite substantial under a more progressive, though possibly overly optimistic scenario.

However, it is crucial to note that the higher TFP growth of foreign-affiliated firms represents only one channel through which FDI affects productivity growth in the host economy. Also important are the effects on domestic firms' productivity through, for example, technological spillovers (i.e., the diffusion of knowledge and technology introduced by foreign multinationals) and the impact of greater competition on market structure and performance. Moreover, FDI may raise social welfare through the introduction of goods and services previously unavailable to consumers in the host country. Especially in the case of services, many of which cannot be traded, FDI represents the only way in which domestic firms are exposed to international competition, and customers can benefit from products offered by foreign firms. Unfortunately, so far, these other effects have either not been examined empirically in a rigorous fashion or they are difficult to quantify. Yet, they are clearly important, and Chapter 6, through a series of industry case studies, will show that, although difficult to measure, such effects can certainly be discerned.

Does Inward FDI Raise Japan's TFP?

Concerning the potential benefits of inward FDI for the host economy, it has frequently been claimed that such investment, and especially green-field investment, generates new employment. It has also been argued that export-oriented firms help to improve the host country's current account balance. However, it is important to note that such arguments are based on a partial equilibrium approach and do not take account of second-order effects throughout the economy. For example, the increased competition from foreign firms may also lead to a reduction of employment at domestic firms. Moreover, exports by foreign firms may lead to an appreciation of the host country's currency and therefore potentially do not help to improve its current account balance. Ultimately, the current account balance of an economy with free international capital flows is determined by the saving–investment balance.

From such a general equilibrium point of view, probably the most important host country benefit from inward FDI is the improvement in productivity brought about by the inflow of intangible assets. Therefore, a key question with regard to FDI, and one that has attracted considerable research interest, is whether foreign-affiliated firms are more productive than domestic ones. A number of studies, on a variety of countries, have been able to show that this indeed tends to be a case;[1] however, such studies also show that the higher labor productivity is typically the result of the greater capital intensity of foreign firms when compared with their domestic counterparts, and TFP analyses suggest that foreign firms' productivity is not necessarily higher if differences in capital intensity are taken into account.[2] These results indicate that, when comparing productivity, it is important to determine the source of any differences before it can be ascertained that foreign firms indeed contribute to TFP growth in the host country. The following sections, relying largely on an empirical investigation by Fukao, Ito, and Kwon (2005), carefully examine the empirical evidence on the relationship between foreign ownership and TFP in Japan.

Comparing the Performance of Foreign and Domestic Firms in Japan

The study by Fukao, Ito, and Kwon (2005) is based on the firm-level panel data underlying the *Basic Survey of Japanese Business Structure and Activities* conducted by the Ministry of Economy, Trade and Industry (METI). This survey provides the most comprehensive annual data on companies

---

[1] Examples include Blomström and Sjöholm (1998) on Indonesia and Griffith and Simpson (2001) on Britain. In their study on the United States, Doms and Jensen (1998) found that U.S. multinational plants had the highest labor productivity, followed by foreign-owned establishments, whereas U.S.-owned nonmultinational plants had the lowest labor productivity.

[2] Studies coming to this conclusion include Ito (2004b) on Indonesia, Ramstetter (2001, 2002) and Ito (2002, 2004a) on Thailand, and Globerman, Ries, and Vertinsky (1994) on Canada.

in Japan, covering all firms with at least 50 employees and ¥30 million of paid-in capital in the manufacturing and mining sectors and several service industries. Unfortunately, however, until around 2000, the coverage of services in the survey was very limited, and important sectors such as banking and insurance and telecommunication still are not included.[3] The study therefore concentrates only on the manufacturing sector – a point that is significant for the discussion later on. Finally, it should be noted that the data cover the years 1994–2000 (1994–2001 in the case of the analysis on M&As),[4] that is, the period during which the surge in FDI in Japan occurred is included only in part.

In the survey, firms were asked what percentage of their paid-in capital was owned by foreigners and whether they had a foreign parent owning more than 50 percent of the firm. Based on this information, the study determined whether a firm was foreign-owned using two definitions of foreign-owned firms: (*a*) a broad definition, where one or several foreigners own 33.4 percent or more of the firm's paid-in capital in total; and (*b*) a narrow definition, where foreign-owned firms are those majority-owned by a single foreign firm. The results reported here principally refer to the narrow definition.[5]

A brief look at the data thus obtained shows how the presence of foreign-owned firms in Japan's manufacturing sector increased during the period 1994–2000 (Table 5.1). Their number grew from 195 in 1994 to 236 in 2000, with 62 exiting and 73 newly entering during this period. In addition, 61 firms that were domestically-owned in 1994 had become foreign-owned by 2000. These firms are regarded as having been acquired by foreign firms. Moreover, during the observation period, the sales of foreign-owned firms nearly doubled from ¥12.2 trillion to ¥23.7 trillion. This increase was mainly due to the 61 M&As, whose sales amounted to ¥14.1 trillion in 2000, which is greater than the total increase in foreign-owned firms' sales of ¥11.5 trillion from 1994 to 2000.

[3] In the service sector, the survey initially covered only retail and wholesale trade. Eating and drinking establishments were added in the 1998 edition. Further industries, including electric, gas and water supply, information services, credit card and loan businesses, etc., were added in subsequent years. Thus, although the coverage is improving, the data available still are insufficient for rigorous empirical analysis.

[4] After some screening of the data, Fukao, Ito, and Kwon's (2005) panel dataset consists of a total of 93,880 observations.

[5] The reason is that there are several Japanese firms where more than a third of issued stocks are owned by foreign institutional investors as portfolio investment; therefore, there is a risk that the broad definition includes such firms.

Table 5.1. *Entry and exit of domestic and foreign firms in the manufacturing sector*

	Number of firms (figures in parentheses are total sales in ¥ billion)					
	1994			2000		
Manufacturing	Total firms	Other firms	33.4% or more foreign-owned	Total firms	Other firms	33.4% or more foreign-owned
Total	13,731 (250,000)	13,536 (238,000)	195 (12,200)	13,486 (265,000)	13,250 (241,000)	236 (23,700)
Firms that exited between 1994 and 2000	4,207 (34,044)					
Breakdown of firms that exited		4,145 (31,900)	62 (2,124)			
Firms that entered between 1994 and 2000				3,962 (32,300)		
Breakdown of firms that entered					3,889 (31,000)	73 (1,221)
Firms that stayed between 1994 and 2000	9,524 (216,000)			9,524 (233,000)		
Breakdown of firms that stayed						
Stayed domestically-owned		9,330 (192,200)			9,330 (205,700)	
Stayed foreign-owned			102 (6,785)			102 (8,285)
Changed from domestically-owned to foreign-owned		61 (13,800)				61 (14,100)
Changed from foreign-owned to domestically-owned			31 (3,215)		31 (4,300)	

Source: Fukao, Ito, and Kwon (2005).

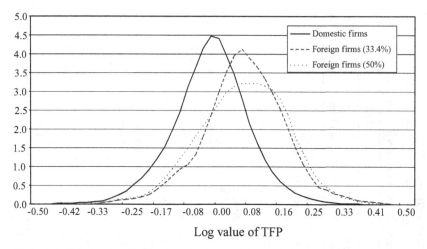

Figure 5.1. TFP density distribution: Foreign and domestic firms
Source: Fukao, Ito, and Kwon (2005).
Note: The figure shows kernel density estimates for the TFP level of foreign and domestic firms. The number of observations is 93,880. "Foreign firms (33.4%)" refers to firms with 33.4 percent or more foreign ownership. "Foreign firms (50%)" refers to firms majority-owned by a single foreign firm.

Comparing foreign-owned firms (foreign firms) and domestically-owned firms (domestic firms) confirms that the former tend to show considerably better performance than the latter. For example, with regard to TFP, foreign firms on average display higher levels than their domestic counterparts, as shown in Figure 5.1, which depicts the histograms of foreign and domestic firms' TFP.[6] However, the distributions are based on pooled data for the entire observation period and determinants of the TFP level other than foreign ownership are not taken into account. It is possible, therefore, that the results of the TFP comparison are biased.[7]

---

[6] TFP in the Fukao, Ito, and Kwon (2005) study is calculated using the methodology developed by Good, Nadiri, and Sickles (1997). Moreover, while several recent studies conducting macroeconomic growth accounting exercises have tried to isolate intangible assets from TFP growth and treat them as a factor input (e.g., Corrado, Hulten, and Sichel, 2005, 2006), Fukao, Ito, and Kwon (2005) take the more traditional approach of not treating intangible assets as factor inputs, because it is very difficult to measure the accumulation of some types of assets at the firm level. TFP therefore includes the contribution of intangible assets.

[7] For example, suppose that the average TFP level grows over time and the presence of foreign firms is also on the rise. In that case, since observations for foreign firms are concentrated in the latter part of the observation period when the average TFP level is higher, in pooled data for the entire period, foreign firms will display higher average TFP than domestic firms even when there is no gap in TFP in any particular year.

To avoid this kind of bias, Fukao, Ito, and Kwon (2005) conducted a regression analysis, in which firms' performance is regressed on the foreign-ownership dummy and other firm characteristics. As a first step, only industry and year dummies were used. The main results (using the narrow definition of foreign ownership) of their regression analysis were as follows:

(1) Foreign firms' TFP is about 8 percent higher and their current profit/sales ratio is 1.5 percentage points higher.
(2) Foreign firms enjoy slightly higher TFP growth.
(3) Foreign firms spend proportionately more on R&D per worker. They also have a significantly higher capital/labor ratio. Probably for this reason, as well as their higher TFP level, the labor productivity of foreign firms is higher than that of domestic firms.
(4) There is no significant difference between foreign and domestic firms in the growth rates of real sales and employment, but foreign firms show a significantly lower growth rate of tangible assets.
(5) Average annual wages per employee are ¥1.28 million higher at foreign than domestic firms.

As indicated, foreign firms tend to conduct more R&D and pay higher wage rates. Their TFP level also tends to be significantly higher than that of domestic firms. However, it is possible that the higher TFP level is the result not of the transfer of managerial resources, knowledge, and so on, from their parent firm overseas, but of their own R&D activities or the (potentially) higher quality of their labor force. To find out which of the two possible explanations is correct, the study also empirically examined the determinants of each firm's TFP level and TFP growth rate. The results suggest that, again, foreign firms display a TFP level that is about 5 percent higher than that of Japanese firms, even after controlling for other factors such as R&D intensity, the percentage of nonproduction workers, the number of years since the firm was established, and firm size (sales) in addition to industry differences and the observation year. When firm dummies are added to the regression model, however, the gap between the TFP level of foreign and domestic firms becomes insignificant, suggesting that the strong correlation between foreign ownership and the TFP level may at least in part be the result of the initially higher TFP level of the firms later acquired by foreigners. Finally, foreign firms also enjoy TFP growth that is 1.4–1.8 percentage points higher than that of domestic firms even after controlling for other factors. Yet, this positive correlation between foreign ownership and the TFP growth rate again becomes insignificant in the fixed-effect models with firm dummies.

Summing up, the comparison between foreign and domestic firms shows that the former had a 5 percent higher TFP level (when controlling for other determinants) as well as higher returns on capital. Moreover, they displayed a higher capital/labor ratio and R&D investment per worker. They also enjoyed a higher TFP growth rate. Probably reflecting the higher levels of capital intensity and technology, foreign companies showed higher labor productivity and wage rates as well, but in the fixed-effect models, no significant positive correlation between foreign ownership and the TFP level or growth rate was found.

M&As and Target Firm Performance

The analysis in the preceding section suggests that there are two possible explanations for the positive correlation between foreign ownership and productivity. The first is that Japanese firms acquired by foreigners benefit from the technologies and managerial resources of their new foreign owners and this transfer of intangible assets boosts their TFP. This mechanism may be called the "technology-transfer effect." The alternative explanation is that foreign firms enjoy greater productivity because foreigners choose firms as M&A targets that already possess higher TFP to begin with. This mechanism can be labeled the "selection effect." Fukao, Ito, and Kwon examine these two possibilities by estimating a probit model that explains whether a firm is chosen as an M&A target based on its TFP performance and other characteristics. In a second step, they then test whether target firms' TFP improved after the acquisition. To determine whether the results obtained are unique to acquisitions by foreign firms or possibly characteristic of M&As more generally, out–in M&As are compared with in–in M&As (M&As involving only domestic firms).

Again using the narrow definition of foreign ownership and the same data as above, but for the period 1994–2001, Fukao, Ito, and Kwon identified 67 cases of out–in and 1,362 cases of in–in M&As.[8] Their estimation arrives at several interesting results. The first is that foreigners indeed tend to choose Japanese firms with above-average performance as acquisition targets as measured in terms of the TFP level and profit rates; they also tend to choose larger firms. In contrast, acquisition targets in in–in M&As tend to display lower profit rates, have greater liabilities, and tend to be smaller.

---

[8] In–in M&As are defined as cases where a firm that did not previously have a parent firm with majority ownership subsequently comes to have a domestic parent firm with majority ownership. For further details on the estimation methodology, see Fukao, Ito, and Kwon (2005).

Second, in the case of both out-in and in-in M&As, target firms' TFP growth rate prior to the acquisition is not a significant determinant of their being selected.

These results imply that foreign firms acquire Japanese firms that already show a better performance at the time of acquisition. It thus seems that at least part of the higher TFP of foreign firms is the result of the selection effect. In contrast, in-in M&As tend to display characteristics of rescue missions. One possible explanation is that in-in M&As in Japan are mainly conducted within vertical and horizontal *keiretsu* networks and financially distressed small firms are salvaged by other member firms through M&As.

The second step of Fukao, Ito, and Kwon's analysis is to examine whether M&As improve target firms' performance. Unfortunately, the data available cover only a relatively short period, so that they can only examine the effect on target firms' performance two and three years after the acquisition – a period that may be too short for the performance-improving effects of technology and managerial resource transfers from parent firms to have any substantial impact on target firms' performance. Nevertheless, the regression results indicate that within that relatively short period of two to three years, out-in M&As improve target firms' TFP level by about 2 percent, an increase that is considerably greater than in the case of in-in M&As (where it is only 0.4 percent after two years and about 1 percent after three years). In addition, during this period, target firms acquired by foreign firms also experience a significant improvement in the current profit/sales ratio, whereas in-in M&A targets experience no such improvement. There are also notable differences in the impact on target firms' employment: although in-in M&As have a positive effect on employment two years after the acquisition, there is no significant effect on employment in the case of out-in M&As.

Summary

In sum, the empirical evidence suggests that foreign firms in Japan indeed show a better performance than their domestically-owned counterparts in terms of a number of indicators. Estimation results indicate that foreign firms' TFP level was about 5 percent higher than that of domestic firms, and their TFP growth rate was about 1.4–1.8 percent faster. They also enjoyed higher earnings and returns on capital and displayed a higher capital/labor ratio and higher R&D intensity. Reflecting their higher TFP and labor-saving production patterns, foreign-owned companies showed higher labor productivity and wage rates as well.

However, at least to some extent, the better performance reflects the fact that foreigners tend to choose acquisition targets that already are more productive and profitable than the average Japanese firm to begin with. But the evidence also suggests that acquisitions by foreigners improve target firms' TFP level and current profit/sales ratio. Moreover, the improvement of target firms' TFP level was found to be larger and quicker than in the case of in-in M&As. Overall, therefore, both the selection effect and the technology-transfer effect appear to play a role in explaining the positive correlation between foreign ownership and productivity. The transfer of intangible assets from foreign firms to M&A takeover targets represents one important avenue by which FDI can help to raise productivity and growth in Japan, and the evidence presented here shows that such transfers are indeed taking place.

The Macroeconomic Impact of Inward FDI

Although the evidence suggests that FDI and the accompanying transfer of intangible assets contribute to productivity growth and hence to Japan's economic performance, it would also be instructive to know how large this contribution (potentially) is. Ideally, therefore, one would try to empirically examine the impact that the inflows of FDI in recent years has had on economic growth and a variety of other macroeconomic indicators. Unfortunately, such an attempt would run into a number of practical difficulties, ranging from a lack of necessary data to problems of how to measure the effects of FDI.[9] Moreover, since despite the increase since the turn of the millennium, FDI inflows relative to the size of Japan's economy have been small, any impact would probably be very difficult to detect.

Therefore, rather than taking such an empirical approach, this section tries to simulate the macroeconomic impact of FDI by using the TFP results reported above and various scenarios regarding the future increase in Japan's inward FDI stock. Since FDI consists of international capital flows accompanied by intangible assets, it is possible to use standard economic theory on the international movement of production factors for the macroeconomic analysis. Details of the specification and assumptions of the simulation are provided in the appendix of this chapter. However, the underlying reasoning of the simulation is quite straightforward: FDI benefits both the home and the host country. The home country enjoys the earnings generated by affiliates abroad, while in the host country, the higher productivity of

---

[9] With sufficient data, it should be possible to examine, for example, whether industry-level TFP growth is affected by inward FDI. Unfortunately, at present, relevant data from the *Establishment and Enterprise Census*, which covers all enterprises in Japan, are available only for 1996 and 2001, while the *Basic Survey of Japanese Business Structure and Activities*, as mentioned earlier, fails to cover a number of important service industries.

foreign firms increases real wage rates and hence benefits workers. Moreover, because of their higher productivity, foreign firms have a higher return on capital, which will induce capital deepening in the host country through capital imports and raise real wage rates further. By employing a standard macroeconomic model to represent these mechanisms, the effects of FDI on macroeconomic variables such as wages and gross domestic product (GDP) as well as the balance of payments can then be calculated.

The simulation is based on calculating the impact that an increase in the presence of foreign firms in the Japanese economy from estimated levels in 2006 would have. As discussed in Chapter 2, the government set the goal of achieving an increase in the FDI stock to 5 percent of GDP by the end of 2010; assuming that this target is met provides the baseline scenario for the simulation. Taking Japan's GDP in 2006 (¥510 trillion) and assuming a nominal GDP growth rate of 2.0 percent, GDP at the end of 2010 should be approximately ¥552 trillion.[10] Five percent of this – the target for the inward FDI stock – amounts to about ¥27.6 trillion. At the end of June 2006, the inward FDI stock was ¥10.6 trillion, or about 2 percent GDP. The simulation therefore calculates the macroeconomic impact of an increase in the inward FDI stock by ¥17.0 trillion. However, rather than basing the estimation of the macroeconomic impact on the increase in the inward FDI stock, it is more appropriate to consider the increase in the presence of foreign firms in the economy this translates into.

In order to do so, it is first necessary to estimate by how much the employment and value added of foreign firms would increase. As indicated in Chapters 1 and 2, the most comprehensive and reliable data on foreign firms' presence in the Japanese economy are provided by the *Establishment and Enterprise Surveys* for 1996 and 2001 (the latest survey available). Using these data and extrapolating the increase in the number of workers employed by foreign firms between 1996 and 2001 taking into account the increase in the inward FDI stock, the number of workers employed by foreign firms in Japan rose from 756,000 in 2001 to an estimated 1,095,000 in June 2006.[11]

---

[10] The figure for Japan's GDP in 2006 is based on the second preliminary estimate published on February 15, 2007.

[11] Based on data from the *Establishment and Enterprise Surveys*, Fukao, Ito, and Kwon (2005) suggest that the number of workers employed by the Japanese affiliates of foreign firms (33.4 percent or more foreign-owned) increased from 1996 to 2001 by 271,000, from 485,000 to 756,000. During the same period, the inward FDI stock increased by ¥3.16 trillion, from ¥3.47 trillion to ¥6.63 trillion. This means that an increase in the inward FDI stock of ¥11.7 million was needed for each additional person employed by a foreign firm in Japan. Assuming that this relationship remained unchanged from 2001 to 2006, the number of employees at foreign firms in Japan as of June 2006 was an estimated 1,095,000 (= 756,000 + (10,600,000 − 6,630,000)/11.7).

Extrapolating further assuming an increase in the inward FDI stock by ¥17.0 trillion from June 2006 to 2010, the number of employees at foreign firms should rise by another 1,453,000. According to this "back of the envelope" calculation, if the government's goal is accomplished, the number of workers employed by foreign firms would more than triple by 2010 compared with the number in 2001, from 756,000 to an estimated 2,548,000.

In 2001, the 756,000 employees at foreign firms created an estimated ¥8.1 trillion of gross value added, or ¥10.7 million per employee.[12] As labor productivity improves, per capita gross value added usually increases over time. Therefore, assuming that the average per capita nominal gross value added of foreign firms increases by 2.5 percent annually from 2001 to 2010, the estimated 1,095,000 employees in 2006 created ¥13.3 trillion of gross value added, equivalent to approximately 2.6 percent of GDP. And in 2010, the estimated 2,548,000 employees of foreign firms would create ¥34.0 trillion of gross value added, which would be about 6.2 percent of Japan's projected GDP in that year.

However, these results do not mean that the increase in foreign firms' contribution to GDP from 2.6 percent to 6.2 percent will raise Japan's GDP by as much as 3.6 percent. A large part of the increase in foreign firms' production will be canceled out by a corresponding decline in domestic firms' production. From this general equilibrium point of view, the major benefit of the new FDI will be the improvement of Japan's TFP.

The empirical results reported in the preceding section suggest that foreign firms' average TFP level is 8 percent higher than that of domestic firms. However, it was also shown that foreign firms enjoy higher TFP levels partly because they purchase Japanese firms that already have higher productivity than the average firm.[13] But the Japanese firms newly acquired by a foreign firm also display a further 2 percent increase of their TFP level in comparison with other domestic firms two years after the acquisition. Because large-scale FDI and out-in M&As are such a recent phenomenon in Japan, and the data used in the empirical investigation reported above only go up to 2001, the time span covered is relatively short. It is therefore difficult at this stage to assess the long-term effect of acquisitions by foreign firms on the TFP level of acquired firms. For the time being, it is therefore assumed that out-in acquisitions raise the TFP level of purchased firms by 5 percent in the long run.

---

[12] See Fukao, Ito, and Kwon (2005).

[13] Because the majority of inward direct investments in developed economies such as Japan are conducted as M&As and not as greenfield investments, it is appropriate to concentrate on the TFP level of acquired domestic firms here.

The stage is now set to consider the simulation of the macroeconomic impact of inward FDI. As a baseline scenario, it is assumed that out-in acquisitions increase foreign firms' share in Japan's GDP by 3.6 percentage points and that, as a result of being acquired, target firms' TFP increases by 5 percent. A 5 percent increase in the TFP level means that Japanese firms purchased by foreign firms can produce 5 percent more output from the same amount of input. This change in itself will raise Japan's GDP. But from a general equilibrium point of view, many other additional changes in the Japanese economy are expected. First, the improvement in TFP raises the demand for labor and increases the real wage rate. Second, the improvement in TFP raises rate of return to capital and will induce new capital accumulation. This capital accumulation will further increase Japan's GDP. Third, the increase in investment will reduce Japan's saving–investment balance, the current account surplus, and capital outflows. Fourth, dividend payments abroad by foreign firms and the fall in Japan's foreign investment income, caused by the decline in capital outflows, mean that the increase in Japan's gross national product (GNP), which includes net foreign investment income, will be smaller than the increase in Japan's GDP.

Based on a general equilibrium model of the economy, the simulation considers the overall effect of inward FDI on Japan's GDP and GNP taking these additional changes into account. It should be noted, however, that the assumption of a 5 percent increase in acquired firms' TFP level is rather conservative. The comparison of the TFP levels of foreign and domestic firms above is based on data for the manufacturing sector only. Yet, studies indicate that labor productivity in Japan's manufacturing sector is more or less on par with that in the United States and the major European economies, meaning that the scope for TFP improvements through FDI is relatively limited; on the other hand, Japan's labor productivity in many nonmanufacturing sectors, including major sectors such as retail and construction, is only about two-thirds or less of the U.S. and European levels.[14] Therefore, FDI from advanced economies in Japan's nonmanufacturing sectors probably yields much larger TFP gains than suggested by the estimates above for the manufacturing sector,[15] and it is in fact in the service sector where most recent FDI has been concentrated (see Table 2.2 in Chapter 2).

---

[14] See, e.g., Baily and Solow (2001), Fukao and Miyagawa (2007), and Chapter 4.

[15] Using the same data source (the firm-level data underlying the *Basic Survey of Japanese Business Structure and Activities*) as Fukao, Ito, and Kwon's (2005) analysis of the manufacturing sector, Fukao, Kwon, and Takizawa (2006) tried to estimate the effect of out-in M&As in the commerce sector on target firms' performance. Although their results showed a large improvement in target firms' labor productivity, they were unable to obtain stable results for TFP.

Moreover, there is also considerable scope for the share of foreign firms' production to increase by much more than 3.6 percentage points. In 2002, foreign firms' share in manufacturing turnover was only 2.6 percent in Japan compared with 20.3 percent in the United States, 24.4 percent in Germany, 35.9 percent in France, and 36.1 percent in Britain. Similarly, in services, foreign firms' share in turnover was only 0.9 percent in Japan, but 7.8 percent in the United States, 8.7 percent in Germany, 9.5 percent in France, and 16.8 percent in Britain (see Figure 2(d) in Chapter 2). Thus, even if foreign firms' share in turnover in Japan were to triple or quadruple from 2002, it would still only be half or less of that in other major economies. Such an increase would probably require a substantial further improvement in Japan's environment for FDI, which, given the current climate, seems unlikely (see Chapter 7). Nevertheless, it is instructive to examine the impact of FDI if foreign firms' share in production were to increase not by 3.6 percentage points but by, say, three times that amount.

Based on these considerations, four different scenarios are examined. The standard scenario shows the potential macroeconomic impact based on the assumption that the TFP improvement and the increase in the presence of foreign firms are relatively moderate in line with the estimation results for TFP and the government target. In addition, three alternative scenarios are considered. The first assumes that the TFP improvement effect in the service sector, and hence overall, is probably much greater than in the manufacturing sector. The second alternative assumes a much larger increase in the presence of foreign firms to illustrate the impact that FDI could have even at levels that would still lag considerably behind those of other advanced economies. The last scenario combines the assumptions of a greater TFP improvement and a larger increase in FDI. Thus, the following four cases are examined:

Case I (standard scenario): a 5 percent improvement of the TFP level and a 3.6-percentage-point increase in foreign firms' share in production.

Case II: a 15 percent improvement of the TFP level and a 3.6-percentage-point increase in foreign firms' share in production (i.e., it is assumed that the improvement of the TFP level is three times as great as in the standard scenario).

Case III: a 5 percent improvement of the TFP level and a 10.8-percentage-point increase in foreign firms' share in production (i.e., it is assumed that the increase in foreign firms' presence is three times as great as in the standard scenario).

Case IV: a 15 percent improvement of the TFP level and a 10.8-percentage-point increase in foreign firms' share in production.

The details of the analysis are reported in the appendix. However, the main assumptions on which the macroeconomic model is based can be summarized as follows:

(1) In order to explain the coexistence of productive and unproductive firms, it is necessary to assume that firms produce differentiated products. It is also assumed that firms operate under monopolistic competition. In such an economy, out-in acquisitions may bring two types of innovation. Using foreign parent firms' technology, domestic firms may improve their production processes (process innovation); or they may increase the variety of products they produce (product innovation). In order to simplify the analysis, it is assumed that only process innovations occur.

(2) The analysis is static, that is, it only examines the long-term effect of a one-time acquisition of domestic firms by foreign firms. In order to simplify the analysis, the employment and production share of foreign firms in the Japanese economy is assumed to increase from zero to 3.6 percent or 10.8 percent.

(3) All products are internationally traded without trade costs. Very smooth international indirect capital flows ensure that Japan's real interest rate is equal to the world real interest rate.

(4) The world equilibrium interest rate and the world price level will not be affected by the increase in Japan's inward FDI.

The results of the simulation analysis are shown in Table 5.2. For Case I, the standard scenario, they show that the 5 percent improvement of the TFP level and the 3.6-percentage-point increase in foreign firms' production share will raise real wages in Japan by 0.17 percent. As outlined above, the higher productivity of foreign firms will directly raise workers wages. In addition, it will also raise the return to capital, inducing capital deepening through capital imports, which will raise real wages further. The 0.17 percent increase in real wages shown in the table is the result of all these effects combined. The increase in the capital stock is also 0.17 percent. The increase in the average level of firms' productivity and the capital deepening induced by the higher rate of return to capital together raise Japan's GDP by 0.24 percent. These increases are permanent, that is, wages and GDP will be higher by the estimated amount every year.

Table 5.2. *Simulation results of the macroeconomic impact of inward FDI*

Assumptions:		Case I	Case II	Case III	Case IV
Foreign firms' TFP level/domestic firms' TFP level		1.05	1.15	1.05	1.15
Increase of foreign firms' output share (percentage points)		3.6	3.6	10.8	10.8
Increase in wages		0.17%	0.42%	0.53%	1.30%
Increase of capital stock		0.17%	0.42%	0.53%	1.30%
Increase of real GDP	a	0.24%	0.68%	0.72%	2.06%
Dividend payments from foreign firms to foreign investors/GDP	b	0.36%	0.36%	1.09%	1.10%
Investment income from Japan's assets abroad received in compensation for the sale of Japanese firms/GDP	c	0.30%	0.21%	0.91%	0.65%
Interest payments abroad for Japan's liabilities created by capital accumulation induced by inward FDI/GDP	d	0.05%	0.11%	0.14%	0.35%
Net change of Japan's international investment account/GDP	$e = -b + c - d$	−0.11%	−0.27%	−0.32%	−0.81%
Increase of real GNP/GDP	$f = a + e$	0.13%	0.41%	0.39%	1.25%

Source: See text.

When it is assumed that inward FDI raises the TFP level three times as much as in the standard scenario (Case II), or the increase in foreign firms' share in production is three times as great (Case III), the impact in terms of the increase in wages, induced capital deepening, and the increase in GDP almost triples in comparison with Case I. That is, the size of the macroeconomic impact is almost proportionate to the magnitude of either the TFP improvement or the increase in inward FDI. In the case of the most optimistic scenario, Case IV, the impact is quite substantial: real wages would rise by 1.30 percent, and GDP would increase by 2.06 percent.

But it is also necessary to take into account the implications for the balance of payments and hence GNP, which includes net foreign investment income. Foreign firms in Japan will pay dividends to their parent firm abroad, while Japan's foreign investment income will fall as a result of the inflow of capital (or the decline in capital outflows), meaning that the increase in GNP will be smaller than the increase in GDP. The table therefore also shows how the increase in GNP will differ from the increase in GDP.

Inward FDI will change Japan's international asset–liability position in three respects. First, foreign investment increases Japan's international liabilities and overseas investors will receive the profits earned by foreign firms in Japan. Under the assumptions of the simulation (see the appendix), dividend payments from foreign firms in Japan to their owners abroad would be 0.36 percent of total GDP in Case I. Second, in compensation for the sale of Japanese firms, Japanese residents will receive foreign assets. It is assumed that Japanese residents use this money as portfolio investment abroad. Investment income from Japan's assets abroad received in compensation for the sale of Japanese firms would be 0.30 percent of GDP. Third, the capital accumulation induced by inward FDI will spur capital inflows and increase Japan's liabilities to nonresidents. Interest payments abroad for Japan's liabilities resulting from the capital deepening induced by inward FDI would be 0.05 percent of total GDP. These three changes in Japan's international asset–liability position will permanently change Japan's balance of payments. Taken together, these effects would reduce Japan's income account surplus by 0.11 percent of GDP in Case I. Thus, subtracting this income account effect from the increase in GDP through inward FDI, the increase in GNP would be 0.13 percent of GDP.

Looking at the other scenarios, in Case III, which assumes that the increase in foreign firms' production share is three times as large as in Case I, the changes in the balance of payments and in GNP are also about three times as large. In contrast, in Case II, which assumes a three times greater TFP improvement, the effect on the balance of payments is slightly less than three times as large and the increase in GNP therefore slightly more than three times as great. Finally, in the most optimistic scenario (Case IV), the change in the balance of payments is relatively large, but the impact on Japan's GNP remains substantial.

Overall, the simulation results indicate that, under the given assumptions, the contribution of FDI to Japan's economy ranges from a modest 0.24 percent of GDP (0.13 percent of GNP) in the conservative baseline scenario (Case I) to a substantial 2.06 percent of GDP (1.25 percent of GNP) in the most optimistic scenario (Case IV). While especially in the baseline scenario, the impact of FDI appears almost negligible, this result should be considered as the lower bound, as other important factors are not taken into account. The first of these is that the assumption of the improvement of target firms' TFP is based on estimation results for the manufacturing sector only. Yet, it is in the service sector where most FDI in recent years has been concentrated and where Japan's TFP most lags behind that of other advanced economies. Consequently, the TFP improvement effect is likely to be much greater than in the baseline scenario. If a greater TFP improvement effect is assumed, as in Case II, then the growth contribution – at an estimated 0.68 percent of GDP (0.41 percent of GNP) – is certainly no longer negligible, taking into account that Japan's annual potential growth rate is probably in the region of 2 percent.

The second important factor not taken into account in the simulation is the impact that the greater presence of foreign firms will have on domestic firms and productivity in the rest of the economy. Two mechanisms in particular deserve to be highlighted. The first is the role of technology and knowledge spillovers from foreign to domestic firms. At least part of the technology and knowledge transferred from foreign parent firms to their affiliates in Japan, on which the higher TFP growth of the latter is based, is likely to spill over to domestic firms through a variety of channels. These include, for example, backward and forward linkages (i.e., interaction with suppliers and customers), the movement of employees and the knowledge and skills they have acquired from foreign to domestic firms, and imitation of processes, products, and services.[16] The second mechanism through which the greater presence of foreign firms affects productivity in the rest of the economy is the greater degree of competition they introduce. This will force their domestic counterparts either to raise their game or cause them to lose market share and, possibly, even exit the market. Thus, although the impact on (some) domestic firms may be negative, overall these dynamics should raise the average productivity in a particular industry (and the economy as a whole) and free up resources for more productive uses. In Chapter 4, it was suggested that part of the reason for Japan's disappointing TFP performance was the low "metabolism" of the economy, that is, the pace with which firms with high productivity growth expand their market share, new firms enter the market, and uncompetitive existing firms exit. The entry and/or greater presence of foreign firms thus should also increase this metabolism and hence help to raise TFP growth throughout the economy. Thus, the fact that technology and knowledge spillovers and the role that the entry of firms with greater TFP growth could play in invigorating the metabolism of the Japanese economy are not included in the simulation gives reason to assume that the impact of FDI is likely to be greater than the estimates suggest.

---

[16] There are quite a number of empirical studies that have attempted to gauge the technology spillover effects from FDI, but to date they have produced no conclusive results. However, this seems to be more a reflection of the difficulties involved in measuring technology spillovers than any lack of such spillovers (see, e.g., Lipsey and Sjöholm, 2004).

Finally, the simulation results based on the assumption of a much greater increase in the presence of foreign firms highlight how FDI could make a tangible contribution to economic growth at levels of FDI penetration that would still lag behind those in other major economies. Case III shows that, even with a relatively conservative assumption regarding the TFP improvement effect, the contribution to economic growth – at an estimated 0.72 percent of GDP (0.39 percent of GNP) – again would be not negligible. Coupled with a more optimistic and possibly more realistic assumption of a greater TFP improvement effect (Case IV), the growth contribution would, in fact, be substantial at an estimated 2.06 percent of GDP (1.25 percent of GNP), which would be roughly equivalent to an extra year of overall economic growth. Admittedly, it seems unlikely that in the near future Japan will be able to attract additional FDI inflows of the magnitude assumed, especially without significant further measures to facilitate FDI. However, the estimate underscores that the gain for Japan is potentially huge and should provide an incentive for policy makers, business leaders, and the wider public to welcome FDI.

Conclusion

The magnitude of the economic gains from inward FDI in Japan unfortunately is difficult to gauge. A key reason is the paucity of data: given that significant inflows of FDI are such a recent phenomenon, the coverage of surveys and statistics in terms of relevant data items, industries, and so forth, is still lagging behind, and it will take years until adequate data for a period sufficiently long for empirical investigation will become available. Against this background, this chapter attempted to pursue an alternative route to assess the potential role of inward FDI by estimating its macroeconomic impact through a simulation based on empirical evidence on TFP and projections of future inward FDI.

The simulation results indicate that even if the stock of inward FDI relative to GDP were to increase to 5 percent, as aimed for by the government, the potential impact on the economy overall would still be very modest. This suggests that the macroeconomic impact of inward FDI to date has probably been even smaller – unless the TFP boost provided by foreign firms in the service sector has been very substantial indeed. In certain service industries, such as retail trade and banking and insurance, this is, in fact, not inconceivable (although – given the lack of data – it is difficult to say with any certainty).

Moreover, the simulation considered only the direct impact of acquisitions on target firms' TFP. Not considered were technology and knowledge spillovers, such as when domestic firms imitate business models and products introduced by foreign firms, as is happening, for example, in the banking and insurance industry. Also not considered was the role of increased competition thanks to inward FDI, which may negatively affect domestic firms by potentially undermining their sales, profits, and so on, but will help to raise the average productivity of all firms in a particular industry and the economy overall. Again, there are plenty of examples demonstrating that indeed foreign firms are exerting competitive pressure on their domestic counterparts in sectors as diverse as automobiles, pharmaceuticals, insurance, and retailing.

The results presented in this chapter represent one important piece in the puzzle to assess the impact of FDI in Japan, illustrating both the transmission channels of this impact and the potential magnitude from a macroeconomic point of view. However, another important piece in the puzzle is the industry dynamics unleashed by foreign investment that shape the macroeconomic impact. These will be addressed in Chapter 6.

Appendix: Macroeconomic Simulation Analysis of the Impact of Inward FDI in Japan

This appendix provides the details of the macroeconomic simulation of the impact of inward FDI based on a model of the Japanese economy with microeconomic foundations.

Basic Assumptions on Market and Technology
The simulation is based on a model with monopolistic competition. It is assumed that in Japan, n commodities are produced by n firms and each commodity is produced by one firm. There are $n\,\theta_F$ foreign firms and $n(1 - \theta_F)$ domestic firms. All products are final goods and internationally traded and there are no trade costs. All consumers, domestic and foreign, have identical homothetic preferences with regard to these goods. Each firm faces the following demand function:

$$X_i = \left(\frac{p_i}{p^*}\right)^{-\frac{1}{1-\sigma}} E \qquad (1)$$

where X_i denotes the demand for firm i's product, p_i is the price of firm i's product, and p^* stands for the world price level. $1/(1-\sigma)$ is the price demand elasticity. It is assumed that $1/(1 - \sigma)$ is greater than one. The parameter E

denotes the size of worldwide demand. It is also assumed that Japan is not a large country and p^* and E can be treated as constant over time.

A Cobb–Douglas constant returns production function is assumed:

$$X_i = a_i L_i^{\beta} K_i^{1-\beta} \tag{2}$$

where L_i and K_i denote firm i's labor and capital input and a_i denotes the TFP level of firm i. Labor and capital markets are competitive so that the cost share of labor is equal to the constant parameter β.

The introduction of managerial resources through out-in acquisitions can be expressed in the model in at least two ways. First, foreign firms can produce with a higher TFP level, a_i (process innovation). Second, foreign firms can produce new goods, so that the number of commodities produced in Japan, n, increases (product innovation). For simplicity, the analysis here focuses on the first type of innovation as a result of managerial resource transfers. In the baseline scenario, it is assumed that foreign firms' TFP level, a_F, is 5 percent higher than domestic firms' TFP level, a_J.

Let r denote the constant world equilibrium real interest rate. Further assumptions are that domestic net saving is zero under r and that there is no capital depreciation.

The Profit Maximization Behavior of Firms

In production function (2), marginal cost does not depend on the production level and can be expressed by

$$\frac{w L_i + r K_i}{X_i} = \frac{B}{a_i} w^{\beta} r^{1-\beta} \tag{3}$$

where w denotes the domestic real wage rate and B stands for $(\beta/(1-\beta))^{1-\beta} + ((1-\beta)/\beta)^{\beta}$. When firms operate under monopolistic competition and the price demand elasticity is $1/(1-\sigma)$, profit-maximizing firms set the price level equal to marginal costs times $1/\sigma$. These conditions yield the following optimal output and factor input levels:

$$X_i = \left(\frac{B}{a_i \sigma p^*} w^{\beta} r^{1-\beta} \right)^{-\frac{1}{1-\sigma}} E \tag{4}$$

$$L_i = \frac{1}{a_i} \left(\frac{r}{w} \right)^{1-\beta} \left(\frac{\beta}{1-\beta} \right)^{1-\beta} X_i \tag{5}$$

$$K_i = \frac{1}{a_i} \left(\frac{w}{r} \right)^{\beta} \left(\frac{1-\beta}{\beta} \right)^{\beta} X_i \tag{6}$$

Foreign firms, which have a higher TFP level, a_F, and can produce output at lower marginal cost, set lower sales prices and produce more output than domestic firms (equation (4)). The total sales of foreign firms are $(a_F/a_J)^{\sigma(1-\sigma)}$ times greater than the total sales of domestic firms. And both foreign firms' share in total sales and their share in labor input in the Japanese economy overall are equal to $\theta_F(a_F/a_J)^{\sigma(1-\sigma)}/(1-\theta_F+\theta_F(a_F/a_J)^{\sigma(1-\sigma)})$.

The Labor Market Equilibrium Condition

The equilibrium condition for the labor market can be expressed by

$$(1-\theta_F)\,nL_J + \theta_F nL_F = L.$$

Using equations (4) and (5) and the equation above yields

$$(1-\theta_F)n\frac{1}{a_J}\left(\frac{r}{w}\right)^{1-\beta}\left(\frac{\beta}{1-\beta}\right)^{1-\beta}\left(\frac{B}{a_J\sigma p^*}w^\beta r^{1-\beta}\right)^{-\frac{1}{1-\sigma}}$$

$$+\theta_F n\frac{1}{a_F}\left(\frac{r}{w}\right)^{1-\beta}\left(\frac{\beta}{1-\beta}\right)^{1-\beta}\left(\frac{B}{a_F\sigma p^*}w^\beta r^{1-\beta}\right)^{-\frac{1}{1-\sigma}}=L \quad (7)$$

where L denotes Japan's total labor endowment, which is assumed to be constant. The domestic real wage rate is determined by equation (7), which shows that inward FDI (an increase in θ_F) will increase the demand for labor and raise the equilibrium real wage rate. Because the price level p^* remains unchanged, the level of workers' welfare will be improved by inward FDI.

Capital Accumulation Induced by FDI

Productive foreign firms enjoy higher returns to capital and this fact will induce capital accumulation. Under production function (2), the following equation holds:

$$\frac{wL}{rK}=\frac{\beta}{1-\beta} \quad (8)$$

where L and K denote Japan's total endowment of labor and total input of capital. Under the assumption of perfect international capital mobility, the capital input level, K, is endogenously determined by equation (8). Therefore, the increase in capital input is proportional to the increase in the real wage rate.

Japan's GDP Before and After Inward FDI

Using the model just developed it is possible to determine how inward FDI changes Japan's GDP. To simplify the analysis, an equilibrium without inward FDI ($\theta_F = 0$) and another equilibrium with inward FDI ($\theta_F > 0$) are compared.

When there is no inward FDI, all firms have the same productivity level and produce the same amount. Therefore, the real GDP level can be expressed by

$$\sum_{i=1}^{n} X_i = n a_J \left(\frac{L}{n}\right)^{\beta} \left(\frac{K_0}{n}\right)^{1-\beta} = a_J L^{\beta} K_0^{1-\beta} \quad (9)$$

where K_0 denotes the total input of capital stock in Japan. When FDI occurs and $\theta_F n$ firms are purchased by foreign firms, the real GDP level can be expressed by

$$\sum_{i=1}^{n} X_i = \theta_F n a_F (L_F)^{\beta} (K_F)^{1-\beta} + (1 - \theta_F) n a_J (L_J)^{\beta} (K_J)^{1-\beta} \quad (10)$$

where foreign and domestic firms' factor inputs can be expressed by

$$L_i = \frac{\left(\frac{a_F}{a_J}\right)^{\frac{\sigma}{1-\sigma}}}{1 - \theta_F + \theta_F \left(\frac{a_F}{a_J}\right)^{\frac{\sigma}{1-\sigma}}} \frac{L}{n} \quad \text{for } i \in \mathbf{F} \quad (11)$$

$$L_i = \frac{1}{1 - \theta_F + \theta_F \left(\frac{a_F}{a_J}\right)^{\frac{\sigma}{1-\sigma}}} \frac{L}{n} \quad \text{for } i \in \mathbf{D} \quad (12)$$

$$K_i = \frac{\left(\frac{a_F}{a_J}\right)^{\frac{\sigma}{1-\sigma}}}{1 - \theta_F + \theta_F \left(\frac{a_F}{a_J}\right)^{\frac{\sigma}{1-\sigma}}} \frac{w_1}{w_0} \frac{K_0}{n} \quad \text{for } i \in \mathbf{F} \quad (13)$$

$$K_i = \frac{1}{1 - \theta_F + \theta_F \left(\frac{a_F}{a_J}\right)^{\frac{\sigma}{1-\sigma}}} \frac{w_1}{w_0} \frac{K_0}{n} \quad \text{for } i \in \mathbf{D} \quad (14)$$

where $\mathbf{F}$ and $\mathbf{D}$ stand for the set of foreign firms and the set of domestic firms, respectively. w_0 and w_1 denote the wage rate before and after the inward FDI, which can be calculated using equation (7).

Assumptions on Parameter Values

By setting the parameter values, it is possible to simulate the macroeconomic impact of inward FDI. The cost share of labor, β, is assumed to be equal to 2/3 and the price demand elasticity, $1/(1-\sigma)$, to be equal to 5 (this means that the mark-up rate will be $(1/\sigma - 1)^*100 = 25$ percent). As explained in the text, four cases are examined. Here, the calibration for Case I is explained in detail. In Case I, it is assumed that foreign firms' TFP is 5 percent higher than domestic firms' TFP, that is, $a_F/a_J = 1.05$. The ratio of foreign firms to total firms after the inward FDI, θ_F, is set at a level that satisfies the following condition:

$$\theta_F(a_F/a_J)^{\sigma/(1-\sigma)}/(1 - \theta_F + \theta_F(a_F/a_J)^{\sigma/(1-\sigma)}) = 0.036$$

The equation above means that, after the inward FDI takes place, foreign firms' share of total sales and of labor input in the Japanese economy overall will be equal to 3.6 percent. The solution of the equation above is $\theta_F = 0.0298$.

Simulation Results

The results of the simulation analysis are shown in Table 5.2. They suggest that the increase in inward FDI assumed in Case I will raise the real wage rate and total capital input by 0.17 percent and lift GDP by 0.24 percent. Wages and GDP will be permanently higher by this amount.

The Effects on Japan's Balance of Payments

Dividend payments abroad by domestic firms and the fall in Japan's foreign investment income caused by the inflow of capital (or the decline in capital outflows) mean that the increase in Japan's GNP (which includes net foreign investment income) will be smaller than the increase in Japan's GDP. Table 5.2 shows how the increase in GNP will differ from the increase in GDP. Inward FDI will change Japan's international asset–liability position in three respects. First, inward foreign investment will increase Japan's international liabilities, since foreign investors will receive part of the profits earned by foreign firms in Japan. Typically, foreign investors receive only part of the profits because when the foreign capital participation rate in a particular firm is less than one, then domestic investors will also receive their share. In addition, the Japanese government will receive corporate income taxes from firms in Japan. Second, in compensation for the sale of Japanese firms, Japanese residents will receive foreign assets. It is assumed that Japanese residents use these funds for portfolio investment abroad. Third, capital accumulation induced by inward FDI will cause capital inflows and increase Japan's liabilities to nonresidents. These changes in Japan's international asset–liability position will permanently change Japan's balance of payments. In the simulation, the effects of these changes are calculated as follows:

(1) Dividend payments to foreign owners
In the model, 20 percent of GDP is monopolistic rent. To simplify the analysis, it is assumed that firms pay the entire rent to their stockholders as dividends and all the real capital accumulation is financed through indirect financing. If the conditions for the Modigliani–Miller theorem hold, then firms' financial structure will not change the results. It is assumed that the average capital participation rate of foreign parent firms in their Japanese affiliates is 50 percent. It is also assumed that there is no corporate income tax. In Case I, after the FDI, foreign firms' market share is 3.6 percent. Therefore, foreign parent firms receive $0.5 \times 0.2 \times 0.036 \times \text{GDP}_1$ in annual dividends, where GDP_1 denotes Japan's GDP after the inward FDI. Therefore, given the simulated increase in GDP as a result of inward FDI by 0.24 percent and using the relationship $\text{GDP}_1/\text{GDP}_0 = 1.0024$, dividend payments to foreign owners in terms of GDP_0 are $0.5 \times 0.2 \times 0.036 \times \text{GDP}_1 = 0.0036 \times \text{GDP}_0$.

(2) Foreign income from Japan's portfolio assets abroad received in compensation for the sale of Japanese firms
Before the inward FDI, the total value of Japanese firms' stocks is $0.2 \times \text{GDP}_0/r$, where r denotes the world equilibrium interest rate. 50 percent ownership of θ_F percent of Japanese firms is sold to foreign firms. In exchange, Japanese residents receive $0.5 \times \theta_F \times 0.2 \times \text{GDP}_0/r$ in foreign assets. The annual investment income from these assets will be $0.5 \times \theta_F \times 0.2 \times \text{GDP}_0 = 0.003 \times \text{GDP}_0$.

(3) Interest payments abroad for Japan's liabilities created by the capital accumulation induced by inward FDI
Adding the simulated increase in Japan's capital stock through FDI of 0.17 percent to the existing capital stock $(1 + 0.0017)$, the share of the foreign capital stock as a result of this FDI is 0.17 percent (i.e., $0.0017/(1 + 0.0017) = 0.17$ percent). Interest payments abroad for these liabilities on Japan's part are $0.0017 \times r \times K_1$. Since the cost share of capital is 0.3333 and the

mark-up rate is 25 percent, the interest payments are equal to $0.0017 \times 0.3333 \times 0.8 \times GDP_1 = 0.0005 \times GDP_0$.

Taken together, these effects will reduce Japan's income account surplus by $0.36 - 0.30 + 0.05 = 0.11$ percent of Japan's GDP. Therefore, the increase in GNP will be $0.24 - 0.11 = 0.13$ percent of GDP.

SIX

The Impact of Foreign Direct Investment in
Japan: Case Studies of the Automobile, Finance,
and Health Care Industries

Although the amount of foreign direct investment (FDI) in Japan relative to
gross domestic product (GDP) or other countries has been rather small, this
does not necessarily mean that its role has been negligible. In fact, quite the
opposite is true: in a number of industries, foreign-owned firms now account
for more than 10 percent of total employment and have become an integral
element of the business landscape.[1] What is more, as their presence has
grown, foreign-owned firms are increasingly having an impact in shaping
the business dynamics of some these industries.

The purpose of this chapter is to examine such industry dynamics in
greater detail through a series of case studies. Doing so not only provides
concrete examples of how foreign acquisitions help to raise the performance of acquired firms, thus illustrating the total factor productivity (TFP)
improvement effects discussed in Chapter 5. It also yields at least anecdotal
evidence of some of the knowledge spillovers and competition effects taking
place as a result of inward FDI. To this end, the individual case studies examine the particular structure of an industry, the regulatory framework (where
this has played a role in shaping the industry), and recent changes therein
relevant for FDI. The case studies then consider the role of FDI in the sector,
hone in on prominent cases of FDI, and show how the presence of foreign
multinationals in one way or another has affected domestic firms or the
industry as a whole.

Sectors examined in detail include the automobile industry, banking and
insurance, and the health care sector (pharmaceuticals, medical devices, and
health care services). The wholesale and retail sector and telecommunications will also be considered briefly. As this list indicates, the scope of sectors

---

[1] See Table 2.1 in Chapter 2 for sectors in which the employment share of foreign-owned
firms now exceeds 10 percent.

137

covered is quite broad, ranging from manufacturing to services and from industries wide open to FDI to those in which government regulations in effect continue to make FDI impossible. The analysis thus covers a fairly representative cross section of Japanese industry.

The remainder of the chapter is organized as follows. The next section looks at the automobile industry, focusing in particular on Renault's acquisition of Nissan and the growing presence of foreign suppliers in Japan. This is followed by an analysis of the financial sector, in which the areas of investment banking, retail banking, and insurance are examined in detail. Next, the health care industry is discussed, concentrating on the pharmaceutical and medical devices industries, but also considering health care services, a sector in which FDI remains impossible because of the entry regulations on corporate providers. The next section then presents a brief examination of two other sectors – wholesale and retail and telecommunication – which have attracted substantial amounts of FDI but cannot be considered in detail here. A synthesis of the case studies is provided in the final section.

Automobile Industry

There is probably not a more suitable industry with which to begin the sectoral analysis of FDI in Japan than the auto industry. This is by far the country's most internationalized industry: motor vehicles and parts account for a large share of all Japanese merchandise exports, and overseas production by the car industry is far ahead of that of any other Japanese industry.[2] Conversely, foreigners have been able to invest in the sector for decades, and General Motors (GM) and Ford acquired substantial stakes in Japanese automakers in the early and late 1970s, respectively. As a result, even before the wave of FDI in the late 1990s, the auto industry was already the sector in Japan with the highest share of employment by foreign-owned companies (see Table 2.1 in Chapter 2).

Yet, at the same time, even this relatively internationalized sector has remained essentially Japanese. Although foreign companies have acquired

---

[2] In 2006, motor vehicles and parts accounted for 20.3 percent of Japan's total merchandise exports. The overseas production ratio of the Japanese car industry reached 36.0 percent in 2004, followed by the electronics industry with an overseas production ratio of 21.3 percent (Overseas production ratios from: Ministry of Economy, Trade and Industry, *Kaigai Jigyo Katsudo Kihon Chosa, Dai-35-kai (2005)* [The 35th Survey of Overseas Business Activities], online: <http://www.meti.go.jp/statistics/downloadfiles/h2c412hj.pdf> (accessed March 5, 2007).

controlling stakes in a number of Japanese automakers, no foreign cars are manufactured in Japan;[3] foreign parts makers have only recently begun to penetrate the market; and foreign brands continue to be relatively exotic. Though fiercely competitive, the Japanese market has been and continues to be dominated by domestic carmakers. Imports of foreign cars account for less than 5 percent of total domestic sales. Compare this with the situation in Europe or the United States, where both imports and local production by wholly-owned foreign subsidiaries have long commanded considerable market shares. In Europe, for example, non-European makers alone accounted for about 36 percent of new car registrations in 2006.[4]

What is more, until recently, foreign participation in Japanese carmakers had little impact on the way the Japanese car industry operated. Despite substantial shareholdings by GM and Ford, the "Suzuki production system" or the "Mazda production system" have not been very different from the famous "Toyota production system" characterized not only by just-in-time production and lean manufacturing (now copied by most Western competitors), but also by a number of other Japanese business practices, such as close and long-term ties with dedicated (Japanese) suppliers, lifetime employment, and the reluctance to close factories in difficult times.[5] Thus, although the car industry appears relatively internationalized by Japanese standards, in comparison with other countries it still remains very much a home-grown affair.

Nevertheless, the Japanese car industry today looks quite different from a decade ago, as a number of international and domestic factors have paved the way for foreign companies to gain a greater foothold in the Japanese market. On the international side, factors include the resurgence of volume producers in Europe and the United States during the 1990s as the former managed to strengthen brand images and the latter achieved

---

[3] For this reason, the Japan Automobile Manufacturers Association (JAMA) has no purely foreign members, since a prerequisite for membership is to have manufacturing operations in Japan. However, this distinction is also increasingly difficult to make with Volvo's acquisition of a 100 percent stake in Nissan Diesel.

[4] This figure counts the sales in Western Europe of Japanese and Korean makers and of the core brands of the American auto giants Ford and GM (Opel/Vauxhaul; Chevrolet is also included). Authors' calculation based on statistics retrieved from the European Automobile Manufacturers Association website: <http://www.acea.be> (accessed March 5, 2007).

[5] However, it should be noted that not all car manufacturers have used this "Japanese" production system with equal success. Research by Ito (2004c) and Ito and Fukao (2001) indicates that some assemblers were much better than others at squeezing cost reductions out of their suppliers during the early 1990s. Although information for individual companies is not available, it seems almost certain that Toyota was much more successful at this than other firms such as, for example, Nissan.

quality improvements that diminished the competitive advantage of
Japanese carmakers. At the same time, the 1990s were a period of global
industry consolidation as carmakers entered vertical and horizontal alliances
for the complementation of vehicle types and marketing areas.[6] All the while,
global capacity was growing and Japanese manufacturers were not always
well positioned to react to shifts in consumer tastes (such as the growing
popularity of light trucks in the United States). Factors on the domestic side
include the prolonged malaise of the Japanese economy and the maturation
of the Japanese car market – annual car sales in Japan dropped from a peak of
5.1 million units in 1990 to a trough of 4.1 million in 1998 – as well as difficulties at some companies in adapting to the new environment.[7] International
and domestic factors combined to erode the competitiveness of Japanese
carmakers and meant that the industry consolidation that was sweeping the globe around the turn of the millennium eventually also reached
Japan.

By far the most conspicuous cases were the acquisition of a controlling
interest in Nissan by the much smaller French firm Renault and the tie-
up between DaimlerChrysler and Mitsubishi Motors Corporation (MMC),
which made headlines worldwide. But, as shown in Table 6.1, there were also
a number of other, less conspicuous deals involving car and truck assemblers
around this time. Ford increased its shareholding in Mazda to 33.4 percent,
the ownership share required to gain a measure of management control, and
GM progressively increased its stakes in Suzuki and Fuji Heavy (Subaru) to
20 percent each (although GM has since sold most of its shareholdings in
its Japanese partners, because of financial problems at home). Meanwhile,
in an entirely domestic tie-up, Toyota boosted its investment in Daihatsu
to 51 percent. What is more, foreign investment in the sector has not been
confined to final assemblers as foreign parts suppliers have also increased
their presence in Japan. Examples include Bosch (Germany), Valeo (France),
Autoliv (Sweden), and Mahle (Germany), all of which have acquired stakes
in Japanese parts suppliers in recent years.

Case Study: The Renault–Nissan Alliance
Before examining changes in the Japanese car industry more generally, it
is useful to have a closer look at the alliance between Renault and Nissan.

---

[6] Development Bank of Japan (2000).
[7] Car sales have recovered somewhat from the low in 1998, reaching around 4.7 million units
in 2005. Figures from Japan Automobile Manufacturers Association, *The Motor Industry
of Japan 2006*, online: <http://www.jama-english.jp/publications/MIJ2006.pdf> (accessed
May 5, 2007).

Table 6.1. *Japanese carmakers and their owners (owners and their ownership share in parentheses)*

1995	2004	2007
Toyota	**Toyota**	**Toyota**
Hino (Toyota: 50.5%)	Hino (Toyota: 50.1%)	Hino (Toyota: 50.1%)
Daihatsu (Toyota: 16.6%)	Daihatsu (Toyota: 51.1%)	Daihatsu (Toyota: 51.2%)
Honda	**Honda**	**Honda**
Nissan	**Nissan (Renault: 44.3%)**	**Nissan (Renault: 44.3%)**
Nissan Diesel (Nissan: 39.8%)	Nissan Diesel (Nissan: 23.8%; Renault: 17.8%)	
		Nissan Diesel (Volvo: 100%)**
Mitsubishi	**Mitsubishi (Daimler: 18.8%)**	**Mitsubishi**
	Mitsubishi Fuso* (Daimler Chrysler: 85%; Mitsubishi group companies: 15%)	
		Mitsubishi Fuso (Daimler Chrysler: 85%; Mitsubishi group companies: 15%)
Suzuki (GM: 3.3%)	**Suzuki** (GM: 20.0%)	**Suzuki** (GM: 3.0%)
Fuji Heavy (Subaru) (Nissan: 4.2%)	**Fuji Heavy (Subaru)** (GM: 20.0%)	**Fuji Heavy (Subaru)** (Toyota: 8.7%)
Isuzu (GM: 37.5%)	**Isuzu** (GM: 11.9%)	**Isuzu** (Toyota: 5.9%)
Mazda (Ford: 24.5%)	**Mazda** (Ford: 33.4%)	**Mazda** (Ford: 33.4%)

* Mitsubishi Fuso was established in 2003.
** Volvo acquired a 13 percent stake in Nissan Diesel from then-parent Nissan Motor Co. in March 2006 and obtained another 6 percent of Nissan Diesel's shares in September of that year. Following a takeover bid in February 2007, the Swedish firm's stake was to be raised to 100 percent.
Source: Compiled by authors from *Kigyo Keiretsu Soran, Japan Company Handbook*, company websites, and press reports.

Not only has this been the foreign investment in Japan that has received by far the most attention, it is also the one that has probably had the greatest impact on the Japanese car industry and beyond.

Before the alliance with Renault, Nissan was a company in long-term decline: the Japanese carmaker's share of both the domestic and the global market was dropping, production volumes were falling, and the company was on the verge of bankruptcy, having registered losses in six of the seven years between 1992 and 1999, including the record loss of almost ¥700 billion in 1999. This desperate state meant that the new management team from

Renault led by Carlos Ghosn had considerable leeway to undertake drastic restructuring measures.

The most publicized and controversial among these was the reduction of excess capacity by closing five factories in Japan and cutting the global workforce by 21,000, with 16,000 jobs axed in Japan. Similarly controversial was the dissolution of Nissan's *keiretsu,* that is, the sale of many of the company's nonstrategic assets, including stakes in the large majority of its more than 1,100 suppliers. This step went hand-in-hand with a streamlining of supplies. Whereas Nissan's purchases of parts and materials had previously been organized by country or region, they were now to be organized on a global scale and combined with those of Renault through the newly established Renault Nissan Purchasing Organization. Internal comparisons between Renault's and Nissan's purchasing costs had revealed that Nissan was paying a substantial premium on identical parts and components, and the use of common purchasing represented one way in which it was possible to lower costs. Another step was the reduction in the number of suppliers for parts and materials to 600, allowing those suppliers that continued to do business with Nissan to enjoy economies of scale.

A further area in which operations were streamlined and global best practice was introduced is Nissan's financial operations. Nissan had no chief financial officer until 1996 and when one was introduced, he did not have access to all necessary information.[8] As a result, Nissan did not know whether a particular car it was selling was making money for the company or not. In addition to the sale of noncore assets, one pillar in the effort to reduce Nissan's crippling debt burden consequently was to make the management of the company's financial operations a top priority, centralizing financial functions in Tokyo, and repatriating debt to Japan.

But the overhaul of the way Nissan does business did not stop there. Other areas affected were the company's employment policies, where merit-based promotions and remuneration replaced the traditional seniority-based system; the introduction of outside talent not only from Renault, but also from other Japanese companies such as the new head of design, who came from rival carmaker Isuzu; and the company's communication with the press, shareholders, and employees, establishing a culture of corporate transparency.

What many of the measures have in common is that they instilled a profit orientation into Nissan's operation that was previously lacking and turned the company from one that only had a strong worldwide presence

---

[8] Ghosn and Riès (2005).

into one that actually coordinates all its activities from a global perspective. This approach is most visible in the reorganization of Nissan's purchasing policy and the relationship with its suppliers, but it can also be seen in the company's financial operations, its product design strategies, and the deployment of assets.[9]

The outcome of the restructuring effort is well known: a turnaround from the record loss in 1999 to successive record profits six years in a row and industry-leading operating margins. In addition, the declining trend in domestic sales was reversed and Nissan was able to steal market share from rivals Honda, Mazda, and Mitsubishi, the latter having suffered a collapse in sales due to ongoing quality problems.[10] And even the number of employees, which had shrunk following the drastic restructuring measures, has been gradually increasing again.[11]

Renault–Nissan: The Repercussions

The repercussions of the alliance between Renault and Nissan go considerably beyond its immediate impact on the Japanese carmaker itself, its suppliers, and its rivals. From the start, the Renault–Nissan case has been in the public eye like few other foreign investments, meaning that it has played an important role in shaping public perceptions of foreign companies and their business methods in Japan. For example, cutting the global workforce by 10 percent, closing five factories in Japan, and selling most of Nissan's shareholdings were drastic steps by Japanese standards. But because they were quickly vindicated by greatly improved business results, they have probably helped to make such measures more acceptable, though so far no other major car manufacturer, none of which has been in similarly dire straits, has followed suit.

Turning to the impact of the alliance on Japan's auto industry, it would be difficult to claim that Renault's investment in Nissan has led to greatly increased price competition or introduced qualitatively new products in the

---

[9] For example, design units in Japan and the United States now work closely together to build a global brand identity. And almost at the same time that Nissan was closing factories in Japan, where it was suffering from excess capacity, it was building a new factory in the United States for the production of pick-up trucks for the North American market.

[10] However, Nissan's impressive recovery somewhat ran out of steam in 2006: profits dropped for the first time in seven years and the company had to cede the position of Japan's second-largest automaker to Honda.

[11] On a nonconsolidated basis, i.e., looking just at Nissan's core operations in Japan, the number of employees dropped from 41,300 in FY1996 to 30,400 in FY2001, but has since grown again to 32,200 in FY2005 (*Source:* Nissan annual reports).

market. Of course, Nissan's renewed strength exerts pressure on its rivals, but, as already mentioned, Japan's car industry is used to fierce competition at home. Similarly, Nissan's revival, of course, in part owes to newly developed products that appeal to consumers, but these do not represent a genuinely new type of product previously unavailable in Japan.

However, there are at least two areas in which the Renault–Nissan alliance has had an impact on its peers and the wider industry. The first of these is managements' focus on profitability. For much of the postwar era and continuing well into the 1990s, Japanese business strategies tended to focus on market share; in contrast, profitability often was a secondary objective. In recent years, though, a greater emphasis on profits and profitability can be observed. For example, in Toyota's annual report for FY2000, the word "profitability" appears only three times, and each time only in a general discussion of what factors might affect the company's financial results. But that number increases to twelve in the FY2004 annual report, which is littered with statements such as: "[O]ne of the major management tasks that Toyota faces today is the optimal deployment of its existing management resources to facilitate business expansion, *strengthen profitability*, and train personnel" [emphasis added].[12] No similar linguistic shift can be observed at Nissan's and Toyota's main rival, Honda: the term "profitability" does not occur once in its annual reports, but they do carry statements such as: "[W]e consider redistribution of profits to shareholders as one of our most important management issues."[13] An important reason for the growing emphasis on profitability and shareholder value probably is the increasing ratio of shares held by foreign portfolio investors.[14] However, another contributing factor is likely to have been Ghosn's single-minded focus on bottom-line results at Nissan. Not only has this increased the pressure on other companies to do likewise, Nissan's industry-leading operating margins have also raised the bar for its competitors.

The other area where the Renault–Nissan alliance has had wider repercussions is in the supplier industry. As mentioned earlier, the reorganization of Nissan's parts purchases consisted of two elements: first, the streamlining of such purchases on a global scale through the Renault Nissan Purchasing Organization. Traditionally, Nissan had placed orders for the same part with more than one *keiretsu* supplier. Now, however, mass orders were to

---

[12] *Toyota Annual Report 2004*, p. 11.
[13] *Honda Annual Report 2004*, p. 3.
[14] The percentage of shares held by foreign investors in Toyota in March 2006 was 26.6 percent, while the corresponding figure for Honda was 35.6 percent.

be placed with one global supplier. For Renault and Nissan, this meant they were able to exploit synergies and gain bargaining power vis-à-vis suppliers as a result of the increased scale of orders, while suppliers were able to exploit economies of scale, helping them to lower costs. But for Nissan's traditional *keiretsu* suppliers, the new arrangement also meant increased competition and screening out as the number of Nissan's suppliers was halved from around 1,200 to about 600.[15]

The second element in the reorganization of parts purchases was the dissolution of Nissan's *keiretsu*, that is, the sale of its stakes in all but four of the 1,394 companies in which Nissan held stocks. Rather than indiscriminately offloading its shareholdings, though, Nissan typically sought to arrange tie-ups with other Japanese or with foreign companies.[16] The most important among the domestic tie-ups was that between Calsonic and Kansei, creating a global player that has been able to boost sales by 70 percent from a combined ¥405 billion before the merger (2000) to ¥715 billion in 2005.[17] Meanwhile, the car electronics business of Unisia Jecs, another major *keiretsu* supplier, was sold to Hitachi (which turned the company into a wholly-owned subsidiary in 2002), while the transmission division was sold to Valeo of France, one of the biggest parts makers in Europe and the largest parts suppliers to Renault.[18] Valeo was also encouraged by Ghosn and his team to acquire Nissan's shareholdings in Ichikoh Industries, which in turn invested capital in Valeo.[19] Other international tie-ups involving major Nissan suppliers were the sale of seat maker Ikeda Bussan to Johnson Controls of the United States and of a 30.8 percent equity stake in suspension maker Yoruzu to Tower, also of the United States.

The dissolution of the Nissan *keiretsu* thus has allowed a number of foreign companies to become suppliers to Nissan for the first time. More than that: it has provided them with production bases in Japan through the joint ventures and capital tie-ups they entered with former Nissan affiliates.

---

[15] See Ikeda and Nakagawa (2002) and Magee (2003).
[16] In selling its stakes in suppliers, Nissan was careful not to let suppliers fall into the hands of its Japanese competitors. This explains why a large number of suppliers were sold to foreign companies. For the same reason, suppliers were also not sold to financial firms, because these might resell them to domestic competitors. See Economic and Social Research Institute (2005).
[17] Figures from annual reports.
[18] Further examples of domestic tie-ups involving Nissan suppliers abound, including the acquisition of a 6.5 percent stake in Kinugawa Rubber by Toyo Tire and Rubber (1999), a 23.4 percent stake in Exidy by Aisin Seiki (2001), a 23.7 percent stake in Fuki Kiko by Koyo Seiki (2001), etc. *Source:* JETRO (2005a).
[19] Ikeda and Nakagawa (2002).

But the alliances also provide benefits for the Japanese side. The tie-up between Valeo and Ichikoh, for example, includes the shared utilization of plants, thus giving the latter a foothold in Europe and elsewhere, helping it to meet Nissan's requirement for suppliers that are competitive on a global scale.

Finally, following the reconfiguration of the supplier network, restructuring continued in 2006 with the sale of Nissan's and Renault's stakes in Nissan Diesel to Swedish truckmaker Volvo, which subsequently made the Japanese company a wholly-owned subsidiary in 2007. The divestiture formed part of Nissan's strategy to focus on the company's core passenger vehicle and light commercial vehicle business,[20] while for Nissan Diesel, which had been struggling for years, the takeover by Volvo promised the injection of badly needed funds. Thus, even almost ten years after the initial transaction, Renault's acquisition of Nissan was still having repercussions.

Suppliers and the Keiretsu

The tie-ups between former Nissan *keiretsu* members and foreign parts makers represent only a fraction of the growing tide of collaborations between Japanese suppliers and foreign counterparts. Between 1997 and 2004, there were at least 24 cases in which foreign parts manufacturers acquired stakes in Japanese companies or entered joint ventures.[21] This development forms part of a worldwide trend toward modularization and systematization, in which suppliers deliver parts to auto manufacturers in the shape of partially assembled units (modules) and functionally integrated units (systems), with parts suppliers assuming responsibility for design and development as well as assembly, and which, in turn, has led suppliers to broaden their capabilities through joint ventures and mergers and acquisitions (M&As).[22] Driven largely by American and European megasuppliers such as Delphi and Visteon (the former in-house part-manufacturing departments of GM and Ford), Bosch (Germany), ZF Sachs (Germany), and Valeo (France), the supplier industry has thus seen a trend toward global integration similar to the car assembly industry itself.

Despite the size of Japan's car industry, only two of the country's suppliers, Denso and Aisin Seiki, both affiliates of Toyota, rank among the global top

[20] Nissan press release, "AB Volvo to acquire Nissan's remaining 6% stake in Nissan Diesel," September 25, 2006; online: <http://www.nissan-global.com/EN/NEWS/2006/_STORY/060925-02-e.html> (accessed March 14, 2007).
[21] Based on JETRO (2005a: 70–1), Figure 49.
[22] Development Bank of Japan (2000).

ten. Most other suppliers, though strong in specialized niche markets, lack the scale of their foreign competitors, as indicated by their respective sales, which for many Japanese parts makers are in the order of several hundred ¥ billion (several US$ billion), compared with several ¥ trillion (tens of US$ billion) for the likes of Bosch, Delphi, or Visteon.[23] This means that many Japanese suppliers are struggling to muster the financial and managerial resources to provide the global supply capacity and enhanced development capability required by carmakers today.[24] While some Japanese parts makers have acquired foreign affiliates, accepting foreign capital through M&As or entering joint ventures often represents the best way to respond to globalization and the need for modularization and systemization.

The dismantling of the Nissan *keiretsu* with the aim not only of returning Nissan's balance sheet to an even keel, but also of creating a network of world-class suppliers that can shoulder greater responsibilities in terms of independent design and development of modules clearly fits in with this pattern. However, it is important to note that the issue of supplier–manufacturer relationships is not a question of "superior" Western management techniques versus "outdated" Japanese practices. A case in point is Toyota, which has gone from strength to strength, overtaking Ford as the world's second-largest automotive manufacturer in terms of sales (if the sales of truck maker Hino are included). Yet, Toyota has gone in the opposite direction from Nissan, raising its shareholding in compact carmaker Daihatsu to a majority stake in 1998 and making truck maker Hino a subsidiary in 2001, while its closest affiliate and former parent, Toyoda Automatic Loom, increased its ownership of Toyota's most important suppliers, Denso and Aisin Seiki.[25] Such steps have been interpreted as defensive moves to reassert control over *keiretsu* members at a time when these large suppliers were becoming increasingly independent-minded and foreigners were acquiring stakes in parts makers that were also important suppliers to Toyota.[26] Yet, it is interesting to note that Nissan, too, has recently moved to strengthen its ties with remaining *keiretsu* suppliers again. Having at one

[23] Calsonic and Kansei, the two former Nissan *keiretsu* suppliers, for example, had sales of ¥280 billion and ¥130 billion, respectively, in 2000, the year before their merger. Even after the merger and rapid growth, the sales of about ¥700 billion in 2005 reached only about a quarter of Delphi's or Bosch's (automotive technology only), which were in the region of US$30 billion.

[24] Development Bank of Japan (2000).

[25] Hino website; Ahmadjian and Lincoln (2001).

[26] See *Purchasing.com*, "Supplier landscape shifts as companies seek global strategies," January 13, 2000.

point considered selling its stake in Calsonic to Delphi, Nissan raised its shareholding in the merged Calsonic Kansei in November 2004 from 27.6 percent to 41.7 percent, turning it into a consolidated subsidiary to retain close control over a supplier that provides the company with key technology.[27] Thus, it remains to be seen what kind of supplier network configurations will prove more successful in the future. What is clear, though, is that the growing presence of both foreign carmakers and parts suppliers has led to a greater diversity in organizational arrangements.

The Toyota example also shows that the *keiretsu* and traditional supplier–assembler relationships continue to matter in large parts of Japan's automotive industry. One important reason that Toyota has strengthened the relationship with its suppliers is that it wants to retain close control over product development for parts and components. This type of strategy, however, has also led to complaints from foreign parts companies that suppliers are still expected to "build-to-print" the traditional Japanese way, suggesting that they continue to face difficulties in doing business in Japan as a result of the reluctance to outsource product development on a global basis.[28] Similarly, even though European suppliers have been able to expand their sales in Japan, the supplied parts and components are largely for vehicles destined for export to European markets only and not for models sold in Japan, the United States, or other overseas markets. While this helps Japanese car manufacturers to meet European standards and reduce political friction, it limits European suppliers' prospects in Japan.[29]

Finally, another illustration of the continuing importance of the *keiretsu* is provided by the hapless DaimlerChrysler–Mitsubishi Motors alliance. MMC's membership of the larger Mitsubishi *keiretsu*, the core of which includes Tokyo Mitsubishi Financial Group, Mitsubishi Corporation, and Mitsubishi Industries, is generally considered to be a major reason why the alliance failed. Not only did the tightly knit *keiretsu* relationships make it more difficult for the new German management to overhaul supplier relationships, the knowledge that in an emergency the other group companies would come to the rescue, as they eventually did, also meant that at MMC there was much less of a sense of crisis and much greater resistance to change

---

[27] Economic and Social Research Institute (2005) and *The Nikkei Weekly* (online), "Ghosn recasting keiretsu supplier," January 24, 2005. The latter quotes Ghosn as saying: "Not everything about the *keiretsu* is wrong. It simply did not function properly under Nissan in the past. From now on, we need stronger ties."

[28] *Autoasia*, Q1, 2004, p. 68.

[29] A. N. R. Millington, Director General of the Tokyo Office of the European Automobile Manufacturers Association, interview on May 13, 2005.

than at Nissan. Following scandals involving cover-ups of defective vehicles and mounting losses, DaimlerChrysler decided to abandon MMC in August 2004, although the German-American firm did retain its 85 percent stake in the truckmaker Mitsubishi Fuso.

Summary

The globalization of the car industry has proceeded rapidly over the past decade or so, and today, most major players operate, either directly or through alliances, in the major markets of North America, Europe, Asia, and beyond. Among Japan's industries, too, the automotive sector has been at the vanguard of internationalization, both through exports and overseas production. Yet, as recently as the late 1990s, Japan's car industry remained much less globalized than its counterparts in Europe and the United States. Not only were there no wholly-foreign carmakers manufacturing vehicles in Japan; if the Nissan case is representative, Japanese companies, although operating internationally, had also been slow to adopt an integrated global business perspective.

At least to some extent, this has begun to change. Foreign companies have been able to make inroads, entering equity participations or joint ventures with Japanese companies and, in the case of Volvo's acquisition of Nissan Diesel in 2007, even turned a Japanese vehicle manufacturer into a wholly-owned subsidiary. In the process, foreign firms have introduced advanced management techniques (such as in Nissan's financial operations) and Western-style employment practices (such as performance-based promotion and remuneration). They have also contributed to a shift in the management objective of Japanese companies from market share to profitability and shareholder value.

But probably the most important area in which foreign companies have been a catalyst for change is in industry structure. The dissolution of the Nissan *keiretsu* has meant that, on the one hand, about half of the company's traditional suppliers have lost (one of) their main customer(s). On the other hand, the reorganization of parts procurements at Nissan has helped some traditional suppliers, such as Calsonic Kansei, to expand, and has opened the door to new, often foreign suppliers. But consolidation in the supplier industry has not been confined to Nissan *keiretsu* members, as a growing number of foreign companies have acquired stakes in other Japanese counterparts or entered joint ventures. This not only has made the composition of the car industry in Japan more international but also has helped Japanese suppliers to strengthen their global capabilities to serve customers worldwide.

Banking and Insurance

Long cosseted by government regulation and structural entry barriers, the banking and insurance sectors provide a vivid illustration both of the substantial changes that have taken place in Japan over the past decade-and-a-half and of the remaining challenges ahead if the country is to develop globally competitive service industries. To be sure, much of the transformation of Japan's financial sector is the result of domestic forces and foreign companies have at best played a marginal role. Yet, in those areas where foreign players have gained a foothold, their impact is clearly visible.

However, to understand the role of FDI in this sector, it is necessary to make a brief digression and consider banks' and, to a lesser extent, insurance companies' place in Japan's economic system. Financial institutions have been at the heart of what, by the 1980s, often came to be referred to as "Japan Inc.," the monolithic *keiretsu* system with the banks and insurance companies at the center of tightly knit webs of cross-shareholdings. A central element of this arrangement, in turn, was the main-bank system, characterized by strong established ties between domestic banks and their corporate clients. Loans from city banks (commercial banks) would typically provide the main source of external funds for most companies and banks often held significant equity interests in their corporate clients, getting closely involved in companies' managerial affairs in times of financial distress. Similarly, insurance companies would be major long-term shareholders in firms belonging to the same business grouping. Under this arrangement, stringent government regulation of the financial sector and the "convoy system" – meant to guarantee stability by preventing laggards from falling behind and leaders from moving too far ahead – thwarted competition and innovation in products and services, and conventional lending to corporate clients provided the major source of income for Japanese banks. Likewise, insurance companies all tended to offer the same standardized services and products.

However, the traditional system came under substantial strain as a result of the prolonged economic malaise, financial deregulation, and other economic reforms. In the banking sector, nonperforming loans – a hangover from the burst of the bubble economy – and failure on the part of the government to decisively deal with the problem meant that, by the end of the 1990s, the entire financial system was teetering on the brink of collapse. Between 1997 and 2003, a number of securities firms, including one of the country's Big Four, Yamaichi, two of the three long-term lending banks, Long-Term Credit Bank and Nippon Credit Bank, and several regional banks, including

Hokkaido Takushoku, Kofuku, and Ashikaga banks, went bankrupt and, in most cases, were nationalized.

The life insurance industry was similarly creaking under the burden of negative carrying costs – the shortfall between guaranteed payouts to customers on insurance products and the minimal or negative return on assets resulting from the Bank of Japan's zero-interest-rate policy and slumping stock and real estate markets. All in all, a total of 20 banks, 27 credit unions, 181 credit associations, 7 life insurers, 2 property and casualty insurers, and 7 securities companies went bankrupt between 1992 and 2003.[30]

A complete meltdown of the financial system was averted only through the injection of massive government funds, resulting in the quasi-nationalization of a large part of the banking sector and providing the impetus for substantial industry consolidation across traditional *keiretsu* lines. The Industrial Bank of Japan, Fuji Bank, and Dai-ichi Kangyo Bank, for example, merged to form the Mizuho Financial Group, while Sumitomo Bank and Sakura Bank joined forces to become the Sumitomo Mitsui Banking Corporation. The mergers were made possible by a series of financial sector reforms commonly labeled as Japan's "Big Bang" in reference to Britain's financial market deregulation in 1986. The reforms, for the first time since before World War II, allowed Japanese firms to form holding companies and led to further financial sector consolidation in other areas, such the securities industry.

But the Big Bang reforms were intended to achieve much more than to aid industry consolidation, aiming, as they did, at turning Tokyo into a global financial center on par with London and New York. To this end, controls on foreign exchange transactions, fixed share-trading commissions, and government-stipulated uniform insurance premiums were abolished. In addition, for the first time, banks were allowed to enter the securities business, and barriers between the insurance business and banking, securities, and trust banking were lifted.

While it is debatable whether these reforms deserve the Big Bang label,[31] they certainly form part of a long-term transition in Japan's financial system from a bank-centered to a financial market-centered one. The beginnings of this trend date back to the late 1980s, when large Japanese corporations began raising external funds through foreign and domestic bond issues. Since then, bank debt as a source of funding for large, publicly trade firms has declined

---

[30] Horiuchi (2004: 43).
[31] See, e.g., *The Economist*, "Bang, pop or splutter?" May 7, 1998.

further in importance.[32] Shrinkage and consolidation in the banking sector therefore are likely to continue. On a brighter note, however, Japanese banks have made substantial progress in the disposal of nonperforming loans – one important reason why the economic gloom over Japan has finally lifted.

FDI in the Financial Sector – An Overview
Foreign direct investment trends clearly reflect the changed conditions in Japan's financial sector. Government regulations and close ties between banks and corporate customers have meant that foreign financial institutions have long struggled to penetrate the Japanese market, and until the mid-1990s, banking and insurance accounted for less than 5 percent of total FDI inflows. Since then, however, FDI in the sector has skyrocketed, accounting for 41 percent of total inflows between 1997 and 2004, making banking and insurance by far the leading industry in every year, with the sole exception of 1999, when it was eclipsed by the car industry.[33] As a result, financial intermediary services and insurance today are the industries with by far the highest share of employment by foreign-owned companies in the service sector in Japan (see Table 2.1 in Chapter 2).

Three major reasons for the increase in foreign investment in the banking and insurance sectors can be identified. The first and most obvious is deregulation. Although foreign banks continue to complain that Japan's financial industries remain more heavily regulated than their American or British counterparts,[34] the Big Bang reforms have broadened the areas in which foreign financial institutions can bring their expertise to bear. The same is true for the insurance sector, where deregulation has allowed life and non-life insurers to enter each others' business, abolished government-stipulated premium rates, and streamlined the approval of new insurance products (see below). The second reason is the gradual transformation of Japan's financial system from a bank-centered to a capital-market-centered one. As securities markets gain in importance as an alternative source of funding, the role of

[32] See Hoshi and Kashyap (2001), chapter 7.
[33] Based on Ministry of Finance (MOF) notification statistics. Data for 2005, which are not consistent with the notification statistics, suggest that FDI in the finance and insurance sector remained strong but, partly because of withdrawals, was eclipsed by transportation, wholesale and retail, and communication in the service sector and chemicals and pharmaceuticals and electric machinery in the manufacturing sector. In 2006, the finance and insurance sector was again in the lead, especially because a number of other sectors saw large-scale withdrawals.
[34] A frequently cited example of remaining obstacles is Article 65 of the Securities and Exchange Law, which separates the banking and securities business.

established main-bank relationships is diminishing, removing one of the major obstacles for foreign banks operating in Japan.

But in and of themselves, these two factors probably would not have been sufficient to draw the substantial amounts of FDI actually witnessed. Instead, they provided the backdrop to the third major event: the deepening economic and financial crisis that produced a significant number of takeover targets. Generally reluctant to take over operating banks and insurance companies because of the heavy risks involved, foreign investors were much more willing to acquire failed institutions and, as indicated above, they were spoilt for choice. In the banking sector, Merrill Lynch, for example, took over the distribution network of Yamaichi Securities; a group of foreign investors, led by Ripplewood Holdings, bought the failed Long-Term Credit Bank of Japan, since revived as Shinsei Bank; and Nippon Investment Partners, a special-purpose fund set up by the Asia Recovery Fund, bought the operations of Kofuku Bank, a regional institution that collapsed in 1999 and has since been reopened as Kansai Sawayaka Bank (KS Bank). Meanwhile, in the insurance sector, foreign investors snapped up five of the nine life insurers that failed between 1997 and 2001. (In contrast with the banking sector, there were also four instances in which foreign insurers bought Japanese counterparts that had not (yet) gone bankrupt. See Table 6.2.)

Although foreign-owned firms continue to account for only a fraction of the banking and insurance business overall, they have been able to carve out significant market shares in some areas, which, moreover, are typically growing much more rapidly than the traditional segments in which domestic firms dominate. Much of this success owes to the global capabilities, professionalism, and sophisticated risk management techniques that foreign multinationals have developed while operating in the more advanced and deregulated markets of the United States and Europe. The presence of such global players as well as the products and services they offer have affected their industries in various ways. The following sections examine this impact in greater detail, looking at investment banking, retail banking, and the life insurance industry, respectively.

Investment Banking

The banking and finance sector spans a wide range of services, including retail and commercial banking, investment banking, securities trading, and asset management. It is in the latter areas – investment banking, securities trading, and asset management – that foreign financial institutions have made by far the greatest inroads into the Japanese market. What is more, although most of the major international players have been in Japan since the 1980s, it is only since the second half of the 1990s that they have begun to make their presence felt. This success has been based on a combination of the developments already described – deregulation, the transition to a capital-market-based financial system, and economic malaise – and foreign investment banks' expertise, which has allowed them to compensate for what they lack in local knowledge and access – the bases of traditional relational banking – with transactional and technical know-how.

The following examples illustrate the interplay between structural change, the demand for investment banking services, and the role of foreign companies providing such services. Even before the Big Bang, the ongoing recession created what is often called the "distress business," such as the disposal of bad loans, the unwinding of cross-shareholdings, the raising of capital from foreign investors for cash-strapped companies, and the development of derivatives that provided firms with ways to offload risk or disguise financial problems. Requiring extensive technical expertise and access to foreign institutional investors that would buy these sophisticated financial products, foreign investment banks were often the only ones able to provide such services.[35]

Structural change and economic reforms have also led to a large increase in M&A activity in Japan since the mid-1990s. Not only have out–in M&As as the preferred means of market entry for foreign firms jumped with the overall rise in FDI, but there has also been a substantial growth in domestic M&A activity, and foreign investment banks have been able to gain a large share of this business as well, based on their international experience in M&A deals. In 2006, seven of the top ten financial advisors for M&A deals were foreign investment banks.[36]

The transition from a bank-centered to a capital-market-based financial system, meanwhile, means that companies increasingly access capital markets directly to meet their financing needs by issuing bonds and equities. Although in most cases, the main underwriter of such securities still is Japanese, foreign investment banks often are joint book runners thanks to their superior access to international investors.[37] Such access to international

---

[35] *The Economist*, "Rich pickings for the gaijin," May 14, 1998.

[36] *Source:* Thomson Financial, "Mergers & Acquisitions Review," online: <http://www.thomson.com/pdf/financial/league_table/ma/150587/4Q06_MA_Global_Finl_Advisory> (accessed March 7, 2007).

[37] According to Bloomberg, the top ten underwriters of stock and convertible bond sales in Japan in the first quarter of 2005 were ranked as follows: Nikko Citigroup (then jointly owned by Citigroup and Nikko Cordial, which has since been acquired by Citigroup) led the pack with a market share of 27.3 percent and 15 issues, followed by Nomura, Daiwa, and

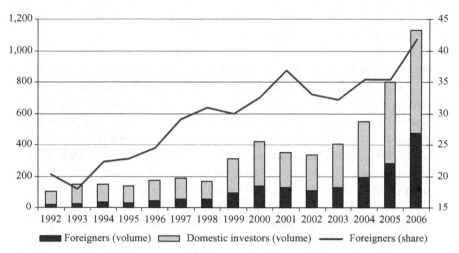

Figure 6.1. Trading value and proportion of trading value by type of investor on the First Section of the Tokyo Stock Exchange (¥ trillion; percent)
Sources: For 1992–2004: Japan Securities Dealers Association, *Fact Book 2002* and *Fact Book 2005*; online: <http://www.jsda.or.jp/html/eigo/publi_i.html> (accessed March 7, 2007). For 2005 and 2006: authors' calculations based on data from the Tokyo Stock Exchange, "Investment Trends by Investor Category," online: <http://www.tse.or.jp/english/data/exotic/sector/index.html> (accessed March 7, 2007).

investors, in turn, has grown in importance as foreigners have been the most important net buyers of Japanese shares in recent years.[38] In fact, to a large extent as a result of the unwinding of cross-shareholdings, the percentage of Japanese shares held by foreign investors has risen from only 4.7 percent (in terms of market value) in 1990 to 26.7 percent in 2005.[39] What is more, foreigners tend to be more active shareholders than their Japanese counterparts, buying and selling shares more frequently, so that foreigners now account for about two-fifths of all trading on the Tokyo Stock Exchange (Figure 6.1). And since foreign investors prefer dealing with foreign firms,

---

Mizuho with a combined market share of 50.0 percent and a total of 57 issues. Among the remaining six firms of the top ten, only one was Japanese (Shinko Securities, market share: 1.9 percent, 13 issues), while the other five were foreign: Morgan Stanley, Goldman Sachs, JPMorgan, UBS, and Merrill Lynch with a combined market share of 17.9 percent, but only 6 issues (*Bloomberg*, "Nikko Citigroup eclipses Nomura as Top Japan Stock Underwriter", March 30, 2005).

[38] *The Economist*, "The last, best game," October 20, 2005.

[39] Figures from: *2005 Share Ownership Survey*, Table 3, online: <http://www.tse.or.jp/english/data/research/english2005.pdf> (accessed March 6, 2007).

it is widely thought that this trend has helped to lift the share of turnover conducted by foreign securities firms.[40]

Another reason that foreign investment banks have been able to gain a larger share in trading volume is their investment in information technology (IT) and IT skills. Morgan Stanley, for example, has invested heavily in a trading engine that is able to execute trades much quicker and at much larger volumes than most of its competitors, allowing it to offer better prices for its customers, including many Japanese ones.[41] Yet another growth area in which foreign financial institutions have been able to make inroads is asset management. The amount of assets managed by investment advisors has risen fivefold from ¥34.8 trillion in 1992 to ¥145.8 trillion in 2006,[42] but while foreign-affiliated companies have been able to build up assets under management, domestic companies have been losing them.[43]

As these examples illustrate, foreign financial institutions have been able to gain significant market shares in a number of investment banking, securities, and asset management-related areas. There are several reasons that explain this success. The first is that, as Japan makes the transition from a bank-centered to a capital-market-centered financial system, there is a growing demand for the services that investment banks offer. Not only are traditional bank loans, and with them established main-bank relationships, diminishing in importance, while securities markets as alternative sources of funding are playing a larger role; the financial troubles experienced by many Japanese companies also meant that there was ample need for innovative approaches to the restructuring of corporate finances, for example, through the securitization of assets and liabilities.

The second and closely related reason is that, with their global presence and capabilities, foreign investment banks are well placed to capitalize on this shift to capital-market-based corporate financing and other structural changes taking place in the Japanese economy. Investment banking is a business that requires advanced technologies and extensive expertise, including, for example, sophisticated computer software, mathematical talent, and portfolio-modeling capabilities to manage risk and develop innovative financial products – areas in which most Japanese banks have lagged

---

[40] Mitsui Kaijo Kiso Kenkyujo (2001: 49).
[41] Thomas Riley, Managing Director, Morgan Stanley Japan, interview on October 12, 2005.
[42] *Source: Japan Investment Advisers Association*, Statistical Releases, September 2006, online: <http://jsiaa.mediagalaxy.ne.jp/toukei_e/index.html> (accessed March 7, 2007).
[43] *Nikkei Net*, "Market scramble: Foreign asset management firms hone edge," November 20, 2003.

behind.[44] Combining these capabilities with an understanding of global markets, foreign investment banks, according to a foreign industry insider, have introduced a degree of professionalism to the investment process in Japan that was previously missing.[45] In the process, they have developed financial products such as credit derivatives that were previously unavailable in Japan or investment products sold through smaller securities firms that broaden the choice available to private investors.

The third reason that foreign investment banks have been able to gain market share is that Japanese banks have been slow to close the gap with their overseas competitors in this business area. There appear to be several factors explaining why this is the case. The first is that investment banking has been low in Japanese financial institutions' order of priorities, as is illustrated by the importance attached to the various parts of the financial conglomerates. In the case of The Mitsubishi UFJ Financial Group, for example, the holding company takes pride of place, followed by commercial banking (Bank of Tokyo-Mitsubishi UFJ), trust banking (Mitsubishi UFJ Trust and Banking), and only then investment banking (Mitsubishi UFJ Securities).[46] The second and closely related reason why Japanese banks have failed to close the gap is their organizational framework, which continues to be dominated by rigid hierarchies and pay structures.[47] Unable or unwilling to pay competitive salaries, Japanese banks find it difficult to attract the necessary talent, for example, by poaching experienced staff from their foreign rivals.[48] Rather, the flow has generally been one way, with staff from Japanese banks moving to their foreign counterparts. What is more, foreign investment banks in recent years have become one of the most sought-after destinations among high-flying university graduates.[49] A third reason is that, despite the Big Bang, Japan's financial sector continues to be more tightly regulated than its counterparts in the United States and many European countries. Coupled with Japanese banks' weak presence in more advanced overseas markets, this means that Japanese banks have little opportunity to develop the skills necessary to compete with their industry-leading Western counterparts.

---

[44] See, e.g., Rapp (1999).
[45] Jean-Francois Minier, Chairman of the EBC Banking Committee, interview on May 11, 2005.
[46] The authors are grateful to Jean-Francois Minier, Chairman of the EBC Banking Committee, for this point.
[47] *The Economist*, "Rich pickings for the gaijin," May 14, 1998. Though dating from 1998, this observations applies as much today as it did back then.
[48] This, of course, assumes that they would be interested in doing so in the first place.
[49] *The Nikkei Weekly*, "Foreign investment banks flourishing from local talent," May 2, 2005.

Compare this not only with the large American investment banks, with their home base in the world's most advanced financial market and a presence in all major financial centers, but also with some of the Swiss, German, or Dutch banks. Even though the financial markets of the latter's home base may not be as large or advanced, they have a strong presence in New York and London, providing exposure and hence learning opportunities in the most sophisticated markets.

That Japanese financial institutions do not accord a higher priority to investment banking and revise organizational hierarchies and pay structures to attract high flyers indicates that Japanese banks either continue to be preoccupied with bringing their core business – commercial lending – into order; or that, to date, foreign investment banks are not perceived as a threat. The latter hypothesis is supported by a Japanese report on the effect of foreign competition in the financial industry on domestic players, which comes to the conclusion that, with the exception of foreign-currency-related business and share and bond issues, at present there is little direct rivalry between foreign and domestic institutions – they live in different "habitats."[50]

The same report also suggests that the presence of foreign banks has provided little direct stimulus to Japan's financial industry as a whole – simply because the overlap is so small.[51] Nevertheless, the products, services, business models, and employment practices of Japanese banks are becoming more like those of their Western competitors. Japanese banks, for example, have become active in areas such as project finance and derivatives trading and have adopted risk management techniques and more meritocratic salary schemes. What is more, although Japanese banks continue to lag behind in the development of innovative financial products, they have actively copied such products developed by foreign companies and in the process have learned from them. In other words, there are knowledge spillovers from foreign investment banks through product imitation. Thus, even if the gap in terms of technical expertise and innovative capabilities persists, the presence of foreign banks is raising the level of capabilities in Japanese financial institutions.

But given the important role financial institutions play in the allocation of capital, it is important to look beyond the impact of foreign investment banks on the Japanese banking industry alone. One of the problems plaguing the Japanese corporate sector in recent decades has been the poor return

---

[50] Mitsui Kaijo Kiso Kenkyujo (2001: 54).
[51] Mitsui Kaijo Kiso Kenkyujo (2001: 55).

on capital. Although the effects are difficult to quantify, it seems fair to say that the products and services offered by foreign banks have helped to put capital resources to better use. One example is the services related to the restructuring of corporate finances, such as through the purchase and resale of distressed debt through securitization or, similarly, the purchase of poorly managed real estate, the introduction of professional management, and its resale through real estate funds, helping firms to return to financial health.

In sum, rather than entering the low-margin corporate lending business, foreign banks in this segment appear content to concentrate on more profitable areas in which they can overcome whatever handicap they suffer from their lack of long-term relations through superior products, services, and technology previously unavailable in Japan. While this means that their activities remain confined to the investment banking business, this is a field that is bound to continue to grow as Japan makes the transition to a capital-markets-based financial system. And although the impact of foreign players on Japan's banking sector has remained limited, their products and services contribute to the ongoing restructuring of the country's corporate sector more generally.

Retail and Commercial Banking

Whereas the investment banking, securities, and asset management business has lured dozens of foreign firms to Japan, the number of foreign investments in the retail and commercial banking sector can be counted on one hand. What is more, the small number of cases there are fall into two distinct groups. The first consists only of Citibank as the sole foreign bank to have established retail operations in Japan. Citibank, in fact, traces its origins in Japan as far back as 1902, when its progenitor, the International Banking Corporation, opened a branch in Yokohama.[52] The second category, on the other hand, is made up of four Japanese banks that failed during the financial crisis in the late 1990s and that were purchased and subsequently revived by foreign investors: Shinsei Bank (formerly Long-Term Credit Bank of Japan), Kansai Sawayaka Bank (KS Bank, formerly Kofuku Bank), Tokyo Star Bank (formerly Tokyo Sowa Bank), and Aozora Bank (formerly Nippon Credit Bank).[53] Despite their very different histories, these two groups have

---

[52] Harner (2000: 181).

[53] Aozora's case is somewhat different from the three other failed banks in that the rescue was initially led by Japan's Softbank. However, in 2003, the U.S. investment fund Cerberus, which had already held a minority stake in the bank, also acquired Softbank's share, bringing Cerberus' total stake to 62 percent.

a number of features in common that distinguish them from their domestic counterparts.

The first of these common features is that their operations are comparatively small. Citibank,[54] for example, operates only 25 branches in the whole of Japan (most of them in the Tokyo area), Shinsei Bank has 38 branches (including seven subbranches), and Tokyo Star Bank has 33 branches (and one subbranch), all in the capital.[55] These figures compare with the hundreds of branches that Japan's city banks operate throughout the country. A second common feature is the attention paid to innovative (by Japanese standards) customer services. For example, as any foreign visitor to Japan will soon notice, even today it is difficult to find automated teller machines (ATMs) that operate 24 hours and/or accept foreign-issued debit or credit cards. Citibank, followed by a number of the resuscitated banks, has been the first to introduce such services, typically without the charges levied by the city banks for the use of cash dispensers outside business hours. Other ways in which these banks distinguish themselves is by offering bright, modern branches (with the back office hidden from the customer) and by introducing new products and services, including personal financial advisors, multipurpose and multicurrency accounts, and, in the case of Citibank, services directed at internationally oriented customers, such as commission-free overseas cash withdrawals.

A third common feature is that both Citibank and the revived smaller banks pursue more focused business models than their large Japanese counterparts, and one important area on which they have concentrated is consumer lending. Consumer finance is a segment that banks in Japan were historically barred from entering because of the government's determination to channel scarce financial resources to investment rather than consumption during the country's postwar industrialization drive. This situation gave rise to a vibrant consumer finance industry, which, however, has enjoyed a dubious reputation due to the high rates of interest charged and tabloid stories of overborrowing by low-paid workers and housewives.[56] In recent years, however, banks have started to move into consumer finance as well, with Citibank and the revived banks leading the way. Following the

---

[54] The discussion here does not consider Citigroup's acquisition of Nikko Cordial in early 2007, which is going to raise the American firm's presence in Japan substantially and is likely to have far more wide-ranging implications than its operations so far. See, e.g., *Nikkei Net*, "Citigroup to launch new era of competition in Japan" (May 1, 2007).

[55] As of March 2007. In fact, a significant reduction in the number of branches was one of the measures to turn the failed banks around.

[56] Harner (2000).

rescue by foreign investors, KS Bank, for example, streamlined its business to concentrate on lending to small and medium retailers and on consumer lending.[57] Similarly, Tokyo Star Bank has focused on business with high profit margins, such as credit cards, car loans, housing loans, and small- and medium-business loans,[58] areas into which the major banks are now beginning to follow.

This clear focus has helped Citibank and the resuscitated banks to be profitable at a time when Japan's other banks have found it difficult to derive much value from their retail banking and commercial lending operations. However, focus provides only part of the explanation and this is where the stories of Citibank and the resuscitated banks part. Citibank's operations in Japan form part of a long-term commitment to the Japanese market that has gradually evolved over the decades. Reentering Japan as soon as World War II had ended, the bank handled foreign currency-related business on behalf of local counterparts during the 1950s, lent foreign currency to Japanese companies during the 1960s, and became involved in providing corporate loans and trade finance during the 1970s. It was not until the 1980s, following the first wave of financial deregulation in Japan, that Citibank began to move into retail banking. Expanding only gradually at first, Citibank's retail operations received a significant boost as a result of the deepening financial crisis and weakening yen during the late 1990s, when worried savers flocked to the bank to open foreign currency accounts.[59] As a result, the deposit base more than quadrupled in the space of only a few years.[60] And in probably its biggest coup yet, Citigroup acquired Nikko Cordial in the spring of 2007 – a move that means that, for the first time, a foreign bank will offer comprehensive financial services in Japan. If successful, the impact on competition and other aspects of Japan's financial sector may be far-reaching.[61] In sum, Citbank's position as the only foreign bank with retail operations in Japan is the result of unrivaled dedication to the Japanese market coupled with the ability to continuously innovate, adapt, and exploit niches as they presented themselves.

Compared with Citibank, the resuscitated banks represent FDI of an altogether different nature. Consisting of the purchase of existing, albeit bankrupt, banks, the acquisitions were backed, not by foreign banks that

---

[57] ACCJ, FDI Case Studies, Kansai Sawayaka Bank (KS Bank), online: <http://www.accj.or.jp/document_library/FDICaseStudies/1069040587.pdf> (accessed March 8, 2007).
[58] *Nikkei Net*, "Tokyo Star Bank makes weak debut on price concerns," October 25, 2005.
[59] Harner (2000: 181–90).
[60] Harner (2000: 189).
[61] See, e.g., *Nikkei Net*, "Citigroup to launch new era of competition in Japan" (May 1, 2007).

wanted to gain a foothold in Japan, but by private equity funds whose aim was to turn the banks around to sell them off again at a profit. Because of this focus on short-term gain, such funds, feeding off the "carcasses" of failed firms by stripping their assets, have often been labeled as "vulture funds."

Taking a closer look at the cases of Kofuku/KS Bank, LTCB/Shinsei Bank, and Tokyo Sowa/Tokyo Star Bank, however, yields a less negative picture. The first thing to note is that in each of these instances, private equity investors, by overhauling management, introducing a more focused business model, investing in information technology and cutting costs, were able to restore these bankrupt banks to profitability. At Tokyo Star Bank, for example, almost half of the branches were shut and back-office operations were centralized in a Tokyo suburb. Staff levels were cut from 1,100 to 700, but have since increased again to about 1,070. As a result of these and other measures, profits jumped from ¥7.3 billion in 2002 to ¥14.0 billion in 2006. Once turned around, KS Bank was subsequently sold to the Bank of Kansai in 2003, while Shinsei Bank and Tokyo Star Bank successfully returned to the stock market in 2004 and 2005, respectively. This outcome provides a stark contrast with the situation only five years earlier, when the government was hard-pressed to find investors to take the nationalized banks off its hands.[62]

But it is also important to note that this turnaround could not have been achieved had the government not assumed a large portion of the banks' bad loan burden. Nor were the new management methods without controversy. In particular, Shinsei's refusal, in 2000, to participate in the debt-forgiveness scheme for ailing retailer Sogo earned the bank much criticism from the political establishment. What is more, doubts remain regarding the long-term prospects of Shinsei – despite its successful initial public offering (IPO) in 2004 – and Aozora, the other former long-term credit bank.[63]

Considering that taxpayers shouldered a large part of the bad-debt burden, whether the large gains that the private equity funds were indeed able to pocket upon the (partial) sale of their investments are justified remains a moot point.[64] Leaving such questions aside, what is clear, however, is that

---

[62] See, e.g., *The Economist*, "Hard bargains," June 24, 1999.

[63] On Shinsei, see, e.g., *The Economist*, "Reborn, remade, resold," January 15, 2004.

[64] In the case of Tokyo Star Bank, the offering of about 30 percent of outstanding shares was estimated to more than double Lone Star's initial investment, and including the unsold portion, Tokyo Star was worth about seven times the initial investment (*The Standard*, "Tokyo Star IPO set at top of range," October 18, 2005). WL Ross is said to have earned an 85 percent return on its $220 million investment when it sold most of its stake to Bank of Kansai (*BusinessWeek Online*, "Tokyo Star Bank is on the rise," February 23, 2004). And

under foreign ownership, these banks have brought a breath of fresh air into Japan's banking sector. Offering innovative services and consumer financial products, Citibank and the revitalized banks have led the way in providing consumers with greater choice and convenience – moves that some of the city banks are slowly beginning to copy.[65] They have also broken with the mold of providing almost automatic debt forgiveness. In the Sogo episode, Shinsei Bank's refusal to participate in the debt write-off led the government to attempt a bailout of the stricken retailer. However, following a public outcry, the government was forced to abandon this plan, resulting in Sogo's collapse. The practice of keeping zombie firms alive nevertheless continued.

Overall, although foreign-owned banks have introduced novel ideas and practices to Japan and, on occasion, have created quite a stir, their impact on the Japanese banking sector or the corporate world beyond has been rather limited. This is not surprising given their relatively small size. Even the largest of the revived banks, Shinsei Bank, which in its former incarnation as LTCB at one stage was the ninth-largest in the world, today only has a fraction of the assets (¥10 trillion) of Japan's biggest, Mitsubishi UFJ Financial Group (¥186 trillion).[66] And even taking Citibank and the other four foreign-owned banks together, their branch networks pale in comparison with those of the country's leading financial institutions. Therefore, the role of foreign-owned retail and commercial banks in Japan is at best marginal and is likely to remain so, given that it is highly improbable that foreigners will want to or be able to purchase any of the country's large city banks.

Insurance

In many ways, Japan's insurance industry has traditionally shared many of the characteristics of the banking sector. Like the banks, insurance companies in Japan were at the heart of the *keiretsu* system, acting as long-term stable shareholders in companies belonging to the same business group. Insurance companies also fell under the supervision of the Ministry of Finance, enjoying – like the banks – an explicit government guarantee but also having to submit to strict regulation. Analogous to the separation of business fields in the banking sector, there used to be strict barriers between the life and non-life insurance business. And just as there were restrictions

Ripplewood's ¥120 billion investment was estimated to be worth ¥1.5 trillion at the time of flotation in 2004 (*The Economist*, "Reborn, remade, resold," January 15, 2004).
[65] See, e.g., *The Economist*, "At your service," September 25, 2003.
[66] As of 2006. Sources: *Shinsei Bank Interim Report 2006, Mitsubishi UFJ Financial Group Annual Report 2006.*

on the range of financial products available in the banking sector and commissions were fixed, insurance products and premium rates were subject to approval by the Ministry.

As in the banking sector, these arrangements created an industry in which the range of products offered was limited, innovation was stunted, companies tended to be weak in managing risk, and competition followed its own peculiar logic. One major business area for insurance companies, for example, was the so-called *dantai hoken* (group insurance) covering all employees of a particular firm in one contract. Because insurers were unable to compete on price or through product differentiation, one important way in which they strove to secure such business for themselves was through *keiretsu* shareholdings, thus providing one important explanation for this central feature of the Japanese economy. Another example of the type of inefficient competition that government regulation of the insurance sector gave rise to is the door-to-door sale of life insurance products through the so-called "bicycle ladies" who make up about 90 percent of the sales staff at life insurance firms.[67] In 2005, Japan's largest life insurer, Nippon Life, alone employed 53,000 such women.[68]

What is more, operating in a large and, until the mid-1990s, growing home market, Japanese insurers neither saw the need nor possessed the skills to become international players.[69] At the same time, although foreign insurance companies were allowed to operate in Japan in principle, licenses for new entrants were only granted if they introduced novel products, which, however, were subject to lengthy approval procedures. The outcome was not that there was an absence of foreign insurers operating in Japan. On the contrary, American Insurance Group (AIG) entered Japan as early as 1946, followed by American Family Assurance Company of Columbus (AFLAC) and Prudential in the 1970s, and each of these companies was able to build a successful business in the country. But once established in Japan, these foreign players became as much part of the system as their domestic counterparts, barred from offering insurance products in rival business areas but also protected on their own turf from outside competition. Thus, despite some foreign participation, Japan's insurance market was largely sheltered from full international competition.

---

[67] *Nikkei Net*, "Nippon Life to hire more men for sales positions," March 3, 2005.

[68] *Nikkei Net*, "Nippon Life to hire more men for sales positions," March 3, 2005.

[69] Even today, the overseas insurance business of Japan's largest life insurer, Nippon Life, for example, remains limited to relatively minor operations in the United States, China, the Philippines, and Thailand.

Much of this has changed dramatically since the mid-1990s, however. As in the banking sector, deregulation and financial problems brought on by the deterioration of asset prices provided the trigger. Starting in 1996, the government introduced a series of amendments to the Insurance Business Law (the first modifications of the law in 56 years) that allowed life and non-life insurers to enter each other's business, lifted the ban on insurance holding companies, changed product registration from an approval to a notification basis for many types of insurance, and streamlined the approval process, thus allowing greater product competition and innovation.[70] During the same period that these regulatory changes were enacted, insurance companies – and especially the life insurers – were falling on increasingly hard times. Having suffered a decade of losses caused by high guaranteed pay-outs to policy holders and dismal investment returns, nine life insurance companies and two non-life insurers collapsed between 1997 and 2001. Most of the failed life insurers were snapped up by foreign competitors, as were four life insurers that were bought before they went bankrupt (see Table 6.2). In addition, a number of foreign insurers established subsidiaries in Japan, meaning that most global players now have a presence in the country.

In contrast with the banking sector, the entry of foreign firms in the insurance sector is contributing to substantial structural and other changes in the industry. One important reason is that in the banking sector, foreign investments have generally been confined to the establishment of subsidiaries in specialized niche markets (e.g., investment banking) or the acquisition of collapsed banks by private equity funds aiming to turn them around and then sell them on. (At least this was the case until Citigroup acquired Nikko Cordial in spring 2007, which was too recent to be considered here.) In contrast, foreign investments in the insurance industry, especially in the life insurance sector, primarily consisted of the acquisition of failed or struggling insurers by companies from the same industry aiming to gain a presence in the market.

The most immediate measure of the impact of FDI in the insurance sector is foreign firms' market share, which has grown rapidly in recent years. In the life insurance business, foreign companies' market share in Japan in terms of premium income has risen from less than 5 percent in 1997 to 25 percent

---

[70] For a detailed chronology of deregulation measures, see *The Life Insurance Association of Japan,* "Deregulation and Liberalization of the Japanese Life Insurance Market," online: <http://www.seiho.or.jp/english/publication/2005-2006/2006_04-4.pdf> (accessed March 8, 2007).

Table 6.2. *Bankruptcies and acquisitions in the Japanese insurance industry*

Company	Year collapsed	Buyer	Country of buyer	Year bought
Nissan Mutual[a]	1997	Artemis	France	1999
Heiwa Life[b]	–	Aetna (ING)[c]	USA (Netherlands)	1999
Toho Mutual	1999	GE Capital[d]	USA	2000
Nihon Dantai Life[b]	–	AXA	France	2000
Nicos Life[b]	–	Winterthur Group	Switzerland	2000
Daihyaku Mutual	2000	Manulife	Canada	2001
Daiichi Mutual Fire & Marine[e]	2000	–	–	–
Orico Life[b]	–	Prudential	UK	2001
Taisho Life	2000	Yamato Life	Japan	2001
Chiyoda Mutual	2000	AIG	USA	2001
Kyoei Life	2000	Prudential Financial	USA	2001
Tokyo Mutual	2000	T&D Financial	Japan	2001
Taisei Fire and Marine	2001	Sompo Japan	Japan	2002

[a] Following Nissan Mutual's collapse, the company's life insurance business was transferred to Aoba, which is the name of the entity that Artemis bought. Aoba was subsequently sold on in 2004 to Prudential.
[b] Did not collapse.
[c] Aetna, an American subsidiary of the Dutch financial services company ING, subsequently sold Heiwa Life to MassMutual of the United States.
[d] GE Capital's Japanese life insurance business was subsequently bought by AIG in 2003.
[e] No buyer was found.
Sources: Various press reports.

in 2004 and around a third in 2005.[71] What is more, foreign life insurers have been able to enjoy growth at a time when the overall life insurance market has been shrinking.[72]

---

[71] Sources: *Nikkei Net*, "Foreign insurers seek novel policies," May 12, 2003; *Nikkei Net*, "Foreign Life Insurers Grab 25% Share of Domestic Market," December 1, 2004; *Nikkei Net*, "Foreign life insurers saw slower premium revenue growth in FY05," May 31, 2006; NLI Research Institute, "Financial Overview of Life Insurance Companies in Fiscal 2003," online: <http://www.nli-research.co.jp/eng/resea/life/li040913.pdf>, Figure 1 (accessed March 8, 2007).

[72] Life insurance business in force in Japan peaked in 1996 and has been steadily shrinking ever since. See The Life Insurance Association of Japan, *Life Insurance Business in Japan, 2005–2006*, p. 34, online: <http://www.seiho.or.jp/english/publication/2005–2006/2006.pdf> (accessed March 8, 2007). Against this background, annual premium income in the Japanese life insurance industry shrank until 2002, but has registered slight increases since. Foreign insurers registered a particularly large jump in their combined premium income of 38 percent in 2004, which slowed to 8 percent in 2005. See: *Nikkei*

Foreign life insurers' success in Japan greatly owes to their dominant position in the so-called third sector. Comprising products such as medical and nursing care insurance that fall between the traditional categories of life insurance on the one hand and property and casualty insurance on the other, the third sector was long a niche market that only in recent years has grown in popularity, accounting for about 30 percent of new policies in 2004. In contrast, death benefit products, the staple of Japanese life insurers, have steadily fallen out of favor.[73]

A number of factors have contributed to foreign insurers' strong position in the third sector today. The first is that third-sector insurance products in Japan were in fact pioneered by foreign companies, with AFLAC being the prime example. When AFLAC entered Japan in 1974, it was the first company to offer cancer insurance in a country where the disease was surrounded by social taboos and awareness was limited. Almost single-handedly creating a market for such a product in an effort that spanned more than two decades, AFLAC held 80 percent of the cancer insurance market by the late 1990s.[74] In addition to introducing cancer insurance to Japan, AFLAC was also the first company to offer further innovative third-sector insurance products such as nursing care and specialized medical care insurance as supplements to Japan's national health care system.[75]

In addition to leadership in product innovation, a second factor behind foreign insurers' success in Japan is price competitiveness. Foreign insurers generally have been able to offer products at low premiums that, moreover, are easy for customers to understand, whereas Japanese companies tend to sell more complex products with various additional benefits.[76] As a result, AFLAC's medical insurance, for instance, is almost 40 percent cheaper than similar products available from the major domestic firms.[77] Underlying this cost competitiveness is the much greater degree of foreign insurers' specialization. AFLAC's concentration on third-sector products is in stark contrast with traditional life insurers in Japan, which tended to be much less focused. In fact, imitating Nippon Life, the country's largest life insurer,

---

Net, "16 Foreign Life Insurers Boost Premium Income 38% in FY04," June 7, 2005; *Nikkei Net,* "Foreign life insurers saw slower premium revenue growth in FY05," May 31, 2006.

[73] See, e.g., *Nikkei Net,* "6 Major Foreign Life Insurers' Premium Revenue Up 15% in FY04," May 31, 2005.

[74] *Nikkei Net,* "Foreign Insurers Cut Deeply Into Japanese Market," February 9, 2004.

[75] Harner (2000: 238).

[76] *Nikkei Net,* "6 Major Foreign Life Insurers' Premium Revenue Up 15% in FY04," May 31, 2005.

[77] *Nikkei Net,* "6 Major Foreign Life Insurers' Premium Revenue Up 15% in FY04," May 31, 2005.

168   *Foreign Direct Investment in Japan*

they would typically offer the entire product range, from A to Z, even if only a dozen policies of a particular type of insurance were sold.[78] Following deregulation and increasing competition, Japanese life insurers have been trying to become more focused, but this is a slow process because the largest proportion of business by far is with existing customers.

Finally, AFLAC and other foreign companies have also benefited from a controversial deal struck between the Japanese and U.S. governments in 1996 that delayed the entry of Japanese firms into the third sector by first- and second-sector companies until 2001. Since complete liberalization in 2001, however, competition in the third sector has increased considerably, with major domestic life insurers offering specifically targeted third-sector products.[79] The third sector is thus turning into a primary battleground in the life insurance industry.

In other areas, too, Japanese life insurers are now trying to develop original and innovative products. They have begun to become more flexible in the premium discounts offered to individual customers, started to add various riders to traditional life insurance products, and developed investment-type life insurance products that were previously unavailable. In addition, life insurers are trying to improve their services, allowing customers, for example, to use ATMs at post offices and banks for insurance-related transactions.[80]

But product innovation and price competition are only two of the areas in which deregulation and increased foreign participation have led to a transformation of the industry. Other important areas include skill requirements, services, sales and distribution channels, and employment. These issues are obviously closely related. To stay with the example of third-sector medical insurance, both the development and the marketing and sales of such products require skills that many Japanese insurers used to lack. Consequently, Nippon Life, for instance, in 2005 set up a new medical research unit that,

---

[78] Hitoshi Morita, President and CEO, PCA Life, interview on May 17, 2005.

[79] In 2004, Asahi Mutual Life, for example, began selling medical plans that cover operations to prevent varices, while Dai-ichi Mutual Life introduced lifelong medical care insurance that does not require premium payments if policy holders need nursing care (*Japan Times*, "Insurers race to get into medical policies as population ages," February 26, 2005). Other traditional life insurers that have begun offering medical insurance products or life insurance products that also provide hospitalization and surgery benefits include Sumitomo Life, Nippon Life, and Meiji Yasuda Life. See, e.g., JETRO (2005b); *Nikkei Net,* "6 major foreign life insurers' premium revenue up 15% in FY04," May 31, 2005.

[80] The Life Insurance Association of Japan, *Yearbook 04/05*, "Changes in life insurance products in Japan," online: <http://www.seiho.or.jp/english/pdf/2004–2005/2005–04-a.pdf> (accessed November 21, 2005).

consisting of a staff of 19, including seven physicians, is responsible for analyzing medical data with a view to developing new forms of medical insurance.[81]

The proliferation of new insurance products and the decline in sales of standard life insurance products also requires more professional sales forces. Nippon Life, for example, has found that the sales performance of its "bicycle ladies" has plummeted.[82] But again it is foreign companies that have been leading the way in the professionalization of sales forces at the Japanese insurers they acquired, cutting the number of traditional sales agents, retraining personnel, hiring experienced salespeople from other industries, and moving to a sales system based on consulting services and "financial planners."[83] Following its acquisition of Daihyaku in 2001, Manulife, for instance, embarked on halving the number of sales agents at the Japanese company but was at the same time retraining remaining sales staff and recruiting 100 new sales people every month. One corollary, and gauge, of this professionalization is that the number of male sales staff is on the rise. Following the cue of foreign insurers, Sony Life, a relatively new market entrant, is stepping up insurance sales by male employees, who now account for more than 10 percent of overall insurance sales staff. Similarly, Nippon Life was planning to hire men with sales experience in real estate and other sectors and train them to sell life insurance. Beginning with 200 such personnel, the company was intending to eventually increase this number to 1,000.[84]

Similarly, again as a result of deregulation and led by foreign companies, insurers have been broadening their marketing channels. A number of them, including the AIG affiliates in Japan (Alico Japan, AIG Star Life, and AIG Edison Life), have expanded into direct marketing, including internet sales.[85] More important are the alliances that foreign insurers have forged with major as well as smaller second-tier and regional banks to sell individual pension insurance policies. Such ties have flourished since the ban on banks

---

[81] JETRO (2005b).

[82] *Nikkei Net*, "Nippon Life to hire more men for sales positions," March 3, 2005.

[83] See, e.g., *The Economist*, "Cautionary tales," June 5, 2003; *Nikkei Net*, "Foreign life insurers overhauling Japanese sales forces," October 16, 2003; *Nikkei Net*, "Foreign insurers contribute to rise in male sales staff," January 22, 2005.

[84] *Nikkei Net*, "Nippon Life to hire more men for sales positions," March 3, 2005; *Nikkei Net*, "Foreign insurers contribute to rise in male sales staff," January 22, 2005.

[85] See, e.g., *Nikkei Net*, "16 Foreign Life Insurers Boost Premium Income 38% in FY04," June 7, 2005.

However, the extent to which direct marketing adds to insurers' bottom line seems questionable because of high advertising costs. PCA Life President and CEO Hitoshi Morita, for example, therefore thinks such efforts are primarily an attempt to raise brand awareness (interview, May 17, 2005).

to sell insurance policies was lifted in October 2002 and foreign life insurers have teamed up with more than 200 financial institutions. Alico Japan, for instance, has signed up with eighty-one banks, including all three mega-banks. But other foreign insurers are not far behind. Having established ties with regional banks earlier, ING Life in 2004 linked up with Mizuho and UFJ Bank (now The Bank of Tokyo-Mitsubishi UFJ, BTMU), while AXA joined forces with Bank of Tokyo-Mitsubishi (now BTMU). BTMU also sells policies for Manulife, with which it has an equity tie-up.[86] Providing insurers with new marketing channels while allowing banks to diversify their insurance offerings, such tie-ups are one major factor behind the expansion in foreign life insurers' market share in Japan.

The tie-ups also demonstrate that in the insurance sector foreign firms have become an established part of the landscape. Not only are they forging links with domestic financial institutions; consumers also do not appear to make any distinction between domestic and foreign providers.[87] Or, if considerations of nationality do play a role, this may actually play into the hands of overseas insurers given the failure of domestic providers around the turn of the millennium.

Thus, comparing the role of foreign companies in the insurance and the banking sector, substantial differences can be observed. In the latter, the presence of foreign banks has only had a limited impact on their domestic counterparts. The insurance sector provides a stark contrast. Here, foreign companies have rapidly gained significant market share, contributed to increased price and product competition, and led the way in corporate restructuring. Operating in a deregulated and more competitive environment, Japanese insurers have been forced to follow suit, introducing third-sector products and upgrading skills by investing in product-development capabilities and professionalizing sales forces. In other words, the entire *modus operandi* of the Japanese insurance industry has been transformed as a result of deregulation and foreign participation. In addition, with prices, product differentiation, and service levels now the defining competitive parameters, and a considerable number of insurers now in foreign hands, long-term shareholdings and *keiretsu* relationships, too, no longer play the role they once did. Thus, although there are of course many other reasons for the unwinding of cross-shareholdings among Japanese corporations, the competitive transformation of the insurance sector has been one factor

---

[86] *Nikkei Net,* "Foreign life insurers expand sales network through bank alliances," July 25, 2005.

[87] Hitoshi Morita, President and CEO, PCA Life; interview on May 17, 2005.

contributing to the demise of this defining feature of the country's postwar economy.

The realignment of the Japanese insurance industry is likely to continue apace. Despite their success as a group, not all foreign insurers are thriving in Japan and their number shrank from a peak of 18 of 41 life insurers operating in Japan in 2003 to 16 in 2005. At the same time, however, the total number of life insurers in Japan is very small compared with the 354 companies found in the United States, the 455 in Germany, and the 400 in the United Kingdom.[88] Thus, there seems to be considerable room for more competitors in Japan.

Health Care

Health care is a sector of vital importance in any economy. Not only does it account for a significant proportion of economic activity, especially in industrialized countries; it also has an important impact on social welfare. In Japan, total expenditure on health accounts for 7.9 percent of GDP. Although substantial, this figure is in the lower range of comparable Organisation for Economic Co-operation and Development (OECD) countries, indicating that Japan has managed to contain health care costs more effectively than other developed nations.[89] What is more, this has been achieved while providing comprehensive health coverage to all citizens and without the rationing seen, for example, in Britain. And although health care is of course only one contributing factor, the Japanese today enjoy the highest life expectancy in the world.[90]

Yet, despite its apparent success, Japan's health care sector has its fair share of problems. Peculiarities in the country's health care system and health care regulation have fostered an environment in which competition from foreign firms in the pharmaceutical and medical devices industries was limited, leading Japan's manufacturers to fall behind their international rivals. Other areas, in particular health care provision (i.e., doctors, hospitals, clinics), have been even more sheltered from competition, so that, according to one study, the productivity of the Japanese health care system is only about 75 percent of the level in the United States.[91] What is more, these problems

---

[88] JETRO (2005b).

[89] Health expenditure amounts to only 8.1 percent of GDP in the United Kingdom, but to 10.5 percent in France, 10.6 percent in Germany, and 15.3 percent in the United States. Data are for 2004. Source: *OECD Health Data 2006*.

[90] United Nations Development Programme, *Human Development Report 2006*.

[91] McKinsey Global Institute (2000).

are compounded by the demographic challenge – the aging and shrinking of the population – which is going to impose a growing burden on the national health care system and hence government finances. Already, the copayment share of employees covered by the national health insurance has had to be successively raised from 10 percent in the 1990s to 30 percent today.

The health care sector makes an interesting case study of FDI in Japan for several reasons. First of all, it spans a number of subsectors with very different characteristics, regulatory regimes, and patterns of foreign participation. Potential areas to look at include pharmaceuticals, medical equipment, medical diagnostics, blood products, and health care services. This section considers three of these: pharmaceuticals, medical equipment, and health care services. Including two manufacturing industries and a service sector, these three categories are fairly representative of the entire health care spectrum.

A glance at two of these sectors, drugs and medicine and medical services, for which separate data on employment accounted for by foreign affiliates as a share of total employment are available (see Table 2.1 in Chapter 2), shows a stark contrast in the extent of foreign penetration: together with the car industry, drugs and medicine is, in fact, the segment with the highest share of foreign employees of any industry in Japan. In contrast, in the medical services, health and hygiene segment, foreign companies are almost nonexistent and account for less than 0.2 percent of total employment in the sector. Although this is not a sector that readily lends itself to FDI in any country, the figure for Japan is less than a tenth of that for the United States.

The reasons for this contrast between the pharmaceutical industry and health care services are easy to find. Whereas FDI in the pharmaceuticals sector has been possible for decades, current regulations prohibit for-profit companies from providing health care services. The health care service sector therefore provides a useful illustration of a "sanctuary" where the absence of FDI is not the outcome of any discriminatory policies against foreign companies but rather the result of more general entry barriers that also inhibit the entry of domestic operators. This lack of competition in health care services – in areas where competition is appropriate – is an important factor contributing to the observed low productivity in Japan's health care system.

But it is not only in the area of services that the regulatory framework has had detrimental effects. Heavy regulation has also been responsible for delaying the introduction of new drugs and treatments developed overseas and for fostering pharmaceutical and medical devices industries that were largely inward looking. Regulatory and other changes in the 1990s have since made it much easier for foreign companies to introduce drugs in Japan and, as the following sections show, the impact has been far-reaching.

The Pharmaceutical Industry

At first glance, Japan's pharmaceutical industry seems to present a paradox. At almost US$60 billion in 2004, the country's drug market is the second largest in the world, behind only that of the United States (ca. US$230 billion), and about twice as large as third-ranked Germany's.[92] Japanese firms have long dominated their home market,[93] and given such a strong domestic demand base, one might expect Japan's drugmakers to be among the leading pharmaceutical companies in the world. Yet, not one Japanese firm ranks among the global top ten in the industry, and the country's three largest (ranked fifteenth, sixteenth, and twentieth) together account for less than 4 percent of global sales.[94] What is more, this figure obviously includes sales in Japan. The country's export market share (calculated as the share of total OECD exports in the sector) is smaller still and even shrinking, having fallen from 3.3 percent in 1997 to 1.9 percent in 2004.[95]

Thus, unlike in the car or electronics industry, a large home market has not translated into a competitive advantage abroad. In fact, Japan has consistently run a trade deficit in pharmaceuticals, and this deficit has grown rapidly in recent years (see Figure 6.2). Furthermore, the dominant position of Japanese firms in their home market has been slipping: still controlling 85 percent of the market in 1990, Japanese firms' share had shrunk to less than two-thirds by 2004.[96] And while no foreign firm made it into the top 10 in Japan and only one into the top 20 in 1990, four had broken into the top 10 and another three into the top 20 by 2004 (see Table 6.3).

These figures highlight two major features of Japan's pharmaceutical industry: the dominance of domestic firms in their home market despite their lack of international competitiveness and the inroads by foreign firms into the Japanese market in recent years. How this situation came about, and the role FDI plays in it, can be properly understood only in the context

---

[92] Figures from *Scrip Magazine*, "Growth, in moderation," February 2005.
[93] See, e.g., Thomas (2001: chapter 8).
[94] Figures from *Pharmaceutical Executive*, May 2005 (IMS Health data).
[95] OECD, *Main Science and Technology Indicators*, 2005/1 and 2006/2.
[96] Figures from IMS Health, quoted in Mahlich (N. D.) and Swiss Chamber of Commerce and Industry in Japan, "Pharmaceutical Industry in Japan in 2004," online: <www.sccij.org/reports/pharmaceuticals.html> (accessed December 1, 2005).

Table 6.3. *The top 20 pharmaceutical companies by sales in Japan*

Rank	Company name	Nationality	Sales in US$ billion	Market share in%	Global ranking
1	Takeda	Japan	3.6	6.3	15
2	Pfizer	USA	3.4	5.8	1
3	Roche	Switzerland	2.4	4.2	12
4	Otsuka	Japan	2.4	4.1	24
5	Sankyo	Japan	2.2	3.8	28
6	Novartis	Switzerland	2.1	3.7	7
7	Eisai	Japan	2.0	3.4	19
8	Daiichi	Japan	1.9	3.3	NA
9	Yamanouchi Seiyaku	Japan	1.6	2.8	23
10	Merck & Co.	USA	1.6	2.7	5
11	Mitsubishi Pharma	Japan	1.5	2.7	38
12	Shionogi Seiyaku	Japan	1.4	2.5	39
13	AstraZeneca	UK	1.3	2.3	6
14	GlaxoSmithKline	UK	1.3	2.3	2
15	Fujisawa	Japan	1.2	2.2	27
16	Tanabe Seiyaku	Japan	1.2	2.1	50
17	Sanofi-Aventis	France	1.2	2.1	3
18	Ono	Japan	1.2	2.1	48
19	Sumitomo	Japan	1.1	1.9	NA
20	Kowa Shinyaku	Japan	1.0	1.7	NA

Source: IMS Health, IMS MIDAS^{TM}, MAT Dec 2004, quoted in *Pharmaceutical Executive,* May 2005.

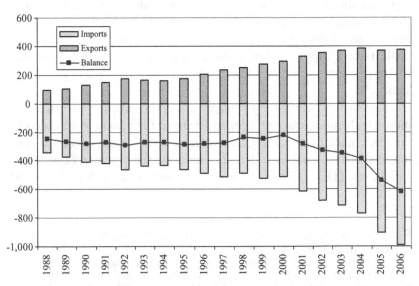

Figure 6.2. Japan's trade in pharmaceuticals (¥ billion)
Source: Japan Customs, online database: <http://www.customs.go.jp/toukei/srch/indexe.htm>.

of the particular "ecosystem" in which the health care industries operate in Japan.[97] This ecosystem is the outcome of political interactions over the years among three key players: the Liberal Democratic Party (LDP), the Japan Medical Association (JMA) representing 156,000 doctors (about 60 percent of all physicians in Japan), and the Ministry of Health and Welfare (MHW; now the Ministry of Health, Labour and Welfare, MHLW). The interplay of these three actors has given rise to a regulatory framework in which the special interests of the medical doctors represented by the JMA have often taken precedence over other considerations, such as economic efficiency, the creation of internationally competitive health care industries, or the welfare of society as a whole.

Critically important elements of the ecosystem this situation has given rise to are the lack of separation (*bungyo*) between the prescription and dispensing of medication and the "doctor's margin": doctors both prescribe and dispense drugs which they purchase from wholesalers at a discount from the official retail price. Since the Ministry of Health reimburses doctors for all drugs at the official retail price, doctors pocket the difference. This system presents doctors with a strong incentive to overprescribe products – Japanese patients have been described as *kusurizuke*, or pickled in drugs – and led to a rapid increase in pharmaceutical demand. In order to keep health care expenditure in check, the government therefore began in 1981 to steadily lower the reimbursement prices for drugs. Drug prices in Japan have fallen by roughly 5 percent a year as a result. Crucially, owing to health ministry regulation, it is prices for established products that drop rapidly, creating incentives for doctors to prescribe the latest and most expensive drugs and for pharmaceutical firms to proliferate many minor, imitative new drugs. As a result, product life cycles in Japan have been much shorter than in the United States, Britain, or Germany, research and development (R&D) resources have been fragmented rather than concentrated on a handful of important products, and Japan has produced few drugs with any likelihood of diffusion overseas.

Another element of the ecosystem in which Japan's pharmaceutical industry has had to operate and which explains its lack of competitiveness is the clinical trial system and drug approval procedures. Based on practices and standards very different from those found in the United States or Europe, results of clinical trials in Japan are "acceptable and respected

---

[97] The term "ecosystem" is borrowed from Thomas (2001) and this brief outline is based on chapters 3 and 4 of his detailed study of Japan's pharmaceutical industry.

almost nowhere else in the world."[98] Japanese firms with global ambitions therefore have typically been forced to conduct clinical trials in the United States or Europe; but lacking financial muscle and marketing know-how, most have chosen to license internationally successful drugs to foreign partners rather than selling them under their own brand name. At the same time, Japan until recently refused to accept clinical trial results from abroad.[99] Foreign firms wishing to introduce a product already being sold around the world therefore had to spend large sums of money and a lot of time (sometimes years) simply to replicate trials already conducted abroad. The effects have been detrimental both to Japan's drug firms and to the country's patients: hampered in their ability to compete overseas and largely insulated from international competition at home, Japan's pharmaceutical industry became increasingly disconnected from advances abroad, while patients failed to benefit from many innovative drugs developed overseas.

A final element that must be mentioned is the distribution system. Over 90 percent of drugs in Japan are distributed by wholesalers, and more than four-fifths of this share are directly dispensed by prescribing hospitals and doctors. Distribution thus is highly complex and fragmented and wholesale prices – which determine the "doctor's margin" – are directly negotiated between wholesalers and doctors, creating the need for large armies of distributors and salesmen. Few wholesalers provide national coverage and many are vertically linked with domestic drug manufacturers. (In fact, many Japanese drug firms evolved out of wholesalers.) The traditional ties between certain wholesalers and manufacturers have made it difficult in the past for other drugsmakers – smaller Japanese as well as foreign ones – to gain access to doctors and most foreign firms operating in Japan have had to team up with one of the five large Japanese firms that used to dominate the wholesale network in the country.[100]

The lack of *bungyo* (separation between prescription and dispensing) and the "doctor's margin," the health ministry's reimbursement pricing scheme, the clinical trial system, the distribution system, and a host of other

[98] Thomas (2001: 52).
[99] It is important to note, however, that this refusal was not based on the fact that these trials were foreign but that they were different. Referring to a specific case in which approval for a drug application by a foreign firm took a total of 44 months (compared with only 5 months for the same drug in the United States), Thomas (2001: 81) observes: "[...] there was no explicit bias against foreign products or even foreign clinical and preclinical trial data here. The expert committee for Taxol never rejected foreign clinical trials because they were foreign, but rather because they were different from established Japanese practice."
[100] Thomas (2001: 59–62).

elements – it is this distinctive ecosystem that explains why Japan's pharmaceutical firms are relatively uncompetitive internationally but still have dominated their home market. The ecosystem also explains why, by the mid-1990s, a significant "drug lag" had opened up between Japan and other developed countries, manifesting itself in the fact that a large number of global products, many of them significant innovations with important therapeutic effects, were not available in Japan.[101] Finally, it also explains why the market share of generic drugs – drugs that are exactly the same as a brand name drug but that anyone is allowed to produce since the original drug's patent has expired – in Japan is so small. Until 1992, the initial reimbursement price for generic drugs was set at 100 percent of the price of the original drug. Since then, reimbursement prices for generics have been successively lowered and now range from 15 to 70 percent of the original drug, with an average of about 50 percent.[102] Nevertheless, reimbursement prices for generics still remain considerably higher than in other comparable countries.[103] In any case, Japan's over-the-counter market is small and doctors, the main dispensers of drugs, face incentives to prescribe more expensive brand drugs rather than low-cost generic alternatives. It is no surprise, then, that the market share of generics in Japan is only 12 percent (on a quantity basis), compared with about 50 percent (in terms of prescriptions written) in the United States, Britain, and Germany.[104]

The stage is now set to consider foreign companies' role in Japan's pharmaceutical sector and recent industry dynamics. The first thing to note is that FDI in the sector has been possible for decades.[105] In fact, part of the implicit protection of Japan's pharmaceutical industry was the requirement that firms wanting to sell drugs in Japan needed to have manufacturing facilities in the country. With takeovers unheard of until the late 1990s, as in the rest of the economy, FDI typically took the form of joint ventures with Japanese partners. Such tie-ups provided foreign firms with access to

[101] Thomas (2001), chapter 1. One indicator of this drug lag is that at the time Thomas wrote his study, 130 of the 230 global drugs since 1985 were unavailable in Japan. One prominent example of a drug unavailable in Japan until only very recently that most of those familiar with Japan will be aware of is, of course, the contraceptive pill. Although used by millions of women worldwide, "the pill" was banned in Japan as a result of pressure by the Japan Medical Association (JMA). Abortion as a principal means of birth control represented a major source of income for Japan's medical profession.
[102] Riku (2005).
[103] Bill Bishop, Director, Corporate Affairs, Wyeth K. K., interview on October 7, 2005.
[104] Figures are for 2002. Source: JETRO (2005c).
[105] Merck, for example, having established a joint venture as early as 1954, gradually began building up a majority stake in its local partner, Banyu, twenty years ago.

local manufacturing expertise as well as help in navigating the complexities of the drug approval process and the distribution system. Given the relative backwardness of Japan's pharmaceutical industry, the overriding motive for investing in the country has been, and continues to be, access to the Japanese market for the sale of drugs developed in the United States or Europe – a fact that is clearly reflected in Japan's persistent and growing trade deficit in pharmaceuticals shown in Figure 6.2.[106] Another avenue for overseas pharmaceutical firms to sell their products in Japan has been through licensing deals, and the distribution of foreign drugs used to be an important source of income for domestic firms.

Beginning in the late 1990s, however, the status quo in Japan's drug industry began to crumble, thanks to regulatory changes that could be labeled Japan's "pharmaceutical big bang." Not only are firms selling drugs in Japan no longer required to have production facilities in the country, but the government also started to introduce measures to simplify and accelerate the approval of marketing applications. Steps were taken to make the use of foreign clinical trial data easier and a new, better-staffed regulatory body, the Pharmaceutical and Medical Devices Agency (PMDA), was set up with the aim of reducing the review of drug applications to less than 12 months.

The implications of these regulatory steps are far-reaching. In effect largely removing the hurdles that had hitherto afforded Japanese firms a degree of protection, the measures have led to a rapid realignment in the industry. Simply by introducing drugs long established overseas, Western multinationals have been able to gain significant market share and earn a tidy profit – in some cases, thanks to the lack of competition from generics, even on products whose patents have already expired. As a result, even though the Japanese pharmaceutical market has more or less stagnated over the past decade or so as a result of the government's reimbursement pricing policy, the same policy at present is providing foreign drugmakers with ample profit opportunities.

The new opportunities have also led to an increased interest in investing in Japan. In line with patterns observed in other sectors, acquisitions of Japanese companies became a common mode for foreign companies to establish or expand their presence in Japan. In addition to headline-making cases, which are presented in Table 6.4, many Western firms have been buying out former joint ventures with domestic manufacturers to increase

---

[106] It should be noted, though, that Japan runs a surplus in the technology balance of trade in the sector to the tune of ¥149.3 billion (2004), roughly 40 percent the size of its deficit in the merchandise balance of trade in that year. The figure for the technology balance of trade for the pharmaceutical sector is from Ministry of Education, Culture, Sports, Science and Technology, *White Paper on Science and Technology 2006*, Fig. 2–3–16.

Table 6.4. *Acquisitions of Japanese pharmaceutical firms by foreigners*

Date	Companies involved
1996.03	BASF (Germany) acquired controlling stake in Hokuriku Seiyaku.
1999.04	Akzo Nobel (Netherlands) acquired the pharmaceutical division of Kanebo.
2000.01	UCB (Belgium) acquired the pharmaceutical division (prescription drugs) of Fujirebio.
2000.01	Boehringer Ingelheim (Germany) announced a takeover bid for SS Pharmaceutical. SSP became a subsidiary in October 2001.
2001.01	Schering (Germany) acquisition of Mitsui Pharmaceutical Industrial.
2001.03	Abbott Laboratories (US) acquired the pharmaceutical unit of BASF (Germany) and turned BASF-owned Hokuriku Seiyaku into a subsidiary.
2002.10	Nippon Roche merged with Chugai Pharmaceutical.

Source: Japan External Trade Organization (JETRO), "Biotechnology", online: <http://www.jetro.go.jp/en/market/attract/biotechnology/key.html> (accessed March 12, 2007), and press reports.

the recognition of their brands.[107] These developments indicate that foreign drugmakers no longer need their local counterparts and, in fact, go hand in hand with another important trend: foreign pharmaceutical firms have been aggressively expanding their own sales forces in the country in order to sidestep the complex distribution system, obviating the need to pay distribution fees to local rivals, providing greater efficiency, and further enhancing brand recognition. In early 2004, the top five foreign pharmaceutical firms, led by Pfizer from the United States and AstraZeneca from Britain, had a combined sales force of 9,030 in Japan, compared with 6,500 for the top domestic manufacturers.[108]

Meanwhile, Japanese companies are struggling. Not only are they losing their licensing business because Western firms increasingly sell their drugs on their own; there is also little they can do to respond to the onslaught of competition in a stagnating market. Because of the nature of the domestic ecosystem, Japanese companies have invested less in R&D than their foreign peers and have few promising products in the "pipeline." What is more, despite dwindling profits, they have long resisted consolidation even as their European and American rivals have grown bigger through M&As and devoted ever larger sums to R&D. However, this began to change in 2005

---

[107] An example is Wyeth's gradual acquisition of Takeda's stake in their joint venture in Japan, Wyeth K. K.

[108] IMS Global Insight, "Sumos wrestle into Japan," online: <http://www.imshealth.com/web/content/0,3148,64576068_63872702_70261002_70960269,00.html> (accessed March 12, 2007).

180   *Foreign Direct Investment in Japan*

with the merger of Yamanouchi Pharmaceutical and Fujisawa Pharmaceutical to form Astellas Pharma, followed by similar tie-ups between Sankyo and Daiichi Pharma, Dainippon Pharmaceutical and Sumitomo Pharmaceutical, and Teikoku Hormone and Grelan (with the latter becoming Aska Pharma).[109] Yet, doubts remain whether these mergers will create sufficient synergies to overcome underlying weaknesses in the development of blockbuster drugs and create sufficient financial muscle to compete on a global scale.[110] Moreover, the alliances have been seen, in part, as preemptive moves in anticipation of the introduction of the so-called triangular merger scheme in 2007 allowing foreign companies to acquire Japanese firms by using stock swaps.[111]

Overall, the outlook for most Japanese drug manufacturers is bleak. At best a handful are expected to be able to compete internationally, and to do so, they have to become much more globally oriented, quickly. Many already have set up R&D operations and conduct clinical trials abroad to tap the all-important U.S. market. What is more, some of the larger players, led by Takeda, are in the process of expanding their sales forces abroad to avoid missing out on overseas profits on drugs sold under license, as has happened in the past.[112] Medium-sized companies, on the other hand, are likely to find it much more difficult to survive. If not swallowed by a bigger domestic or a foreign firm, they may quit the brand-name drug business and instead concentrate on generic drugs or drug-manufacturing services for other companies. As in other industries, there is a growing division of labor among increasingly specialized firms, and liberalization, begun in 1997 and continuing today, is gradually removing the barriers for contract sales organizations, site management organizations, contract research organizations, and, most recently, drug-manufacturing service companies – specialized companies that first appeared in Europe and the United States as early as the 1970s and 1980s.[113]

---

[109] See, e.g., *Nikkei Net*, "Drugmakers team up to chase profits," October 3, 2005.
[110] Bill Bishop, Director, Corporate Affairs, Wyeth K. K., interview on October 7, 2005. Also see Pharmiweb.com, "Mergers emerge in Japan," 29 November 2005, online: <http://www.pharmiweb.com/features/feature.asp?ROW_ID = 698> (accessed March 12, 2007).
[111] *Nature Reviews: Drug Discovery*, "Mergers in Japan help firms retain own products," 29 April 2005, online: <http://www.nature.com/news/2005/050425/pf/nrd1744_pf.html> (accessed March 12, 2007).
[112] *Nature Reviews: Drug Discovery*, "Mergers in Japan help firms retain own products," 29 April 2005, online: <http://www.nature.com/news/2005/050425/pf/nrd1744_pf.html> (accessed March 12, 2007).
[113] JETRO (2005c).

Another area in which the presence of Western pharmaceutical firms is clearly being felt is distribution. Bypassing the traditional distribution system by boosting their own sales forces, foreign drugmakers have contributed to the deteriorating profitability of traditional wholesalers, forcing these into mergers and tie-ups. As a result, the number of member companies of the Japan Pharmaceutical Wholesalers Association (JPWA) shrank by 70 percent from 486 in 1985 to 129 in 2007.[114] Merger and reorganization activity accelerated around 1999, leaving only four major drug wholesalers with their various subsidiaries today.[115]

Japan's pharmaceutical sector is at present undergoing a major transition. Leading a sheltered existence in the country's idiosyncratic ecosystem until the late 1990s, Japanese drug manufacturers failed to participate in many of the trends that have been shaping the industry elsewhere. However, as a result of the regulatory reforms initiated over the past seven or eight years, Japan's vast market has become a battleground for the world's foremost pharmaceutical companies, exposing domestic manufacturers for the first time to the full forces of global competition. The presence of foreign companies in Japan thus is a key factor underlying the current transformation of the industry. At least three major trends can be distinguished. The first is globalization, which can be seen not only in the growing market share of foreign companies in Japan, but also in Japanese firms' efforts to expand R&D efforts and sales forces overseas and to build market recognition.[116] The second is consolidation. The number of pharmaceutical companies in Japan peaked at 1,646 in 1993 but then declined to 1,062 in 2003 as a result of market exits and M&As.[117] Market concentration has also gradually been rising, with the sales share of the top 5 drug manufacturers increasing from 21.3 percent in 1990 to 28.6 percent in 2003.[118] The third trend, finally, is the increase in outsourcing of R&D, manufacturing, sales, and site management, leading to growth in the number of firms specializing in these activities.

The most important issue from a Japanese perspective is whether the industry can transform itself quickly enough to ensure its continued

---

[114] Figures from the JPWA website: <http://www.jpwa.or.jp/jpwa/members-e.html> (accessed March 12, 2007).
[115] JETRO (2005c).
[116] See, e.g., *Nature Reviews: Drug Discovery*, "Mergers in Japan help firms retain own products," 29 April, 2005, online: <http://www.nature.com/news/2005/050425/pf/nrd1744_pf.html> (accessed March 12, 2007).
[117] JETRO (2005c).
[118] JETRO (2005c).

existence. The scale of the challenge is formidable. According to one observer, "[n]othing short of a complete merger of every existing Japanese drug firm into a monolith would yield a true competitor to foreign firms such as Merck or Glaxo."[119] Others argue it is difficult to imagine how the industry can survive in the long run without significant further consolidation and partnership with foreign manufacturers.[120] Foreign firms thus are set to play a key role in shaping the future of Japan's pharmaceutical industry.

A final important point that is unrelated to any immediate economic considerations but that forms part and parcel of the presence of foreign firms in Japan is the increase in "product variety" and "consumer choice" they bring with them. In the case of pharmaceuticals, these are particularly valuable gains given that the products in question are drugs that may have a vital impact on patients' well-being. These gains are all the greater because of the size of the gap that had opened up between the drugs available in Japan and overseas, which may have deprived patients of potentially life-saving medication available abroad but not at home.

Medical Devices

In many regards, the situation in the medical devices sector resembles that in the pharmaceutical industry. Japanese firms dominate their domestic market but are relatively weak in the international arena, and their position at home appears increasingly vulnerable: Domestic firms account for 60 percent of sales in Japan, but the country's largest medical device makers, Olympus and Terumo, rank only twelfth and thirteenth in the world. Japan also has a large and growing deficit in the trade in medical devices, with imports more than twice as large as exports (see Figure 6.3). What is more, foreign (that is, American) firms already account for eight of the thirteen leading firms by sales in the country.[121] As in the case of drugs, Japanese firms have been ill-prepared to cope with the increase in competition that gradual deregulation in the medical devices market as part of the wider health care reform effort has brought about.

This lack in competitiveness again is the result of the ecosystem in which the industry has had to operate in Japan. Regulations are one factor. Like

[119] Thomas (2001: 175).
[120] European Business Council in Japan (EBC), "Position Paper: Foreign Direct Investment," 25 May, 2005, online: <http://www.ebc-jp.com/news/2005%20EBC%20Position%20Paper%20on%20FDI%202005%20(English)-May.pdf> (accessed March 12, 2007).
[121] Based on unpublished data obtained from the Japan Medical Devices Manufacturers Association (JMED).

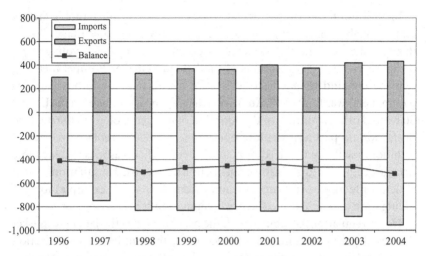

Figure 6.3. Japan's trade in medical devices (¥ billion)
Source: Ministry of Health, Labour and Welfare, *Yakuji Kogyo Seisan Dotai Tokei Chosa*
[Survey on Production Statistics of the Pharmaceutical Industry] (various years).

drugs, medical devices require the approval of the health ministry, and the
Japanese environment is generally considered to be very restrictive, conservative, and highly regulated.[122] Companies – domestic and foreign alike –
have often complained about the cost and time required for product registrations, which in some instances took so long that, by the time products
were approved, they were already outdated,[123] and it seems reasonable to
assume that lengthy approval procedures have acted as a brake on domestic innovation.[124] What is more, approvals do appear to have taken longer
for foreign than for domestic products, although, as in the case of drugs,
this may be less due to any bias against foreign products or clinical evidence per se and more due to differences from established Japanese practice
and the fact that applications by domestic manufacturers tend to be for
incremental innovations, while foreign firms often introduce completely
new technologies.[125]

---

[122] See, e.g., Pacific Bridge Medical, "Opportunities in Japan's medical device market," August
2001, online: <http://www.pacificbridgemedical.com/publications/html/JapanAugust01.
htm> (accessed March 12, 2007).
[123] Takeshi Fujiwara, President, Gambro K. K., interview on June 30, 2005.
[124] Implantable Cardioverter Defibrillators (ICDs), for example, were not approved until these
devices had been in use in other countries for ten years.
[125] Takeshi Fujiwara, President, Gambro K. K., interview on June 30, 2005.

In addition to restrictive regulation, there are other unfavorable factors that are likely to have put Japanese manufacturers at a disadvantage. One of these is that, until the 1980s, Japan's population was relatively young when compared with the populations of the United States or Europe, meaning that the demand for medical devices for age-related conditions (such as pacemakers) was limited.[126] Another is that Japan lags far behind the United States and other countries in the adoption of new technology in the medical profession, in part as a result of doctors' reluctance to replace time-tested techniques with high-tech equipment.[127] Yet another reason is that Japanese firms are reluctant to get involved in medical devices used in situations where patients' life may be in danger (again, pacemakers are an example) for fear of litigation and damage to the firm's reputation.[128]

Heavy regulation, combined with the peculiarities of the Japanese market (such as the difficulties involved in negotiating the multilayered distribution system and the need to provide the free technical support Japanese customers expect), has afforded domestic medical equipment manufacturers some shelter from international competition in their home market. As a result, Japanese firms dominate the domestic market for relatively mature, standardized products in which manufacturing quality and after-sales services are the decisive competitive parameters. Prime examples of such products are dialysis equipment and blood purification products, in which domestic production accounts for more than 80 percent of domestic shipments. On the other hand, imports account for 70 percent or more of total domestic shipments in the case of generic catheters, orthopedic implants, and wound treatment materials and for more than 90 percent in the case of surgical implants and pacemakers and related products. Of 13 categories in total, domestic products occupy a market share of more than 50 percent in five, whereas imports predominate in the remaining eight.[129]

These patterns go hand in hand with another characteristic of Japan's medical devices industry: compared with their international counterparts,

---

[126] Akihiro Yamamoto, Managing Director, Japan Medical Devices Manufacturers Association (JMED), interview on September 12, 2005.

[127] Pacific Bridge Medical, "Opportunities in Japan's medical device market," August 2001, online: <http://www.pacificbridgemedical.com/publications/html/JapanAugust01.htm> (accessed March 12, 2007).

[128] Akihiro Yamamoto, Managing Director, Japan Medical Devices Manufacturers Association (JMED), interview on September 12, 2005; Takeshi Fujiwara, President, Gambro K. K., interview on June 30, 2005.

[129] Based on unpublished data obtained from the Japan Medical Devices Manufacturers Association (JMED).

domestic firms tend to be comparatively small and spend little on R&D.[130] Of course, this does not mean that Japan has no globally competitive firms in this sector. A notable case is Olympus, which in 2001 commanded a 68 percent share in the global market for endoscopes.[131] But Olympus is the exception that proves the rule and its strength in the medical business probably largely rests on electronic and optical technologies honed in other industries.

For foreign companies, Japan is again primarily attractive as a market. Although most multinationals in the industry have established themselves in Japan, the majority concentrate on the import and sale of products manufactured abroad and on after-sales services. Of course, this does not mean that foreign firms do not pursue other activities in the country. A number of foreign firms have been in Japan for decades and have gradually expanded their operations. Becton Dickinson Japan (BDJ), for example, established as a liaison office in 1971, set up its first manufacturing plant and distribution center in 1987; activities in Japan were further expanded in 2002 to include R&D.[132] Other examples include Baxter, which also invested in manufacturing, and Boston Scientific Japan (BSJ), which has set up a training facility to teach doctors how to use the company's products.

Foreign companies' role in the medical devices industry in Japan is only bound to grow as deregulation and the streamlining of product approvals make it easier for them to sell their products. The outlook for domestic firms, on the other hand, is grim. Already lacking in international competitiveness, Japanese firms face the added disadvantage of operating in an environment that is missing many of the ingredients necessary for innovation in this field.[133] Japanese patients (and taxpayers), finally, are likely to benefit from the better treatment options and potential cost savings afforded by the availability of a greater range of more advanced medical devices.

---

[130] According to unpublished data obtained from the Japan Medical Devices Manufacturers Association, a comparison of a sample of Japanese and American firms shows that R&D expenditure for the former is equivalent to only 4.6 percent of turnover vis-à-vis 10.2 percent for the U.S. firms.

[131] Based on unpublished data obtained from the Japan Medical Devices Manufacturers Association (JMED).

[132] JETRO, "Becton Dickinson finds rewards in Japan's health care market", October 2002, online: <http://www.jetro.go.jp/en/invest/success_stories/company/month_2002oct.html> (accessed March 12, 2007).

[133] For example, according to unpublished information from JMED comparing medical engineering-related university education and research in Japan and the United States, there were just twenty-five courses or faculties in this field in Japan versus ninety-six in the United States. The gap in terms of professors, lecturers, and researchers was even greater: 72 versus 450 to 500.

Health Care Services

The provision of health care services is predominantly a local industry and foreign participation is rare in all countries. Nevertheless, it is worthwhile to briefly examine this sector as it provides a vivid example of a "sanctuary" where government regulations, by restricting entry more generally, act as a barrier to FDI. What is more, the sector provides at least one prominent case of a foreign company that is keenly interested in expanding into Japan, but is barred from doing so by current regulations.

A key element of these regulations, which have grown out of the ecosystem described above, concerns the role of for-profit operators in the provision of medical services. As in other developed countries, for-profit operators in Japan are allowed to offer peripheral services (clinical tests, clerical services, meal services for patients, etc.). However, in contrast with the United States and European countries, they are effectively banned from providing the core medical services of diagnosis and treatment (Table 6.5). As a result, whereas in Japan only 0.7 percent of hospitals are operated by for-profit providers, the equivalent share in the United States is 15.1 percent, that in Germany is 19.9 percent, and that in France is 41.6 percent.[134] Coupled with other elements of the regulatory framework, such as reimbursement for each procedure and on a *per diem* basis for hospital stays rather than a flat fee for a particular diagnosed condition, this ban has led to a proliferation of small, unprofitable, and highly inefficient hospitals run by medical doctors with little training in management techniques.[135]

Recognizing the potential gains that greater competition, better choice for patients, and diversification in funding could bring, the Japanese government has recently begun experimenting with allowing companies to manage hospitals in "special zones" if they offer "advanced medical care" in designated fields.[136] However, because such services are not covered by the national health insurance, no such hospitals have sprung up to date. What is more, once nonreimbursed services reach a threshold level of 50,000 procedures, they would be eligible for reimbursement. Thus, any service provider in the "special zones" that is successful would lose its market, because others could offer the service.[137] The government is also trying to attract FDI in peripheral medical services in showcase medical industry development

---

[134] JETRO (2002: 5).
[135] See McKinsey Global Institute (2000) and JETRO (2002) for details. JETRO (2002: 59), for example, reports that 65.4 percent of all hospitals in Japan were losing money.
[136] JETRO (2005d).
[137] The author is grateful to Guy Harris, Chairman of the ACCJ Committee on Healthcare Services, for pointing this out.

Table 6.5. *Possibility of private corporate participation in medical services*

		Japan	US	UK	Germany	France
Medical services	Core services (diagnosis and treatment)	Entry possible for nonprofit operators only	Corporate participation allowed			
	Peripheral services		Corporate participation allowed			

Source: JETRO (2005d).

zones such as the "Finland Health and Welfare Center" in Sendai and the "Kobe Medical Industry Development Project."[138] Crucially, however, the ban on corporate ownership of hospitals and clinics outside the experimental special zones remains firmly in place.

Although health care services represent a sector that is much less internationalized than other service industries, a number of global companies do exist in this field. A case in point is Fresenius Medical Care from Germany, the world leader in renal care that both manufactures dialysis products and runs dialysis clinics around the world. As of 2006, the company was treating 163,500 patients in 2,108 clinics in North and Latin America, Europe, Africa, and the Asia-Pacific region.[139] With approximately 250,000 dialysis patients, Japan is the biggest dialysis market in Asia-Pacific and the second largest in the world, and Fresenius is naturally keen to invest in the country. In fact, the company has been in Japan since 1990 and today has offices on all four main islands of the archipelago. It also has two manufacturing facilities – one in a joint venture with a local company – for the production of dialysis products.[140] Obviously, Fresenius is eager to also open dialysis clinics in Japan, but despite persistent efforts has failed to obtain permission to do so.[141]

Yet, the productivity gains and cost savings from the specialization and economies of scale that corporate providers could generate are potentially huge. Although relying on somewhat dated information, one study suggests center hemodialysis treatment – the kind of treatment Fresenius specializes in – at US$46,800 per patient per year (in 1994) in Japan, costs more

---

[138] JETRO (2005e).
[139] Source: Fresenius Medical Care, patient care statistics, online: <http://www.fmc-ag.com/internet/fmc/fmcag/agintpub.nsf/Content/Statistics> (accessed March 12, 2007).
[140] Fresenius AG, *Annual Report 2005*.
[141] According to people familiar with the case, Fresenius has been trying for years to quietly lobby the government. However, details are difficult to come by as the company is treading carefully so as not to alienate hospital owners, the customers for its dialysis products.

than twice as much as in the United States (US$22,500 in 1990).[142] Apart from renal care services, areas in which allowing corporate ownership could contribute to substantial cost, productivity, and quality improvements in Japanese health care services include the outsourcing of radiation therapy, rehabilitation care, telecare and other health care services that are repetitive and/or pose little risk to patients.[143] Finally, for-profit providers could help to give rise to a cadre of professional hospital managers (as, for example, in the United States) that could transfer best practice thinking from other industries to the hospital sector.[144]

Given the many other distortions in Japan's health care system, lifting the ban on corporate ownership of hospitals and clinics would, of course, only be part of the answer. What is more, even in the United States and most Western European countries, less than one-fifth of hospitals are operated by for-profit providers and foreign participation in the sector is low. FDI in medical services therefore would at best account for a small portion of the overall market in Japan, although there is potential in certain specialized areas, as the Fresenius example illustrates. Yet, a final consideration to take into account is that it is often the corporate sector in which innovations occur, and in the absence of FDI, Japan risks falling (further) behind in the introduction of effective and cost-reducing treatments developed overseas, to the detriment of the country's patients and taxpayers.

Other Sectors

There are, of course, numerous other sectors that would have made instructive in-depth case studies. The chemical industry, business services, but in particular the telecommunications and the wholesale and retail sectors all experienced large inflows of FDI around the turn of the millennium and the growing presence of foreign companies has contributed to important structural changes in these sectors. At the same time, other industries, such as the utilities sector, which has seen considerable cross-border M&A activity elsewhere in the world following recent deregulation, have received little FDI, largely as a result of market entry barriers. Although these industries cannot be examined in detail here, it is nevertheless worthwhile to briefly consider two of these sectors, telecommunications and wholesale and retail.

---

[142] Figures from De Vecchi, Dratwa, and Wiedemann (1999).
[143] The author is grateful to Guy Harris, Chairman of the ACCJ Committee on Healthcare Services, for these examples.
[144] McKinsey Global Institute (2000).

Wholesale and Retail

Ranging from the large-scale outlets of retailers such as Toys "R" Us and Costco to the consumer temples of Western luxury brands in the fashionable areas of Tokyo, retail probably represents the sector in which the presence of foreign companies is most visible to the ordinary consumer. In contrast with many of the other sectors, retail has seen a steady inflow of FDI since the 1980s, although this segment, too, witnessed a rapid increase toward the end of the 1990s. One reason is that deregulation started earlier than in most other sectors. The Large-Scale Retail Store Law, enacted in 1973 and intended to protect small retailers from the incursion of larger retail stores, was amended in 1992 and again in 1994 to facilitate the establishment of large retail outlets.

A pioneering case of FDI in the sector was the opening of a gigantic store (by Japanese standards) of 3,000 m^2 in Ibaraki prefecture near Tokyo by the American toy retailer Toys "R" Us in 1991. The company has since grown into Japan's largest toy retailer with more than 160 stores (including Babies "R" Us stores) all over the country as of March 2007. Like many other sectors in Japan, the toy industry used to be characterized by a multilayered distribution structure in which manufacturers distributed their products through wholesalers to retailers. Toys "R" Us broke with this practice and employed a central buying system for large-lot purchases direct from the manufacturer, passing on the savings to consumers through lower retail prices.

Other foreign retailers and wholesalers have since followed suit. In addition to similarly circumventing the complex distribution system, a number of these have introduced retail business concepts new to Japan, such as membership warehouse clubs (Costco), hypermarkets (Carrefour), and membership food wholesalers (Metro). However, while some foreign retailers have prospered in Japan, others have already exited again, including OfficeMax, Sephora, and Boots, typically because of strategic mistakes and/or a misjudgment of the Japanese market. The most prominent case of these failures is probably Carrefour, which, having entered Japan only in 2001, sold its eight hypermarkets in the country to a Japanese retailer in 2004.

Despite failures such as these, foreign retailers have triggered a transformation of Japan's retail and distribution sector. Domestic rivals have been forced to streamline their own purchasing operations, and although even today, few do business directly with manufacturers, there has been a clear trend toward consolidation in the wholesale sector as a result of increased competition.[145] In addition, superstores have become a common sight in

[145] JETRO (2004a: 44).

Japan, and even though their number has stagnated in recent years following a rapid increase during the 1990s, the sales area per store has continued
to rise.[146] As a result, productivity in the retail sector, which according to
one study toward the end of the 1990s reached only 50 percent of the U.S.
level,[147] is likely to have increased.

Other areas in which foreign retailers have had a significant impact on
the Japanese market is the rise of specialty chain stores – examples of investment cases, in addition to Toys "R" Us, include Sports Authority and Office
Depot – and the luxury segment. In the latter, European and American firms
such as Louis Vuitton, Chanel, Prada, and Coach have gained virtually iconic
status and their products and stores have become an integral part of Japan's
fashion and architectural landscapes.

Today, there is a long list of foreign retailers doing business in Japan that
demonstrate that it is possible to be successful in the country. A closer look
at the failures (whose number is also not insubstantial), on the other hand,
typically shows that the reasons are to be found in strategic management
errors and a lack of understanding of the Japanese market. The retail sector
thus is likely to continue to attract considerable amounts of FDI in the future,
simply because few globally operating retailers can ignore a market the size
of Japan's.

Telecommunication

Having received virtually no FDI until the late 1990s, the telecommunications industry was one of the key drivers of the boom in inward FDI in Japan
around the turn of the millennium. Investments were driven by two coincid-
ing developments. The first was global consolidation in the telecommunications sector. For example, in 1999, Vodafone of Britain acquired AirTouch
Communications of the United States in a deal worth US$60 billion and
then, in the following year, Germany's Mannesmann in what was the world's
largest corporate merger in history, worth US$183 billion. Other large deals
at that time include France Telecom's acquisition of Britain's Orange (worth
US$46 billion) and Deutsche Telekom's purchase of Britain's One 2 One
(worth US$14 billion).

The second important development spurring FDI in Japan's telecommunications sector was deregulation. In World Trade Organization (WTO)
negotiations concluded in 1997, Japan had agreed to remove all foreign investment limitations on Type I carriers (carriers using their own

[146] JETRO (2004a: 13).
[147] McKinsey Global Institute (2000).

infrastructure) except for Nippon Telegraph & Telecom (NTT) and Kokusai Denshin Denwa Ltd. (KDD). Taking effect in 1998, the changes paved the way for the country to participate in the global FDI boom in the sector. On a notification basis, inflows jumped from ¥3.3 billion (about US$27 million at the exchange rate of the time) in 1997 to ¥750.8 billion (approximately US$6.8 billion) in 2000. Although FDI in the sector, in line with global trends, subsided in 2002 and 2003, it picked up again in 2004. On the basis of balance of payments (BOP) data, which are not directly comparable with the notification data, inward FDI in the sector remained strong in 2005, but then turned negative in 2006.

What is interesting about the telecommunications industry case is that the FDI trends in this sector have almost exclusively been shaped by only two cases: the takeover of International Data Communications (IDC) by Cable & Wireless in 1999, and the acquisition of Japan Telecom (J-Phone), first by British Telecom (BT) and AT&T and then by Vodafone. Of the two cases, the latter represents the much larger deal, involving transactions in several stages, in which BT and AT&T sold their share in Japan Telecom to Vodafone, which subsequently increased its stake and then sold the company's fixed-line business to investment group Ripplewood Holdings. Taken together, the various transactions surrounding Japan Telecom account for the large majority of FDI inflows in the telecommunications sector registered in the Ministry of Finance's notification statistics.[148] A second point of considerable interest is that both Cable & Wireless and Vodafone have since withdrawn from Japan, both selling their operations to Softbank – in 2004 in the case of Cable & Wireless and in 2006 in the case of Vodafone. As a result, there are once again no foreign phone companies with significant operations in the Japanese market.[149]

Given that it represents by far the most important investment in the Japanese telecommunications sector, it is useful to concentrate on the Vodafone case in this brief analysis of the role of foreign firms in the Japanese telecommunications sector. The acquisition of J-Phone in 2001 at a stroke had made Vodafone the third-largest mobile phone operator in Japan by number of subscribers. What is more, initially, the company met with considerable success and subscriber numbers continued to increase throughout 2002 and 2003 (Figure 6.4). However, while subscriber numbers at rivals NTT DoCoMo and KDDI (au) continued to rise, Vodafone's stagnated

---

[148] See Chapter 3 for details.
[149] Although a number of foreign companies continue to operate in Japan, they only provide small-scale services to local offices of their compatriot firms.

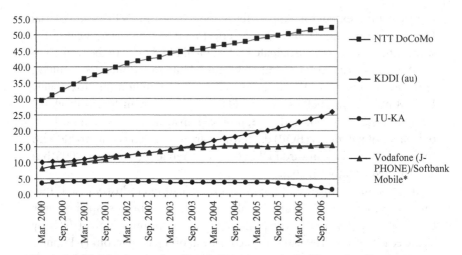

Figure 6.4. Mobile phone subscribers in Japan by carrier (million subscribers)
Source: Telecommunications Carriers Association.
Note:
* Softbank Mobile as of September 2006.

from 2004 onward and the company's market share slipped from a peak of
18.6 percent in the summer of 2003 to about 16.4 percent three years later,
at which point Vodafone decided to pull out of Japan.

   Vodafone's lack of success in the country appears to have been the result
of a number of factors, including the characteristics of the Japanese market,
strategic management errors, and, possibly, government policies. As for
market characteristics, Japan's mobile phone industry since the late 1990s is
generally considered to be a year or two ahead of the rest of the world (with
the recent exception of Korea). Consequently, any foreign entrant would
face a considerable challenge to compete in a market as advanced as Japan's.
In addition, the way in which the Japanese mobile phone industry operates
differs in important ways from patterns found in Europe and the United
States. Whereas in Europe and the United States, customers tend to be loyal
to handset makers rather than providers (a fact encouraged by legislation
to make mobile phone numbers "portable"), mobile phone operators in
Japan have considerably greater power. Working closely with handset makers
and selling their handsets under their own brands, it is the providers that
determine the features and functionality that mobile phones offer. In fact,
this close cooperation between providers and handset makers, together with
strong demand for highly sophisticated products by discerning consumers,
is an important reason for Japan's technological lead.

Entering such a demanding market, Vodafone committed at least two serious strategic mistakes. First, it failed to roll out third-generation (3G) networks and handsets fast enough, falling behind rivals NTT DoCoMo and KDDI, and when it did, it only offered relatively uninspiring services. Second, in an attempt to drive down handset prices, Vodafone introduced handsets that were similar to those in the rest of the world, but offered far fewer features than rival models offered by its competitors.[150] Regarded as "clunky," Vodafone's handsets were ignored by Japanese customers, who migrated to NTT DoCoMo and KDDI instead.

Government policy provides another reason. One area in which Vodafone had been relatively successful is the market for prepaid handsets, a segment that had proved successful elsewhere in the world and where the British company by 2004 had established a leading position in Japan. However, the government identified such unregistered phones as aiding organized crime and threatened to regulate the prepaid market out of business. The dominant position of the NTT group (the former state monopoly) and the failure of government policy to create a level playing field may also have been a factor. The European Business Community in Japan (EBC), for example, has complained about inequalities in spectrum allocation and anticompetitive behavior by the NTT group.[151] However, if such allegations are justified and, if so, to what extent they put foreign operators at a disadvantage, is difficult to assess.

Vodafone's withdrawal and the fact that no other foreign telecommunications provider with major operations remains mean that their impact on the sector in Japan has been limited. One area in which the British company appeared to be shaking things up a bit was Japan's handset industry and market, in which NTT DoCoMo used to call all the shots. Working with a select group of manufacturers, NTT DoCoMo wields considerable influence over the terms on which these manufacturers sell the same handsets to other providers.[152] Although this put Vodafone at a distinct disadvantage, the British company was able to win over newcomers like Sharp, Sanyo, and Toshiba, that were not part of the NTT DoCoMo in-group, and get them to collaborate in the development of Vodafone-specific handsets. It was able to so because of the access to overseas markets that it could offer to these manufacturers, substantially boosting their export sales.[153] However, with

[150] *The Economist*, "Not so big in Japan," September 30, 2004; *The New York Times*, "A major backfire in Japan deflates Vodafone's one-size-fits-all strategy," September 5, 2005.
[151] European Business Community in Japan (2004).
[152] Kushida (2002).
[153] Kushida (2006).

Vodafone no longer operating in the country and handsets by makers such as Sharp and Toshiba making up only a small fraction of the company's international lineup, it seems unlikely that Vodafone's episode in Japan has made any lasting impact on the handset industry.

In order to fully understand why foreign telecommunications providers have failed to establish themselves in Japan would require a much more detailed analysis than is possible here. However, as outlined here, specific reasons probably include the technological gap between Japan and most of the rest of the world and, potentially, government regulation that – whether intentionally or not – makes life difficult for foreign competitors. Management errors on the part of Vodafone, and an insufficient understanding of the Japanese market, as exemplified by the introduction of "clunky" handsets and uninspiring services when 3G services were finally offered, certainly also played a role.[154] However, rather than any one reason in particular, it appears to be the combination of various structural idiosyncrasies of the Japanese telecommunications industry – its technological leadership and the basis for this technological leadership, that is, close cooperation between service providers and handset makers, highly discerning, service-conscious consumers, patterns of competition, and so on – that explains why foreign firms have been unable to gain a foothold in the country.

This interpretation is supported by the fact that, conversely, Japan's telecommunications providers have failed to capitalize on their technological leadership abroad;[155] that is, theirs is a business model that works only in Japan's particular ecosystem. In contrast with other industries, however, this is an ecosystem that is characterized by intense competition, that has served consumers well and, in fact, reflects their preferences which place great value on sophisticated functionality and little emphasis on international compatibility (an important factor in Europe, for example, which, because of the need to agree on common standards, partly explains the technology lag). Thus, the Japanese telecommunications industry appears to be characterized by a situation in which global reach and capabilities are outweighed by (and to some extent, in conflict with) local embeddedness and technological capabilities.

[154] See, e.g., *The Times*, "Vodafone licks its wounds after five years of failure in Japan," March 4, 2006.
[155] NTT DoCoMo, for example, tried to popularize its "i-mode" wireless media platform abroad, but had little success and withdrew from unprofitable overseas ventures, such as its tie-up with Dutch telecommunications provider KPN Mobile in 2005.

Synthesis and Conclusion

The preceding case studies have shown that although the degree of market penetration by foreign-affiliated firms varies across industries, there are by now a number of sectors in which their impact on the Japanese business "landscape" is highly visible. The most dramatic instance of this perhaps is the stunning turn-around at Nissan following the acquisition by Renault. But, as the analyses of the financial and the health care sectors have shown, even where there are no such showcase examples, the presence of foreign multinationals has had an effect on their respective industries and beyond.

In order to synthesize the findings in this chapter, it is useful to consider the impact of foreign companies from five different angles. The first of these concerns foreign firms' effect on the degree of competition in their respective industries – an issue of central importance because of Japan's disappointing TFP performance partly as a result of the lack of competition in a wide range of sectors. By contributing to greater competition, foreign firms force domestic competitors to "shape up" and raise their productivity if they want to survive. In the case studies, the revival of Nissan and the growing market share of foreign insurers and pharmaceutical firms provide clear examples of how foreign companies are turning up the heat on their domestic rivals.

The exposure to global best practice they provide is the second angle from which to consider the impact of foreign companies. Apart from simply raising the number of competitors in a particular industry, foreign multinationals typically also bring with them business expertise and know-how honed in often more advanced and/or competitive markets overseas. Again, the case studies provide a wide array of examples, ranging from purchasing practices and financial operations at Nissan via portfolio modeling, risk management, and product development skills and techniques at foreign investment banks to the R&D capabilities of foreign pharmaceutical firms. In each of these cases, exposure to global best practice has elicited some sort of response by Japanese firms. In the car industry (as in many other sectors), there has been a greater emphasis on profitability; in the financial sector, domestic banks have copied products developed by foreign competitors and have become active in areas such as project finance and derivatives trading; and in the pharmaceutical industry, the introduction in Japan of foreign firms' global blockbuster drugs has forced domestic companies to strengthen their R&D, clinical trials, and marketing efforts overseas.

Foreign firms' contribution to the range of products and services available in Japan represents the third angle from which to consider their impact.

Here, too, the case studies provide numerous examples, ranging from the goods and shopping experience provided by European and American luxury goods makers to previously unavailable third-sector insurance products such as cancer, nursing care, and specialized medical care insurance. In addition, foreign investment banks have provided corporate customers with specialized financial services, helping them to restructure their finances, while banks such as Citibank offer distinct retail services such as 24-hour ATM machines and longer opening hours.

A fourth angle from which to view the role of foreign firms is in terms of their impact on industry structures. In this area, the case studies contain a number of examples where the impact has been rather limited, such as in the telecommunications industry or the banking sector, where, with the notable exception of investment banking, foreign financial institutions have to date failed to make significant inroads. But in other sectors, the impact has been substantial. In the car industry, Renault's acquisition of Nissan was followed by a wider reorganization of the company's supplier network, opening the door to further foreign entrants. In the insurance, wholesale and retail, and pharmaceutical sectors, foreign companies were the first to overhaul or bypass established distribution channels – moves that domestic rivals are beginning to follow and that have triggered a consolidation in the wholesale and retail as well as pharmaceutical distribution sectors. But the clearest evidence of the impact on industry structures can probably be found in the pharmaceutical sector, where the onslaught of competition from foreign drugmakers has set in motion a consolidation process among domestic manufacturers that is likely to accelerate in the coming years.

The fifth angle, finally, from which to examine the role of foreign multinationals in Japan is with regard to employment practices. Although it is hazardous to generalize from just one case, the Nissan example conforms with the widespread notion that foreign firms tend to be more willing to lay off workers when this is necessary. Foreign firms also tend to break with the traditional Japanese seniority-based system and instead rely on merit-based promotions and remuneration. Examples in the case studies illustrating this include again Nissan and the investment banks. Furthermore, although it would be hasty to draw any general conclusions from this without more broad-based evidence, the insurance sector provides an example where foreign companies are leading the way toward greater professionalism by retraining staff and hiring personnel with experience in sales, a move that is gradually being followed by domestic rivals. On the other hand, in the banking sector, despite moves to more meritocratic pay schemes in some domestic financial institutions, they provide no match for the high salaries paid by foreign investment banks.

Another more general trend to which foreign companies are contributing is greater flexibility in employment practices and the labor market as a whole. Whereas only ten or fifteen years ago, foreign firms often found it difficult to recruit personnel, working for a foreign company has gained in popularity in recent years and there is, in fact, a growing number of firms, both Japanese and foreign-owned, that specialize in recruitment services for foreign companies. Two of the industries considered here – the financial and the pharmaceutical/medical sector – are among the busiest for such recruitment consultancies.[156] Thus, "Western style" employment practices are spreading, and although there are other, structural reasons for this, and it is consequently difficult to gauge the extent to which foreign firms are responsible, their growing presence is certainly playing a role.

A final question that it is worth briefly considering is what determines the degree of penetration by and impact of foreign companies in a particular industry. Although the number of case studies presented here is clearly insufficient for a rigorous analysis, they do allow some conjectures. Obviously, FDI is absent in sectors where regulatory entry barriers remain (such as health care service). Apart from that, one factor determining the degree of foreign penetration appears to be the relative importance of "local knowledge" (or embeddedness) versus "global capabilities." In the telecommunications sector, local knowledge and embeddedness, coupled with the willingness and ability to compete in a very specific "ecosystem" appear to outweigh any global capabilities, explaining why the foreign presence contracted again. Similarly, in the banking sector, foreign penetration remains low in areas where local knowledge, such as access to clients through long-term relationships, is important. On the other hand, in the area of investment banking, where global capabilities prevail over the advantages of long-term relationships, foreign penetration is much higher. And in the pharmaceutical industry, foreign penetration remained low as long as local knowledge – the ability to navigate the complex drug approval process – outweighed the importance of global R&D and marketing capabilities, but increased rapidly as regulatory changes simplifying the drug approval process tipped the balance the other way.

Other obvious factors are the strength of domestic companies in an industry and the international competitiveness of that industry more generally. Japan's insurance and pharmaceutical industries for different reasons are

---

[156] Richard Mason, Associate Director, JAC Japan, interview on May 19, 2005.

both relatively weak in international comparison, making it easy for foreign firms to gain market share through superior products. In contrast, Japan leads the world in mobile telecommunications, and foreign firms (mainly Vodafone, but also Cable & Wireless) have failed to establish a lasting presence. The one sector that does not neatly fit into this pattern is the car industry. On the one hand, one of Japan's strongest industries with one of the strongest companies in the world (Toyota), this sector also has the highest penetration of foreign firms of any industry.

A final observation is that deregulation (such as in the financial and the telecommunications sector) and regulatory reform (such as in the pharmaceutical and medical devices industries) clearly have played an crucial role in spurring FDI. However, no clear pattern can be discerned that would suggest that foreign firms have been more successful, or less, in newly deregulated than in other industries. Although they certainly have been very successful in the pharmaceutical and medical devices industries, the same cannot be said for the telecommunications sector.

As the case studies presented in this chapter have shown, FDI can – and in some sectors already does – play an important role in reshaping the Japanese economy. Although the ensuing structural change may be painful for some segments (such as domestic firms in the pharmaceutical and medical devices industries), the presence of foreign firms and the business methods, skills, products, and competition they introduce make a crucial contribution to the revitalization of the industries in which they operate and beyond. At the same time, however, the number of sectors in which the presence of foreign firms has reached sufficient critical mass to bring about such transformation remains limited. There thus remains considerable scope for Japan to benefit more fully from the contribution FDI can potentially make to the economy.

SEVEN

The Prospects for Foreign Direct Investment in Japan

The increase in inward foreign direct investment (FDI) since the late 1990s represents an important development at a time that Japan's economy – despite the recent recovery – continues to face severe challenges. Policy makers recognize, at least in principle, that if the country is to prosper, it will have to embrace globalization more fully. However, whether Japan is truly prepared to do so and, in particular, to provide the kind of environment that attracts foreign firms and allows them to play the same kind of role they do in other advanced economies remains in doubt. On the one hand, the country has certainly come a long way when compared with little more than a decade ago: in the mid-1990s, few would have expected that traditional patterns such as cross-shareholdings and lifetime employment practices would unravel as quickly as they did and mergers and acquisitions (M&As), including cross-border ones, become commonplace. On the other hand, these fundamental changes came about as a result of exceptional circumstances that are unlikely to be repeated, and many other features persist, including pervasive regulation, resistance to a more *laissez-faire* market system, and a low degree of internationalization of society in general.

Against this background, the purpose of the present chapter is to consider the longer-term prospects for FDI in Japan by looking at the factors that determine the country's attractiveness for foreign firms and its willingness and ability to play host to them. Four broad topics are considered. The first of these deals with the factors that draw foreign firms to Japan, the strategic objectives they pursue, their profitability and success, and perceptions of the country as an FDI destination. It will be suggested that the market-seeking objective plays a dominant role and growth prospects are therefore likely to be a key factor determining future FDI flows in the long run. Consequently, the second topic to be discussed is the outlook for Japan's economic growth as well as regional growth prospects more generally.

But the environment for FDI in Japan also depends on political, corporate, and social attitudes toward foreign companies and internationalization, which in turn shape policies and the FDI environment more generally. Another factor is Japan's relations with its neighbors, which affect the likelihood of bilateral or regional agreements that can enhance economic integration and hence FDI. These aspects form the third topic area and, to a large extent, also provide the agenda for the final topic, which addresses steps the Japanese government could take to raise the level of inward FDI.

Japan as an FDI Destination

The attractiveness of Japan, as of any other country, as a host for FDI depends on a range of factors that can be divided into three major categories: economic determinants, the general policy framework for FDI, and business facilitation measures.[1] Economic determinants include fundamental characteristics such as market size, per capita income, market growth, and access to regional and global markets. These determinants are particularly relevant for FDI of the market-seeking variety. In addition, economic determinants include natural and human resources, physical infrastructure, technological and other created assets, and so on, that are of interest in the case of resource- or asset-seeking FDI. Finally, they include the cost of these resources and assets, other input costs, and membership of regional integration agreements that are conducive to the establishment of regional corporate networks – factors relevant in the case of efficiency-seeking FDI. The attractiveness of a country for FDI depends on the particular configuration of these economic characteristics and the extent to which that configuration coincides with the specific market-, resource-, asset- or efficiency-seeking objectives that multinationals pursue.

But in addition to the economic determinants, the policy framework for FDI also plays an important role. This framework includes basic economic, political, and social stability, rules regarding the entry and operations of foreign firms, the standards of treatment of foreign affiliates, policies regarding the functioning and structure of markets (in particular, those pertaining to competition and M&As), international agreements on FDI, trade policies, tax policies, and so on. Lastly, the third category of host-country factors consists of business facilitation measures for foreign companies. Examples of such measures are investment promotion and incentives, measures to minimize hassle costs (i.e., costs related to corruption and administrative

---

[1] See UNCTAD (1998: chapter IV).

efficiency, for example), social amenities (bilingual schools, quality of life, etc.), and after-investment services. The policy framework for FDI and business facilitation measures can be considered as enabling factors that make it possible and/or more attractive for multinationals to invest in a particular country.

Applying these concepts to Japan helps to understand both past inward FDI trends and the outlook for future FDI inflows. For instance, the surge in FDI in Japan witnessed during the late 1990s and early 2000s can be viewed to a large extent as the result of a combination of changes in the economic structure (the unwinding of cross-shareholdings, labor market changes, etc.) and improvements in the policy framework for FDI. These developments removed many, though by no means all, of the implicit and explicit barriers that had obstructed FDI in Japan in the past. Similarly, looking ahead, the concepts help to focus on factors that are likely to be relevant in determining future FDI inflows. For example, although the policy framework for FDI in Japan has improved considerably, certain obstacles remain. Subsequent sections therefore look at the politics surrounding FDI-related policies and consider measures the government could pursue to further improve the environment for FDI.

Yet, although the policy framework is crucial, it is only an enabling factor. Multinationals' decision to invest – or not invest – in Japan first and foremost depends on economic determinants and the extent to which conditions in the country provide the basis for opportunities to expand profits. To begin the assessment of the prospects for FDI in Japan it is therefore useful to first look at the motives multinationals pursue when investing in the country and then to consider the extent to which Japan is viewed as providing the right conditions.

Examining recent FDI patterns in Japan suggests that the overriding objective in the majority of cases has been to gain access to the country's market. One indication of this is that the service sector accounted for almost four-fifths of FDI inflows during the period 1998–2004.[2] In the case of services, not only is establishing a local presence often the only way in which a market can be served. Japan's productivity and international competitiveness in this area are generally low, so that resource-, strategic asset-, or efficiency-seeking motives in most cases were probably of secondary importance. A case in point is finance and insurance, which alone made up half of the service sector FDI during that period. In this industry, foreigners acquired a number of insurance companies that either had failed or were at

---

[2] Based on Ministry of Finance data on a notification basis. The exact share was 78.0 percent.

the brink of collapse. Although these transactions involved the acquisition of local assets, it was not the quality of these assets, or the contribution they could make to regional or global operations, that motivated the purchase, but rather the instant access to the local market they provided.[3] Other major service sectors that attracted FDI during this period were wholesale and retail trade – where the market orientation is quite clear – and telecommunication. With regard to the latter, the dominant case, the acquisition of J-Phone by Vodafone, again primarily served to provide the British company with a presence in the Japanese market, although the strategic asset-seeking motive is likely to have played a role as well, since Vodafone was interested in the firm's mobile technology.

The order of priorities is less clear in the manufacturing sector. The acquisition of Nissan by Renault, for example, is likely to have been based on a combination of efficiency-, strategic asset-, and market-seeking motives, given that, despite its problems, Nissan possessed considerable technological capabilities, and common management of the two companies provided ample opportunity for specialization, economies of scale and scope, and the rationalization of global activities. On the other hand, in the automotive supply industry, access to local customers, the smooth functioning of relationships with them, and the reduction of transaction costs – i.e., market-seeking objectives – are likely to play an important role. As a final example, take the pharmaceutical and medical devices industries. The capabilities of Japanese firms lag considerably behind those of their Western counterparts that have invested in the country, and again, access to the lucrative local market has been the central motive for multinationals to establish or expand their presence.

Another way to look at FDI patterns and motives is in terms of the relative productivity levels of foreign and Japanese firms. Asset-seeking FDI is likely to be concentrated in sectors in which domestic firms display a high level of productivity, such as in the transportation machinery sector. On the other hand, market-seeking FDI is likely to be found in sectors where the productivity of domestic firms lags behind international levels (provided that the productivity gap is not the result of regulations, such as explicit or implicit restrictions on market entry, which would also constrain FDI). Such sectors, which are largely concentrated in the service sector (see Chapter 4), provide foreign multinationals with opportunities to exploit their superior

---

[3] As shown in Chapter 6, there were also a number of acquisitions of failed banks by foreign investment funds for the purpose of turning these around and selling them again at a profit. These cases do not neatly fit into the typology of FDI presented above.

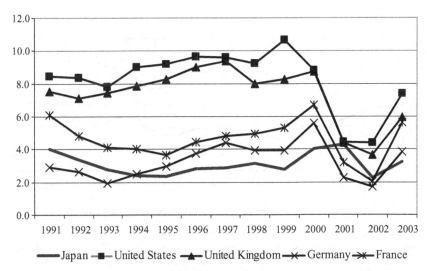

Figure 7.1. Return on assets in the corporate sector (percent, mean weighted by market capitalization)
Source: IMF, *World Economic Outlook*, September 2005, online: <http://www.imf.org/external/pubs/ft/weo/2005/02/chp1data/fig1_14.csv> (accessed April 14, 2007).

productivity and allow them to prosper even if overall economic growth is subdued.

With market-seeking objectives as the main driver of FDI, profit opportunities within the country and the likelihood of success become key determinants of multinational firms' decision to establish themselves in Japan. One way to examine profit opportunities in Japan vis-à-vis other potential host countries is to compare the profitability of all firms in each economy. Measuring profitability in terms of returns on assets, such a comparison shows that firms in Japan tend to be much less profitable than in Western countries (Figure 7.1). Although this suggests that profits are hard to come by in Japan, it also reflects the fact that Japanese firms historically have paid little attention to profitability and have instead tended to focus on growth and market share.

Comparison of the profitability of foreign companies active in Japan with their domestic counterparts shows that the former tend to be considerably more profitable. According to data from the *Financial Statements Statistics of Corporations by Industry* published by the Ministry of Finance, the ratio of ordinary profits to sales of the affiliates of foreign firms in Japan has consistently been about twice as high as that of all incorporated enterprises in the country (see Figure 7.2a). Moreover, profitability has been increasing

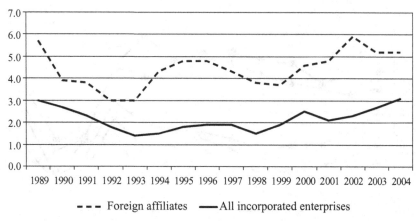

--- Foreign affiliates   ——All incorporated enterprises

Figure 7.2(a). Ratio of ordinary profits to sales (percent)
Sources: METI, "Summary of the 1999 Survey of Foreign Affiliates' Business Activities," July 2000, online: <http://www.meti.go.jp/english/statistics/downloadfiles/h2c201be.pdf> (accessed April 14, 2007); METI, "The 39th Survey of Trends in Business Activities of Foreign Affiliates (Summary)," April 27, 2006, online: <http://www.meti.go.jp/english/statistics/downloadfiles/h2c200he.pdf> (accessed April 14, 2007).

in recent years. Focusing on a different measure, return on equity (ROE), foreign affiliates again show a much better performance than the average of all incorporated enterprises, although the gap has shrunk in recent years and foreign affiliates as a group in fact registered significant losses in 1999 (Figure 7.2b).

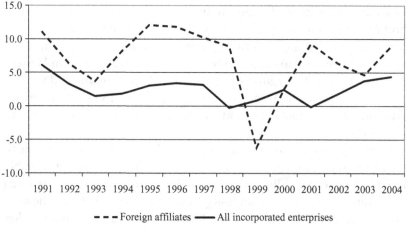

--- Foreign affiliates ——All incorporated enterprises

Figure 7.2(b). Return on equity (ROE) (percent)
Sources: See Figure 7.2(a).

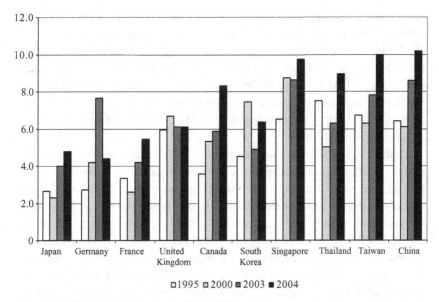

Figure 7.3. Net income/sales ratio of U.S. affiliates by host country (in percent)
Source: Bureau of Economic Analysis, "U.S. Direct Investment Abroad: Operations of
U.S. Parent Companies and Their Foreign Affiliates," online: <http://www.bea.gov/
bea/ai/iidguide.htm#USDIA1> (accessed April 2, 2007).

Finally, it is instructive to compare the profitability of U.S. subsidiaries by
host country (measured in terms of the net income/sales ratio). Although
such a comparison is not without problems because of practices such as
transfer pricing, the overall pattern seems to be consistent with the findings
so far, suggesting that the profitability of U.S. subsidiaries in Japan was
relatively low in 1995 and 2000 but has increased in recent years (Figure 7.3).
Moreover, although lower than in newly industrializing and developing
countries such as Singapore, Taiwan, Thailand, and China, the profitability
of U.S. subsidiaries in Japan in 2003 was more or less on par with that of U.S.
subsidiaries in Germany, France, and Britain, and is likely to have increased
further along with the continued recovery of the economy.

But average profit rates say little about the likelihood that a particular
company investing in Japan will indeed do well and there is some evidence
that the country may still be a difficult place in which to do business. For
example, recent years have seen a number of prominent failures of foreign
firms in Japan, including Carrefour, Boots, Cable & Wireless, and Vodafone.
Arguably, strategic management errors (in particular, a failure to properly understand the Japanese market) have played a role in each of these

cases.[4] But they are no exception: recent research suggests that between 1999 and the first quarter of 2005, on average 170 foreign firms a year exited the Japanese market, and it is particularly young foreign involvements that are affected.[5] Similarly, data published by the Ministry of Economy, Trade and Industry (METI) suggest that the number of firms withdrawing from Japan may be about as high as the number of foreign firms being newly established (Figure 7.4), although the METI figures should be viewed with caution because of the way they are compiled.[6]

That, along with the increase in inward FDI, disinvestments have also been on the rise is confirmed by the balance-of-payments statistics (Figure 7.5). In fact, in 2006, net FDI in Japan even turned negative as outflows jumped and exceeded inflows. To some extent, the outflows reflect the nature of some of the investments in recent years, that is, purchases of ailing Japanese firms by foreign funds, which, having successfully restructured their acquisition targets, recoup their investment by selling them again. Examples include KS Bank, which was sold to the Bank of Kansai in 2003, and Shinsei Bank and Tokyo Star Bank, which listed on the stock market in 2004 and 2005, respectively (see Chapter 6). Outflows have also been inflated by General Motors' (GM's) dissolution of long-standing capital ties with Fuji Heavy Industries (Subaru) and Isuzu and the reduction of its stake in Suzuki (from 20 percent to 3 percent), which appears to be more a reflection of the American carmaker's troubles at home than any problems with its Japanese investments. Given that the jump in disinvestments in 2006 seems to be largely due to two major cases – GM and Vodafone – it may be premature to suggest that

[4] Added to this list may be the dissolution of DaimlerChrysler's ties with Mitsubishi Motors, although the German-American firm did retain its majority stake in Mitsubishi Fuso and it has been speculated that it was Mitsubishi's truck division, which was spun off after the merger, that DaimlerChrysler was interested in in the first place.

[5] David (2006). According to this research, which is based on a careful evaluation of the *Gaishikei Kigyo Soran* published by Toyo Keizai Shinposha, there were 1,056 withdrawals in the period from 1996 to the first quarter of 2005. By age, the highest frequency of withdrawals was observed for foreign investments that were only four years old, indicating a high infant mortality.

[6] The survey (METI, 2006a) reporting these numbers indicates that withdrawals "include [. . .] 'liquidation' and 'reduction in controlling share (controlling share possessed by foreign enterprise drops to one-third or less of the total)" (sic) (ibid.: Note 3), but it is not quite clear whether they are based on all foreign firms in Japan or only those that were subject of the survey. In addition, the survey on which the figures are based suffers from a relatively low response ratio (59.5 percent in the survey published in 2006) and there appear to be other inconsistencies in the data (including differences between the Japanese and the English version of the report). If withdrawals are calculated only on the basis of firms included in the survey, which appears to be the case, the actual number of withdrawals is probably higher still.

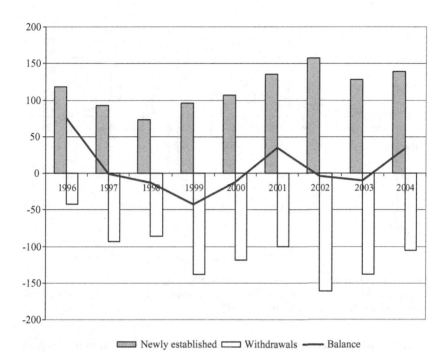

Figure 7.4. Number of newly established foreign affiliates and number of enterprises withdrawing
Sources: METI, "The 37th Survey of Trends in Business Activities of Foreign Affiliates (Main Points)," July 27, 2004, online: <http://www.meti.go.jp/english/statistics/downloadfiles/h2c200fe.pdf>; METI, "The 39th Survey of Trends in Business Activities of Foreign Affiliates (Summary)," April 27, 2006, online: <http://www.meti.go.jp/english/statistics/downloadfiles/h2c200he.pdf> (both accessed April 14, 2007).

it indicates the beginning of a mass exodus from Japan. Nevertheless, combined with the high number of withdrawals, it certainly is a development that should give policy makers cause for concern.

This is especially the case because perceptions of Japan's attractiveness as an FDI destination also appear to be slipping. According to the *FDI Confidence Index* published by a global consulting firm and based on a survey among executives of the world's 1,000 largest corporations, Japan gradually moved up in ranking from twenty-third place in 1998 (the first year of the survey) to tenth place in 2004.[7] However, in 2005, Japan dropped by five places to fifteenth, suggesting that the country was gradually falling out of favor again, ranking behind China, India, the United States, the major

[7] A. T. Kearney (2004).

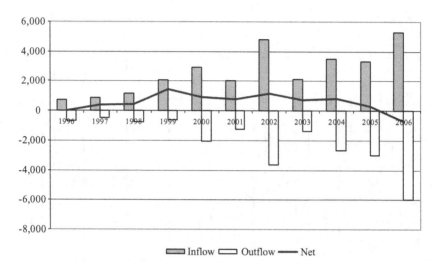

Figure 7.5. FDI in Japan: Inflows and outflows (¥ billion)
Source: Ministry of Finance, online: <http://www.mof.go.jp/bpoffice/bpdata/fdi/efdi2bop.htm#bm1> (accessed April 2, 2007).

Western European economies (Britain, Germany, and France, in that order) and a number of Eastern European countries (Poland, Russia, Hungary, and the Czech Republic).[8] Japan also did not make it into the global top ten FDI destinations listed by multinational corporations in the United Nations Conference on Trade and Development's (UNCTAD's) *Prospects for Foreign Direct Investment*, although among developed economies, Japan was ranked sixth (behind the United States, Britain, Canada, Germany, and France) by a panel of experts and eighth (behind the countries just listed as well as Spain and Ireland) by multinational corporations.[9]

But Japan does rather well in the more broadly based *Global Competitiveness Report* published by the World Economic Forum. Although the report does not explicitly address countries' attractiveness as an FDI destination, it does offer useful indicators of how a country's economic and business environment is perceived more generally.[10] In the 2006–2007 report, Japan

[8] A. T. Kearney (2005).
[9] UNCTAD (2005).
[10] World Economic Forum, *The Global Competitiveness Report 2006–2007*, "Executive Summary," online: <http://www.weforum.org/pdf/GlobalCompetitiveness_Reports/Reports/gcr_2006/gcr2006_summary.pdf> (accessed March 12, 2007). Despite their sophistication, such rankings obviously contain a considerable degree of subjectivity, both in terms of how individual measures are evaluated and how they are weighted. The IMD in its *World Competitiveness Yearbook*, for example, arrives at a very different ranking.

is ranked seventh in terms of global competitiveness overall, which itself is composed of nine "pillars." The country does extremely well, coming first or second, in three of the pillars: health and primary education, business sophistication, and innovation. It is also among the top ten in terms of infrastructure (seventh) and market efficiency (tenth), but for an advanced country only scores a middling place in terms of higher education and training (fifteenth), technological readiness (nineteenth), and institutions (twenty-second), while its macroeconomy earns it only ninety-first place. These indicators suggest that, apart from the macroeconomic situation, Japan offers a business environment that allows its firms to be among the most competitive in the world.

Overall, the picture of Japan as an investment destination that emerges is that the country is of interest primarily for market-seeking FDI, although the efficiency-seeking and the strategic asset-seeking motives have also played a role in some cases. Foreign firms operating in Japan tend to be profitable – and, as a group, in fact more profitable than domestic firms – but the number of withdrawals also appears to be relatively high. Moreover, the country's attractiveness as an FDI destination, which had been improving, seems to have suffered a setback and continues to lag behind the major Western economies. Finally, Japan does reasonably well in an international comparison of national business environments, but has been hampered by its macroeconomic performance. The outlook for the latter is likely to be one important determinant of future FDI flows into the country and will be discussed in detail in the next section.

Macroeconomic Prospects

The increase in FDI in Japan witnessed in recent years can be largely seen as a catch-up process triggered by the removal of barriers that had hitherto hindered market penetration by foreign multinationals. Given the substantial size of this untapped market potential, it mattered little that the Japanese economy was stagnating during this period. (In fact, the economic malaise helped to create the conditions that made many of the investments possible.) What is more, this catch-up process can be expected to continue in the next few years, since even today, the level of inward FDI penetration in Japan remains very low by international standards.

However, in the longer term, given that the great majority of FDI in Japan is of the market-seeking type, the country's macroeconomic performance is likely to be an important determinant of future investment inflows. After all, a vibrant and expanding economy provides far greater profit opportunities than a stagnating one. In this context, it is also useful to consider Japan's economic prospects from a regional perspective. Japan's prolonged economic stagnation and China's stellar economic performance since the early 1990s have gradually shifted attention away from the former and toward the latter. Of course, Japan and China or India (another country that has seen a significant rise in FDI in recent years) are unlikely to be competing for the same kind of investment (as, say, Western European nations often are). Furthermore, especially in the case of market-seeking investment and/or in the service sector, FDI is not a zero-sum game where investments in one country come at the expense of another. Yet, as reflected in the studies mentioned above, it is also clear that it is China (closely followed by India) that is uppermost in business leaders' minds when it comes to foreign investment destinations.[11] On the other hand, taking a long-term view, it is also conceivable that FDI in Japan may benefit from rapid economic development in China, India, and the rest of the Asia-Pacific region, although whether the potential benefits will materialize also depends on Japan's political relations with its neighbors. The following sections take up these various issues in detail.

Japan's Growth Prospects

Japan's economy is finally on the mend. Following two aborted recoveries in 1996 and 2000, annual gross domestic product (GDP) growth has gradually accelerated from only 0.3 percent in 2002 to 2.2 percent in 2006 and by the end of that year had posted eighteen successive quarters of year-on-year expansion.[12] Moreover, unless the policy mistakes following earlier recoveries (premature fiscal and monetary tightening, respectively) are repeated, growth at similarly respectable rates is likely to continue for a while as the economy "catches up" to close the large output gap that opened up during the recession.

Yet, although the short-term outlook for the economy has brightened, Japan continues to face serious long-term challenges. Central among these are demographic trends, that is, the shrinking and aging of the population. Japan's working-age population (those aged 15–64) has been declining since 1996, and the population overall was expected to start shrinking in 2007.[13]

---

[11] China tops both A. T. Kearney's *FDI Confidence Index* and the list of most attractive global business locations named by multinationals in UNCTAD's *Prospects for Foreign Direct Investment.*

[12] The growth figure for 2006 is the second preliminary estimate made public in March 2007.

[13] National Institute of Population and Social Security Research (2002, 2006).

Although there is some room for increased labor force participation by women and older workers,[14] labor input in the economy is expected to shrink in the decades to come and depress output growth. Future economic growth therefore will largely have to come from improvements in productivity.

Estimates of Japan's potential growth rate generally put this at about 2 percent. The Bank of Japan (BOJ), for example, estimates that the potential growth rate, after having fallen to around 1 percent in the 1990s, has recovered to about 1.5 to 2 percent.[15] Similarly, the Council on Economic and Fiscal Policy has raised its estimate of the growth potential from about 1.5 percent to 2 percent.[16] Other observers are even more optimistic, arguing that Japan's potential has risen in the past few years as a result of greater efficiency in the allocation of capital thanks to financial sector reforms, increasing competition such as in the retail and telecommunication sectors, better corporate governance, and deregulation facilitating the establishment of new companies.[17] In addition, there has been a rise in productivity-enhancing investment in information and communications technology, but there also still remains ample room for a further increase in the deployment of information technology in Japan when compared with current levels in the United States.[18] Consequently, the optimists estimate that Japan's growth potential is in the range of 2.0 to 2.5 percent rather than the 1.5 to 2.0 percent suggested by BOJ and government estimates.[19]

Despite their diverging results, which reflect the inherent difficulties in assessing a country's growth potential, these estimates provide a useful indication of Japan's future growth prospects. Although there will clearly be no return to the heady growth rates of the period before the "lost decade" of the 1990s, the coming decades also do not have to be a period of long-term relative decline. Being cautiously optimistic and assuming that GDP growth will indeed be about 2 percent, Japan's economic performance in the coming years will probably not lag much behind that of the member countries of the Eurozone, which grew by an average 2.1 percent in the period from 1995 to 2005 and face similar, although not quite so severe demographic challenges.[20] Moreover, given that Japan's population is going to shrink in the coming decades, per capita incomes are going to rise faster than overall GDP,

---

[14] See, e.g., Council on Economic and Fiscal Policy (2005) for details.
[15] Bank of Japan (2006).
[16] Council on Economic and Fiscal Policy (2005, 2007).
[17] Posen (2001, 2004).
[18] Posen (2001, 2004), Jorgensen and Motohashi (2004), Fukao and Miyagawa (2007).
[19] Posen (2001, 2004), Jorgensen and Motohashi (2004).
[20] Growth figure from OECD online database.

meaning that the Japanese will continue to be among the richest consumers in the world.

In terms of the outlook for FDI, these prospects imply that, although the Japanese market is unlikely to show rapid rates of growth, it will continue to expand, providing opportunities for foreign multinationals particularly in the area of high-end consumer goods and sophisticated services. In fact, much of Japan's future economic growth will have to come from the service sector, whose share in gross value added has gradually expanded from 58.0 percent in 1990 to 69.4 percent in 2004,[21] and in which Japanese productivity lags farthest behind other advanced economies. The service sector thus is the area in which foreign investment can make the greatest contribution to growth and has already been concentrated in recent years.

Regional Growth Dynamics and Their Implications

Japan's growth prospects of course pale in comparison with those of many other countries in East, Southeast, and South Asia, notably China and India. A recent study projects that unless growth in the two largest developing countries is derailed, China's GDP may overtake Japan's as early as 2015, while India's might surpass it around 2030.[22] Such projections are naturally fraught with a high degree of uncertainty,[23] yet, they nevertheless provide a useful scenario to consider the region's growth dynamics and their potential implications for FDI in Japan.

The first thing to note is that the Chinese and Indian economies are likely to expand at rates above or close to 5 percent for another decade-and-a-half or more, even as their potential for catch-up growth diminishes. Besides the large pool of low-cost labor, it is these growth prospects and the associated market potential that draw so many multinationals to these countries. Yet, it is also important to note that, even if the Chinese and Indian economies achieve the rates of GDP growth projected in the study, their level of development will continue to significantly lag behind that of Japan. One indicator of this is per capita GDP projections in U.S. dollar terms: even under the relatively pessimistic growth assumptions for Japan made in the study, the country's per capita GDP in 2030 would still be about five times that of China and more than ten times that of India. Of course, these figures are only averages and already there is a large and growing middle class in China and India whose consumption patterns more and

---

[21] Figures from OECD, *OECD in Figures* (2002 Edition and 2006–2007 Edition).
[22] Goldman Sachs (2003).
[23] The study, for example, projects annual real GDP growth rates for Japan that are well below the 2 percent growth potential that most observers now expect.

more resemble those of consumers in the advanced countries. Nevertheless, Japan will continue to offer the largest market for sophisticated products and services in the region for years to come, with obvious implications for FDI of the market-seeking type.

In addition, the economic advance of China, India, and other countries in the region gives rise not only to potential rivalry but also to great opportunity. At present, Japan finds itself as the only advanced economy in an area of developing countries and therefore does not enjoy any of the benefits that proximity to similarly developed nations provides for cross-border trade and investment. This situation is quite different from that of European countries, for example, and is one of the reasons why FDI has been so low in Japan.

However, as rapid economic development progresses, not only will the gap between Japan and the rest of Asia shrink, but the global economic balance will continue its gradual shift to the region, which is reflected in recent FDI trends: since 1990, East and Southeast Asia's inward FDI stock has grown almost eightfold, from US$157 billion to US$1,439 billion (2005), more than doubling the region's global share from about 9 percent at the beginning of the 1990s to 19 percent at the end of the decade, although this has since dropped again to about 14 percent. The region's outward FDI stock (excluding Japan) has risen even more dramatically, increasing 14-fold from US$68 billion in 1990 to US$827 billion in 2005, and its share in the global total jumped from only 3 percent during the 1980s to approximately 10 percent at the end of the 1990s, although this figure, too, has recently declined again, to about 8 percent.[24]

The regional growth and FDI dynamics may help to boost investment in Japan in two ways. The first is that multinationals from outside the region may decide to serve Asian markets from Japan and/or to locate in Japan functions supporting activities elsewhere in the region. Such functions may range from regional headquarters to R&D centers to logistics and financial operations. In the taxonomy of strategic objectives pursued by multinational enterprises, investments in these types of activities would combine market-seeking motives (the lowering of transaction costs as a result of greater proximity) with efficiency-seeking motives (the rationalization of global activities, international specialization) and thus help to broaden the scope of FDI in Japan.

However, in attracting these support functions, Japan is directly competing with a number of other economies vying to establish themselves, or expand their role, as regional operations centers for multinational

---

[24] All figures are authors' calculations based on the UNCTAD online database.

companies such as Singapore, Hong Kong, Korea, and Taiwan. Singapore, for example, started its Headquarters (HQ) Programme as early as 1986 and further enhanced it in 2003, offering companies that use Singapore as their base for the Asia-Pacific region a preferential tax rate for three years.[25] Similarly, South Korea provides support and various incentives in three free economic zones in an attempt to establish itself as a regional logistics center and business hub for high-value-added services,[26] while Taiwan has spelled out its ambitions in the Asia-Pacific Regional Operations Center (APROC) plan introduced in 1995, which aims to establish the island as a center for manufacturing, sea and air transportation, finance, and telecommunications.[27]

Companies from other parts of the world looking to set up regional head offices or other support functions in Asia thus have a wide range of potential locations to choose from. Compared with these and other alternative investment locations, Japan's attractiveness as a destination for this kind of FDI seems rather limited. Although the country offers certain advantages, such as excellent infrastructure and political stability, its geographic location at the periphery of the continent, the high costs of doing business, relatively heavy regulation in areas such as finance, and other political, cultural, and social factors discussed below put it at a disadvantage.

But there is a second way in which regional growth dynamics may help to boost FDI in Japan: the potential for greater inflows from other Asian countries. Although, at present, FDI from the rest of Asia is still relatively small when compared with inflows from the United States and Europe, it is no longer negligible. The number of out–in M&As by Asian firms jumped from less than 10 annually during the 1990s to about 20 per year during 2000–2002, accounting for about 10 to 15 percent of all out–in M&As in Japan.[28] Moreover, by 2005, Asia accounted for 6.6 percent of the total inward FDI stock in Japan, led by Hong Kong, Singapore, Taiwan, and South Korea (in that order).[29] This trend reflects the fact that the more advanced economies of the region are gradually emerging as source countries of FDI, as is indicated by increase in the combined outward FDI stock of these four

---

[25] UNCTAD (2004: 198).

[26] UNCTAD (2004: 199).

[27] Japan now also appears to be keen to establish itself as a regional hub, as indicated by the government's "Asia Gateway Vision," which, however, is short on detail and does not include any of the tangible benefits for multinationals that Singapore, Taiwan, or South Korea offer. See below for more on the "Asia Gateway Vision."

[28] RECOF (2003).

[29] Authors' calculations based on International Investment Position statistics retrieved from the Bank of Japan website: <http://www.boj.or.jp/en/type/stat/boj_stat/bop/diri/index.htm> (accessed April 2, 2007).

countries from only US$52 billion in 1990 to US$715 billion in 2005.[30] Moreover, even India and China, although still at much lower levels of economic development, have seen substantial increases in outward FDI over the past decade-and-a-half: India's outward stock has risen from only US$124 million in 1990 to US$9.6 billion in 2005, while China's has grown from US$4.5 billion to US$46.3 billion over the same period.[31] Of course, in a global comparison, these figures are still very small, but if the two countries fulfill their economic growth potential, FDI outflows can be expected to rise rapidly. Both countries have already spawned a number of multinationals. Examples include Infosys, an Indian information technology (IT) and business consulting firm with offices around the world (including Japan) and a listing on the NASDAQ stock exchange, Ranbaxy (also from India), which is among the global top ten generic drugmakers and has manufacturing operations in nine countries and offices in forty-nine,[32] and Tata Steel, which in October 2006 took over the Anglo-Dutch steelmaker Corus. Chinese companies are not far behind. In December 2004, Lenovo Group, the country's largest personal computer maker, attracted worldwide attention when it acquired a major interest in IBM's PC-making business. Other firms, many of them state-owned, are also becoming global players, including China National Petroleum Company, Sinopec, and Baosteel.

As Asian countries continue their rapid economic development, regional FDI dynamics will continue to gather pace. Yet, how much of this investment will find its way to Japan depends not only on economic factors, but also on political ones – in particular, the extent to which Japan is able to overcome frictions with neighboring countries, especially China and Korea, and work toward a framework conducive to regional trade and investment. These questions are among the topics addressed in the following sections.

Political, Social, and Cultural Factors

At the outset of this chapter, it was suggested that a country's attractiveness for FDI is determined by a combination of economic and policy factors. The latter include policies explicitly aimed at facilitating FDI as well as policies that affect firms and markets more generally. For example, the surge in FDI in banking and insurance, telecommunications, and pharmaceuticals followed hot on the heels of regulatory changes in these sectors during the latter half of the 1990s. More broadly based measures, such as changes in

[30] Figures from UNCTAD online database.
[31] Figures from UNCTAD online database.
[32] Based on information from the companies' websites.

accounting rules and legislation to facilitate mergers and corporate restructuring also played a role. Yet, although these measures represent important
steps toward making Japan more attractive for FDI, more could be done.
Looking at recent political developments, this section considers the likelihood that further FDI-friendly policies will be forthcoming, while measures
the government could pursue in order to improve Japan's attractiveness for
FDI in the medium- to long-term will be discussed later.

In addition to the political dimension, there is also a social and cultural
dimension shaping the policy framework as well as economic determinants
relevant for FDI. For instance, the past decade or so has seen an important
transformation in social attitudes toward foreign companies and there is
now a greater willingness among Japanese employees – and especially the
young – to change jobs and/or work for a foreign company. This means that
the supply of labor that foreign multinationals can tap into in Japan – and
the cost at which they can do so – has significantly shifted in their favor.
Similarly, hard-nosed employment practices and a clear profit orientation
have become more common among Japanese companies as they struggled
to return to health, making foreign ways of doing business no longer appear
as cold and ruthless as in the past, while M&As have become a regular feature
of the Japanese business landscape as well. Yet, although these developments
play into the hands of foreign multinationals, unease remains strong in some
political circles, a substantial part of the public, and the business community,
so that further change will not come without resistance.

Questions also remain over the extent to which Japan is prepared to fully
embrace and exploit globalization more generally. Japanese society continues to be highly homogenous, a fact that shapes both its willingness to accept
foreigners and foreign ideas and its ability to adapt to the needs of a global
economy. This means that even today, foreign companies operating in Japan
still often find it difficult to hire personnel with the necessary language skills
and international outlook. Finally, political, social, and cultural attitudes
shape Japan's relations with its neighbors and the wider region, affecting
progress in attaining deeper economic integration, with potentially adverse
effects on future FDI in Japan. These political, social, cultural, and international issues are taken up in the following subsections.

Government Policies and Business Attitudes Toward FDI

In contrast with earlier decades, the Japanese government today, in principle,
recognizes the benefits of inward foreign investment. One of the strongest
indications of this are the goals for inward FDI set by Prime Minister Koizumi

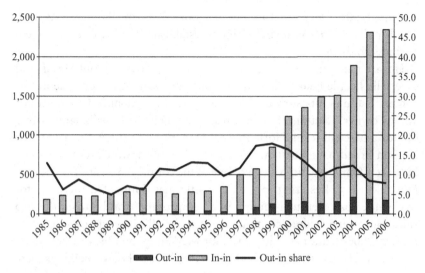

Figure 7.6. In–in and out–in M&As in Japan (number of cases; percent)
Source: RECOF Corporation.

and his immediate successor, Abe.[33] Similarly, the business community has
spoken out in favor of FDI: during the 1990s, the powerful business federation Keidanren, for example, repeatedly called on the government to
deregulate the economy and encourage foreign investment.[34] Yet, along
with the recovery of the economy more generally and of corporate profits in
particular, old patterns are beginning to reappear, indicating that lingering
suspicions of foreign investment, combined with unease over the economic
forces unleashed by recent reforms, remain strong.

Nowhere does this become clearer than with regard to M&As and, in particular, "triangular mergers." As seen in Chapter 3, M&A activity in Japan
has grown substantially in recent years, reflecting wider changes in the country's economy as well as measures introduced by the government to facilitate
corporate restructuring.[35] The number of cases involving a Japanese firm as
the acquisition target rose from less than 300 during the mid-1990s to over
a thousand in 2000 and reached more than 2,300 in 2006 (see Figure 7.6).
In–in M&As make up the bulk of these cases, indicating that Japanese firms
have been actively making use of this tool. In addition, the number of out–in
M&A cases has also increased, climbing from around thirty a year during

[33] See Chapter 2 for details.
[34] See Chapter 3.
[35] See Chapter 3 for details.

the mid-1990s to an annual average of about 170 during the 2000s. As these trends indicate, M&As are becoming an established feature of the Japanese business landscape.

However, despite – or because of – this trend, concerns about M&As, and especially hostile takeovers, have also been growing. A key episode in this context is the events surrounding the internet and finance firm Livedoor and its owner, Takafumi Horie. Already having gained media fame with a bid for a baseball team, Horie in 2005 launched a hostile takeover bid for Nippon Broadcasting System (NBS), a radio station, which represented an indirect attempt to gain control of one of the country's private TV stations, Fuji Television. Resulting in a bitter battle that dominated the news for weeks, the spat eventually ended in a compromise deal between the two sides. However, Livedoor continued to make headlines when it was revealed in early 2006 that an affiliate, Livedoor Marketing, had broken disclosure rules and falsified statements and Horie and other board members were arrested.

The Livedoor episode is important because it brought to the surface continuing resistance to the changes sweeping Japan and, at least indirectly, played a role in shaping the environment for M&As and FDI in Japan. Whereas to some, Horie, until his arrest, had been a model of the new kind of entrepreneur the country desperately needed, to others he and his business practices exemplified the "market fundamentalism" and "excesses" unleashed by economic reforms. In particular, Horie's bid for NBS fanned latent fears over hostile takeovers, which featured prominently in the debate leading up the revision of the Commercial Code implemented in May 2006. Reflecting such fears, the revision not only established clearer rules for M&As, but also introduced provisions allowing firms to adopt a variety of antitakeover measures such as "poison pills." Moreover, citing concern over an imminent wave of foreign hostile takeovers, parliament postponed the lifting of the ban on triangular mergers for a year.

Following this, albeit temporary, setback for foreign firms wishing to invest in Japan, efforts by Japan's business community to protect themselves against unwanted takeovers intensified in the run up to the lifting of the triangular merger ban at the new date in May 2007. To understand the significance of triangular mergers, one needs to be aware that most large-scale M&A deals in Western countries are at least partially financed by equity swaps. In Japan, however, foreign firms have been effectively barred from using this method because firms wishing to pay for the acquisition of another firm with their own shares could only do so if they were listed in Japan. Yet, as of December 2006, only 25 foreign firms were listed on the Tokyo Stock

Exchange, and their number in fact has been shrinking in recent years (the current figure compares with 127 in 1991), with IBM and Pepsi among the latest firms to exit.[36] Hence the importance of the triangular merger scheme, which allows a foreign firm to issue its shares to a special-purpose company it owns in Japan, which then merges with the Japanese company for legal purposes. Shareholders of the Japanese company receive the newly issued shares in an effective swap.

Although triangular mergers cannot be used for hostile takeovers,[37] the two are often mentioned in the same breath and – intentionally or unintentionally – confused, reflecting the apprehension with which Japan's business community has viewed the lifting of the ban. In a last-minute attempt, the Keidanren, for example, called for more stringent takeover rules, arguing that the country's "overall legal provisional framework [was] inadequate for the blocking of corporate merger and acquisition attempts that are detrimental to corporate value or that harm the national interest through the outflow of technology."[38] In an encouraging sign, however, the ruling Liberal Democratic Party (LDP) dropped a proposal that would have imposed tougher shareholder approval requirements for triangular mergers on the grounds that such requirements would make it virtually impossible to conduct such mergers.[39]

At the same time, though, firms are coming up with other ways to protect themselves against hostile takeovers. By February 2007, nearly 200 firms had adopted antitakeover measures such as issuing share warrants to trust banks or other "friendly" outside parties.[40] In addition, firms have started resorting to cross-shareholdings again. Since bottoming out in 2004, shareholdings by nonfinancial firms have increased by about 30 percent.[41] Nippon Steel, for example, has strengthened its alliance with Sumitomo Metal Industries and Kobe Steel by increasing cross-shareholdings with the explicit aim of fending

---

[36] *Source:* Tokyo Stock Exchange website. The delisting of foreign firms itself of course should be cause for concern given the government's stated ambition of making Tokyo a global financial center on par with New York and London.

[37] By law, the board of the company to be acquired must approve the transaction before it goes to shareholders for their final approval, thus precluding any takeover against the will of the board.

[38] Nippon Keidanren, "Further Revision of M&A Legislation is Needed," December 12, 2006, online: <http://www.keidanren.or.jp/english/policy/2006/085.html> (accessed April 11, 2007).

[39] Nikkei, "LDP nixes stricter triangle merger rules," March 12, 2007.

[40] Nikkei, "Nearly 200 firms introduce measures to foil hostile takeover bids," February 23, 2007; Nikkei, "Firms erecting anti-takeover defenses also raising transparency," March 29, 2007.

[41] Nikkei, "Cross-holding revives as takeover shield," January 29, 2007.

off any takeover attempt.[42] Likewise, following a failed hostile takeover attempt by Oji Paper, Hokuetsu Paper Mills entered cross-shareholdings with Daio Paper, while Nippon Paper Group and Rengo announced a similar move.[43]

Overall, therefore, it appears that at the same time that the triangular merger scheme, long-awaited by the foreign business community in Japan, is going ahead, the Japanese business community – having regained some confidence on the back of the country's economic recovery – is reverting to traditional patterns. As much as fending off potential foreign suitors, anti-takeover measures seem to be designed to protect the interests of incumbent managers, as is illustrated, for example, by the vigorous fight put up by Hokuetsu Paper Mills to ward off Oji Paper in an entirely domestic hostile takeover attempt. Although it is unlikely that the developments described here will result in a return to the economic structures of earlier decades, they clearly indicate that resistance in the Japanese business community to "Western" business practices and acquisitions by foreign firms remains widespread. Combined with anecdotal evidence suggesting that it remains difficult for foreign firms to find suitable and willing acquisition targets,[44] this may explain why the number of out–in M&As has been stagnating in recent years and has actually been falling as a share of all M&As involving Japanese target firms (see Figure 7.6).

It is important to note that there are also voices in Japan criticizing this continuing resistance and urging the country to welcome globalization in general and foreign investment in particular. The *Nikkei Shinbun*, Japan's leading economic daily, for instance, has become a staunch supporter of inward FDI.[45] At the same time, however, politicians' enthusiasm for inward FDI has been waning since Koizumi's departure. The Expert Committee of the Japan Investment Council, for example, which under Koizumi used to hold four or five meetings a year, did not meet once under Abe, and although

---

[42] Reuters, "Nippon Steel, two others eye anti-takeover defence," March 29, 2006.

[43] Nikkei, "Cross-holding revives as takeover shield," January 29, 2007.

[44] According to a survey by the Economist Intelligence Unit, for example, 60 percent of M&A deals since 1998 involving foreign firms have related to unlisted Japanese companies, and often these were small deals with firms or subsidiaries where relationships already existed (Economist Intelligence Unit press release, "Threat of hostile takeovers hangs over Japanese companies," July 14, 2005, online: <http://www.eiuresources.com/mediadir/default.asp?PR=360001836>; accessed April 12, 2007).

[45] Examples of representative editorials include "Foreign capital must be welcomed amid rapid globalization" (March 5, 2007) and "Make Japan a global nation of lofty aspirations" (January 7, 2007).

he had promised to strive for the early fulfillment of Koizumi's FDI goal, no new initiatives that could help to achieve this were launched.

This apparent lack of interest in inward FDI appears to reflect a different set of priorities more generally. Koizumi explicitly ran on a platform of economic reform, making an economics professor, Heizo Takenaka, who held important posts in all five Koizumi cabinets, his right-hand man and calling a snap election to gain popular backing for his plan to privatize the postal-savings system. Although Abe at the beginning of his premiership had indicated that he wanted to bring about more far-reaching structural change, his main interests lay in the foreign policy arena, while the domestic policy debate was largely dominated by the issue of income equality (*kakusa shakai*), a topic forced onto the government's agenda by the opposition.

Looking at business and political trends taken together, it seems that as Japan's economy is regaining strength, the enthusiasm for reform, structural change, and inward FDI is dampening. In large parts of the business community, foreign investment continues to be viewed as a threat rather than an opportunity, prompting the adoption of antitakeover measures that are likely to put a brake on future FDI inflows. As for the government, recent signals have been mixed, with the LDP nixing proposals to impose more stringent requirements for triangular mergers, but also no new measures on the table. Against this background, the way the triangular merger scheme works in practice – which only time can tell – will provide a crucial test of the government's stance on FDI. Measures to ensure that triangular mergers indeed become a useful tool for FDI in Japan, as well as other steps the government could take to promote foreign investment, are discussed further below.

Social and Cultural Aspects

Japan's "closedness" to FDI in the past to a large extent is a reflection of the closedness of the country more generally. Unlike the United States and Australia, or, more recently, Britain and other Western European countries, Japan has no history of large-scale immigration. Foreign nationals account for only 1.5 percent of the population, compared with 4.5 percent in the United Kingdom (which, in addition, has a large number of naturalized immigrants) and 8.9 percent in Germany, while foreign-born nationals make up 11.8 percent of the U.S. population.[46] Ethnically, culturally, and linguistically, the Japanese remain one of the most homogenous people in

[46] Figures from the OECD online database.

the world, and for this reason, FDI poses as much a social and cultural challenge as it is an economic and political one.

In fact, many of the implicit barriers to FDI in the past, such as closed labor market institutions (in particular, the lifetime employment system) or constraints on M&As, contain a social and cultural dimension. Similarly, adapting to the needs of a global economy requires skills and attitudes that are shaped by social and cultural factors. Thus, although economic prospects and policies toward foreign firms are likely to be the key determinants of future FDI inflows into the country, the extent to which Japan as a society is willing and equipped to provide a home to foreign multinationals will also play a role.

In this regard, Japan certainly has come a long way. Despite lingering unease, most Japanese appear to accept the need for a more market-driven economy and see foreign companies in a positive light. For example, according to a survey conducted in 1995, 97 percent of managers thought that it is *stake*holders who own companies. But by 2005, this had completely changed, with 90 percent of managers replying that it is the *share*holders who own companies.[47] Similarly, foreign companies are increasingly seen in a positive light. A recent survey involving 3,000 ordinary Japanese suggests that roughly a third of respondents had a positive or somewhat positive image of foreign firms in Japan, while only 6.6 percent held a negative or somewhat negative opinion.[48] In addition, 30.2 percent of respondents answered that their image of foreign firms had improved, while only 8.9 percent indicated that it had become worse.[49] This pattern is more or less confirmed by foreign companies themselves, who believe that their image has improved in recent years and that they are generally perceived in a positive light.[50]

The majority of respondents who expressed an opinion also thought that foreign companies had a positive effect on the Japanese economy (47.3 percent), whereas only a small minority thought the effect was negative (7.7 percent).[51] Among those who held a negative opinion of foreign firms, about half thought that foreign companies were only after a quick profit,

---

[47] Survey cited in METI presentation "M&A Rules in Japan" dated May 2005 and available online at: <http://www.meti.go.jp/policy/economic_oganization/pdf/rontenkoukai_gaiyou_eng.pdf> (accessed April 3, 2007).

[48] Nomura Soken Kenkyujo (2005: 2). The rest either had no particular impression or no particularly positive or negative image of foreign firms.

[49] Nomura Soken Kenkyujo (2005: 2). 47.7 percent reported no change in their opinion, while 13.2 percent did not know.

[50] Nomura Soken Kenkyujo (2005: 46–7).

[51] Nomura Soken Kenkyujo (2005: 3). The rest did not know (12.0 percent) or said that it was impossible to say (33.0 percent).

aiming to buy Japanese firms cheaply only to sell them again after a brief period.[52] Yet, overall the number of such respondents was less than 4 percent, indicating that the identification of foreign firms with "vulture funds" that can sometimes be found in the press is not widely shared.

One problem faced by foreign firms setting up in Japan in the past was the difficulty to recruit employees. Yet, the survey indicates that about 20 percent of respondents either are already working for a foreign company or would like to do so, roughly the same share as those who say they do not want to work for a foreign company, and a further 45.5 percent replied that they could not say.[53] Interestingly, a larger share of women than men indicated they would like to work for a foreign firms (21.5 percent versus 17.2 percent). Moreover, not surprisingly, it is particularly the young that would like to work for a foreign firm, and the most important motivation is to develop a global outlook (cited by 52.1 percent of those wanting to work for a foreign firm), followed by the high pay and the opportunity to test one's ability. These survey results suggest that, on the whole, the Japanese today are well disposed toward foreign firms, and especially many of the young are willing to embrace the opportunities they provide.

Yet, although the acceptance of foreign companies is increasing, Japan's potential as a foreign investment destination is likely to also depend on the extent to which society is equipped and willing to accept and respond to internationalization and all that implies. As in most countries, there is little enthusiasm for allowing more immigration (despite the fact that this would help to ease population trends). Similarly, many Japanese remain uneasy about what an influx of foreigners would mean for their community. For example, in the same survey referred to above, 48.1 percent of respondents thought that having foreign residents live in the same area helps to give it an international character, but an almost equal share (47.8 percent) was worried that it might lead to problems, and a third feared that communication might be difficult.

Nevertheless, the government has recognized that Japan needs to attract not only foreign business, but also foreign talent. For this reason, the country's strict visa regulations have been gradually relaxed: the duration of a standard work visa, for example, was extended from one to three years and foreign students, who previously would have lost their residence status upon graduation are now granted visa extensions to allow them time to find

[52] Nomura Soken Kenkyujo (2005: 16).
[53] Nomura Soken Kenkyujo (2005: 20). The remaining 12.2 percent either did not want to work for a company (11.7 percent) or provided no answer (0.5 percent).

a job.[54] In addition, the government has been actively seeking to expand the number of foreign students studying in Japan. In fact, a "Plan to Accept 100,000 Foreign Students" was formulated as early as 1983 and this goal was reached in 2003 following an increase in the number of foreign students between 1998 and 2003 by 54 percent.[55] As a result, Japan today is the sixth most important destination for students studying abroad (behind the United States, the United Kingdom, Germany, France, and Australia, which together account for 70 percent of the global intake of foreign students).[56]

At the same time, however, at 2.2 percent, the share of foreign students in tertiary enrollments remains much lower than the Organisation for Economic Co-operation and Development (OECD) average of 6.4 percent. And although the number of foreign students who stay on in Japan to work after graduating has increased in recent years, their number, at 5,264, is still very small.[57] What is more, almost two-thirds of those obtained visas to work as interpreters or language teachers,[58] that is, probably not in their field of study. One reason why the number of foreign students remaining in Japan to work is so small appears to be "the negative mindset of Japanese firms toward employment of international students."[59] Another possible reason is that many suffer unpleasant experiences while in Japan. In a comprehensive survey involving almost 5,000 foreign students in Japan, roughly half complained about "Japanese peoples' prejudice and closed-mindedness toward non-Japanese people."[60] And 53.0 percent felt that when it comes to the type of non-Japanese person Japanese people like, it was typically "Americans, Europeans, blonds, people with blue eyes, people who speak English, people from advanced countries, rich people, etc." Yet, more than 90 percent of foreign students in Japan are from the rest of Asia (with Chinese students accounting for 59.7 percent and South Korean students for 22.0 percent of the total).[61] On the other hand, the survey among foreign students is somewhat dated – it is from 1995 – and anecdotal evidence suggests that Japanese

---

[54] JETRO (2005f).
[55] JETRO (2005f: 32) and OECD (2005b: 267)
[56] OECD (2005b: 254).
[57] JETRO (2005g).
[58] JETRO (2005g). Of the remainder, 23.4 percent received visas for work in mechanical engineering, 7.4 percent obtained visas to teach at university, 2.4 percent received visas to work as researchers at government institutions or private corporations, and 1.0 percent obtained visas to serve as business/investment managers. Of the students who remained in Japan to work, 94.9 percent were from Asia.
[59] JETRO (2005f: 8).
[60] Cited in Keizai Doyukai (2002: 24). The survey was conducted by Sumiko Iwao.
[61] OECD (2005b: Table C3.2). Figures for 2003.

attitudes are changing. For example, there has been a visible increase in TV programs featuring foreigners, and pop culture from other Asian countries, particularly from South Korea, has gained great popularity in Japan – trends which, it may be assumed, reflect and contribute to an environment in which foreign students, especially those from other Asian countries, can feel more comfortable.

The relatively low degree of internationalization of Japanese society – in terms of the overall number of foreigners living in the country, the number of foreign students studying and staying on to work in Japan, and the extent to which this provides the Japanese with experience in interacting with foreigners – is relevant for inward FDI because it plays a role in determining the ease with which foreign multinationals can find employees with the right skills, attitudes, and experience. For example, although more and more Japanese are willing to work for a foreign company, in a survey of foreign firms, 35.5 percent of firms indicated that they still had difficulties in finding qualified personnel, with language being by far the most important reason.[62] The shortage of qualified personnel is also the most frequently cited issue when it comes to setting up outside the main business regions of the Kanto and Kansai areas.[63] And the European Business Council in Japan observes:

One of the greatest difficulties European firms continue to face doing business in Japan is securing internationally qualified Japanese employees for their Japanese operations. Unfortunately, Japan's education and certification system does not effectively address the widening gap between competency levels and the needs of employers in today's increasingly global economy, especially for skills in areas such as legal services, engineering, biotechnology, financial accounting, and IT.[64]

These observations are confirmed by anecdotal evidence that, especially in highly specialized fields, the pool of candidates is very small. For instance, according to the educated guess of the Japanese CEO of a foreign-affiliated insurance firm, there may be only about 1,000 actuaries in Japan, and of these, only ten possess sufficient language skills to be able to communicate with a foreign head office over the phone.[65]

Yet another survey, this time among foreign financial institutions operating in Japan, provides further instructive results.[66] Asked to compare Tokyo as an international financial center with London, New York, Hong Kong,

---

[62] Nomura Sogo Kenkyujo (2005: 52 and 55).
[63] JETRO (2004b).
[64] European Business Council in Japan (2005).
[65] Hitoshi Morita, President and CEO, PCA Life, interview on May 17, 2005.
[66] Japan Center for International Finance (2004).

and Singapore, foreign financial institutions overwhelmingly indicated that employing and securing personnel competent in international finance was more difficult in Tokyo than in both the two Western and the two Asian financial centers. Individual comments cited in the survey highlighted the difficulty of "securing personnel that have a good command of English and can give advice from a global viewpoint" and that "not only internationalization of the financing business but also internationalization of the entire Japanese society, and thus fundamental educational system reforms are needed."[67]

These social factors, coupled with high operating expenses (such as office rents, labor costs, and property costs), high taxes and heavy regulation put Tokyo at a clear disadvantage vis-à-vis the other international financial centers and 18 of the 29 institutions subject of the survey indicate that their Tokyo unit is and has been handling transactions only in Japan. What is more, another three replied that they had transferred or were planning to transfer part of the major operations of their unit in Tokyo to some other unit(s) in Asia, which in all three cases was Singapore.

Although this survey covers less than three dozen firms from one particular sector, the results highlight the difficulties Japan faces not only in turning Tokyo into an international financial center on par with London and New York, or even Hong Kong and Singapore, but also in attracting the regional support functions of foreign multinationals more generally. Unless firms have a strong market-seeking motive for investing in Japan, they are unlikely to base themselves in the country as a result of the high costs, the heavy regulation, and the low degree of internationalization of Japanese society when compared with many other countries in region.

Japan's Relations with Its Neighbors
Although at present, outward FDI by Asian countries other than Japan remains relatively small on a global scale, regional growth dynamics mean that it is only a matter of time until countries like Taiwan, South Korea, and eventually China will emerge as significant sources of FDI. Given the role that geographic proximity plays in determining investment flows, as gravity models show, this trend may have important implications for future inflows of direct investment in Japan. However, political tensions with South Korea and, in particular, China mean that economic integration with these two countries and in the region more generally is being hampered, with potentially adverse effects on FDI.

---

[67] Japan Center for International Finance (2004: 9).

Economic relations between Japan and its two neighbors have deepened rapidly over the past few decades. The volume of trade with South Korea has managed to keep pace with the growth in Japan's overall trade, hovering at about 5–6 percent of the total, while trade with China has accounted for an ever-increasing share that reached 17 percent of Japan's total trade volume in 2006. Together, South Korea and China thus now account for almost a quarter of all Japanese trade and, in 2003, China overtook the United States as Japan's most important source of imports. In addition, China has become a major destination for Japanese outward FDI and in 2006 was the third-most important recipient country, behind only the United States and Britain.[68] Japanese firms now employ more than one million people in China.[69]

However, in contrast with the deepening commercial relations, political relations with South Korea and China have, if anything, deteriorated in recent years. Overshadowed by history, Japan's relations with the two countries have been difficult even at the best of times. In South Korea, ill-feeling remains strong over Japan's harsh colonial rule of the Korean peninsula from 1910 to 1945 and the perceived failure of Japan to properly atone for its deeds. Relations between the two countries had warmed following the announcement by the world football governing body Fédération Internationale de Football Association (FIFA), in 1996, that Japan and South Korea were to jointly host the 2002 World Cup. Leaders of both countries met frequently and in 1998, Japan issued a written apology to South Korea, which was accepted by Kim Dae-Jung, South Korea's president at the time. In 2002, Korea lifted its formal ban on cultural imports from Japan and in December 2003, the two sides launched official talks on a bilateral free trade agreement (FTA).

However, triggered by Prime Minister Koizumi's annual visits to Yasukuni shrine in Tokyo, where Japan's fallen soldiers are honored but fourteen class A war criminals from World War II are also memorialized, relations deteriorated significantly and tensions have reemerged. Issues of contention include the history textbook controversy, the question of compensation for "comfort women," and a group of islets called Dokdo by the Koreans and Takeshima by the Japanese. Following Koizumi's visit to Yasukuni shrine in 2005, South Korea canceled several high-level meetings, including a summit in Japan scheduled for later that year. The frictions have also overshadowed the FTA negations, which reached a deadlock in November 2004, mainly

---

[68] Based on Ministry of Finance statistics retrieved from <http://www.mof.go.jp/bpoffice/ebpfdi.htm> (accessed April 3, 2007).

[69] METI (2006b).

because of differences over agricultural and fisheries trade, and no progress has been made since.

Japan's relations with China, if anything, have been even worse than those with South Korea. Similarly to the South Koreans, the Chinese feel that Japan has never properly made amends for the invasion and atrocities committed in the 1930s and 1940s and have been incensed by Koizumi's visit to Yasukuni shrine. Tensions have been further fueled by a territorial dispute over the Senkaku islands, called Diaoyutai in Chinese, and a growing sense of rivalry for leadership in the region. China's mounting economic and political clout has gone hand in hand with large increases in defense spending, while Japan has been pursuing an increasingly assertive defense policy, identifying Taiwan as a security concern shared with the United States and describing China as a source of "concern" for Japan in its national defense outline.

Against this background, official contacts between the two countries fell to a minimum during Koizumi's premiership: the last visit to Japan by a Chinese head of state was that by President Jiang Zemin in 1998, while Koizumi's last visit to China took place in 2001. In the spring of 2005, tensions between the two countries came to boil when thousands of Chinese took to the streets in violent anti-Japanese protests in response to Japan's bid for permanent membership of the United Nations Security Council and the Japanese Ministry of Education's approval of school textbooks that play down Japan's atrocities in China in the 1930s and 1940s. Although economic relations between the two countries continued to thrive throughout the period, the political frictions have precluded any attempts to promote further economic integration through formal agreements. A Sino-Japanese FTA, for example, which could have a large potential impact given the size and especially the high complementarity of the two economies, has never been on the table.

Although memories of Japan's deeds during World War II also linger on in other countries in the region, relations with them are generally much better (except, of course, with North Korea). Yet, most of the Southeast Asian countries, for example, are equally wary about Japan as they are about China, with whom several of them have disputes over various islands in the South China Sea and which is a direct competitor for FDI and labor-intensive exports. Reflecting the rivalry, tension, and diverging interests in the region, initiatives such as APEC (Asia-Pacific Economic Co-operation), ASEAN+3 (the Association of Southeast Asian Nations [ASEAN] countries plus Japan, China, and South Korea), and, most recently, the East Asia Summit have produced few concrete results.

In this context, friction with China and South Korea in Japan increasingly came to be seen not only as hampering the country's ability to pursue diplomatic initiatives, but also to harm its economic interests. It is therefore significant that Koizumi's successor Abe on his first overseas trip, in October 2006, traveled not to Washington, as his predecessors had done, but to Beijing and Seoul and that his trip was reciprocated by a visit by China's Prime Minister Wen Jiabao in April 2007. Although it appears that the change in Japan's political leadership has significantly reduced tensions with its neighbors, it remains to be seen whether this will lead to a lasting improvement in relations that will eventually translate into bilateral or regional agreements to facilitate trade and investment.

What the Government Can Do

Government policy toward FDI has certainly come a long way. Following up on the deregulatory measures of the 1990s, the government launched several initiatives to improve the FDI climate in Japan. For example, in 2003, the Japan Investment Council, which is chaired by the prime minister, established the "Program for the Promotion of Foreign Direct Investment in Japan," which identified 74 measures falling under various headings that include the review of administrative procedures, improving the business environment, and providing information on investment opportunities in Japan.[70] What is more, the Program is being followed up in detailed reports tracking the progress being made in implementing these measures. Yet, more could be done and, as will be suggested below, in certain areas, the situation for foreign companies even appears to have become worse. The following subsections will consider in greater detail what the government can do to attract FDI to Japan. To this end, it is convenient to use the classification of FDI determinants introduced at the outset – that is, the economic determinants, the policy framework for FDI, and business facilitation measures – and discuss these in turn.

Economic Determinants
As mentioned above, economic factors determining a country's attractiveness for FDI include aspects such as market size and growth, the supply of different types of resources, the cost of these resources and other inputs, and so on. Many of these factors are not susceptible to policy making or, if so, only in the context of the general policy framework. For example, the size and growth of the Japanese market is subject to policy making only to the

---

[70] See, e.g., Investment in Japan Information Center, "Promotion of Foreign Direct Investment in Japan," online: <http://investment-japan.go.jp/statements/files/20030327–1.pdf> (accessed April 12, 2007).

extent that the government can attempt to steer overall economic growth or the growth of particular industries and markets. Similarly, the supply of different resources and their costs, such as natural resources, skilled and unskilled labor, and so on, are largely given and government policies affect these only at the margin.

Nevertheless, there are certain areas in which the government could conceivably pursue policies that would have a positive impact on economic determinants and help to increase the attractiveness of Japan. The discussion above, for example, highlighted the difficulties foreign firms face in recruiting skilled personnel with an international outlook. To address this issue, the government could devise or strengthen policies that help to foster a workforce that possesses the skills and attitudes required in an increasingly global economy. Relevant policies could span the fields of education, immigration, labor laws, and so on. Although such policies would take time to bear fruit, they would also benefit domestic firms as well as foreign ones.

Another area in which the government could try to influence economic determinants through policy is Japan's high-cost structure, which foreign firms frequently cite as a disincentive. There continue to be a large number of areas, ranging from utilities to transport and distribution, that are highly regulated and as a result contribute to the high cost of doing business in Japan. Again, deregulation in such fields, and the lower costs that would result, would benefit not only foreign firms but domestic firms and consumers as well. Additional possible measures include trade liberalization and efforts toward regional bilateral or multilateral integration agreements (discussed in greater detail in the next subsection), which would not only further contribute to lowering general cost levels in Japan, but also make Japan more attractive as a node in regional corporate networks.

Far-reaching measures such as these that affect labor supply, market structures, and costs, would probably need to be motivated by a broad policy agenda that aims at improving business conditions in Japan more generally rather than simply targeting FDI. Moreover, tangible effects on inward FDI would take time to materialize, but these considerations illustrate that policies that improve the business environment for domestic firms in the long run would also promote inward FDI.

The Policy Framework for FDI
Whereas governments' options to actively shape the economic factors determining their country's attractiveness for FDI may often be limited, this is

certainly not the case when it comes to the policy framework for FDI. Obviously, a favorable policy framework alone will not be enough to attract foreign multinationals if the economic factors are not right; on the other hand, though, unfavorable policies certainly have the potential to deter FDI even if the right economic factors are present. Rules regarding the entry and operations of foreign multinationals, tax policies, policies on the functioning and structure of markets, policies on trade, and international agreements on FDI will all affect the ease with which foreign companies can establish a presence in a particular country. In the case of Japan, each of these areas offers room for measures to raise the country's attractiveness for FDI.

Generally speaking, foreign multinationals enjoy national treatment when investing in Japan. However, a number of exceptions remain, such as in agriculture, fishery, and forestry, mining, telecommunications, air transport, maritime transport, and broadcasting.[71] While lifting the ban on foreign ownership in agriculture, fishing, or mining probably would have little impact on FDI inflows, this cannot be said for some of the other sectors. In Japan, foreigners are banned from owning and operating AM, FM, and TV broadcasting stations (although since 1999 foreigners are allowed to own and operate cable TV facilities). Yet, broadcasting is an increasingly global business and the inward FDI stock in broadcasting in the United States, for instance, amounts to approximately US$28.3 billion, almost on par with retail trade (US$29.7 billion).[72] Similarly, deregulation of the airline industry in Europe has brought significant cross-border investment in its wake and led to an overhaul of the entire industry.[73] These examples suggest that removing the ban on foreign ownership in the domestic air transport business and broadcasting in Japan could have a substantial effect on FDI inflows. Yet another area is the transport of goods and passengers between Japanese ports, which is reserved to Japanese ships. Allowing foreign shipping lines to trans-ship their own overseas cargo on their own vessels in Japan would reduce the need to trans-ship these cargos in other countries and (together with measures to lower port costs through greater competition)

---

[71] See Chapter 2, Table 2.4, for details.

[72] Figures are for 2005. Source: Bureau of Economic Analysis, "Foreign Direct Investment in the United States: Selected Items by Detailed Industry of U.S. Affiliate, 2002–2005," online: <http://www.bea.gov/bea/di/FDI17_0205.pdf> (accessed April 12, 2007).

[73] Intra-European FDI in the airline industry became possible as part of the introduction of the Single European Market in 1993, although ownership restrictions on non-"Community Carriers" remained in place.

232   *Foreign Direct Investment in Japan*

consequently increase Japan's appeal as an entrepôt for regional shipping operations.[74]

In addition to removing remaining outright barriers to the entry of foreign firms, there are various other ways in which the Japanese government could facilitate the entry and operations of foreign multinationals in the country. In this context, policies related to M&As play a vital role, given that M&As represent the most important means by which multinationals enter foreign markets, including Japan. The lifting of the ban on triangular mergers in May 2007 therefore represents a crucial step in the right direction. However, as so often is the case, the devil lies in the details, and the impact of this step greatly depends on the particulars of the rules and regulations and how the government interprets and applies them in practice.

The first thing to note with regard to Japanese regulations is that they permit only one particular type of triangular merger (so-called "forward" triangular mergers), compared with many different versions possible in the United States. Another issue – in fact, the key issue as far as the foreign business community in Japan is concerned – is whether and under what circumstances sellers receiving shares in an equity swap can defer tax payments. Without deferral, sellers face an immediate tax burden that makes it unlikely that the triangular merger would occur in the first place. Deferral rules thus are a central element in determining the extent to which the triangular merger scheme will provide a useful tool for foreign investment in Japan. Although much will depend on how tax rules are applied in practice, members of the foreign business community point out that, as they stand, deferral rules are cumbersome and qualifying for deferral will be especially difficult, if not impossible, for new foreign entrants.

The implications for government policy are obvious: FDI could be greatly facilitated by further reforming M&A regulations. First steps could include relaxing or abolishing conditions that must be met for triangular mergers to qualify for tax deferral, granting foreign firms similar tax deferral treatment as Japanese ones, and increasing the variety of triangular merger mechanisms available. But the foreign business community in Japan has supported the triangular merger scheme only as a second-best approach to facilitating cross-border deals and would have greatly preferred the introduction of direct

---

[74] However, it should be noted that Japan is not alone in imposing domestic (majority) ownership requirements in industries that are deemed to be sensitive. Examples from other countries (as of 2003) include airlines in the European Union and North American countries and coastal and freshwater shipping in the United States (majority domestic ownership required), fishing and energy sectors in Iceland, and the oil sector in Mexico (exclusive domestic ownership required) (OECD 2003: chapter IV).

cross-border stock swaps instead.[75] Such direct cross-border stock swaps are widely used in the United States and Europe and have been employed in some of the biggest and most prominent M&A transactions in recent years, including the Vodafone–Mannesmann, Daimler–Chrysler, and BP–Amoco deals. In sum, M&A rules and regulations represent a key area in which the government could facilitate entry and send a clear signal that it is serious about attracting inward FDI.

Another area in which the government could help to ease the difficulties foreign multinationals face is the availability of qualified workers. Although immigration laws have been relaxed somewhat, this is unlikely to be sufficient. Members of the foreign business community in Japan are therefore calling on the Japanese government to further stimulate the inflow of workers with skills required by foreign firms, such as in the areas of financial accounting, IT, or legal services, by recognizing foreign qualifications and diplomas, and by granting work visas to people with proven skills but without the university diploma or ten years work experience currently required.[76] Closely related to this issue are also the various restrictions placed on qualifying and practicing as a foreign lawyer (*gaiben*) in Japan, hampering not only the operations of international law firms in Japan, but also limiting the supply of lawyers both qualified to practice in Japan and possessing international experience.

Although policies that directly affect the entry and operations of foreign multinationals are important, policies that affect the structure and functioning of markets more generally also play a significant role. The surge in Japanese inward FDI in the 1990s, for instance, owes not only to the removal of some of the remaining formal barriers, but crucially also to deregulation in such key sectors as telecommunications, finance, and retail. Yet, despite some efforts at liberalization, regulations that hamper competition at the expense of new entrants and hence FDI remain widespread.

A case in point is large-scale retailing. Although the Large-Scale Retail Store Law was amended in 1992 and 1994 (and became the Large-Scale Retail Store Location Law) to facilitate the establishment of large retail outlets, there are still no definitive rules for submitting applications for new stores. This is further compounded by the need for building permits and environmental impact assessments, which are often used by local governments to impose new conditions, making the process of opening new

---

[75] See, e.g., EBC, "EBC rejects media reports misrepresenting cross-border swaps in Europe," press release, November 14, 2006.
[76] See, e.g., European Business Council in Japan (2005).

large-scale stores extremely complex. The European Business Council (EBC) in Japan in its annual report on the business environment therefore notes that "[c]ompanies that are new to the market, or companies with less experience and fewer networks at the local level, are disadvantaged vis-à-vis their domestic competitors in this situation."[77] Setting down clear rules and streamlining the application process for large-scale retail stores thus would help to create a more level playing field and facilitate foreign investment in this sector.

Members of the foreign business community and organizations representing their interests, such as the EBC and the American Chamber of Commerce in Japan (ACCJ), cite a substantial number of other areas in which the government could improve regulations and streamline procedures to promote a more level playing field and/or help foreign companies to exploit their strengths. Examples include product approval processes in areas as diverse as insurance, medical equipment, and pharmaceuticals; firewall regulations separating the banking and securities business and restrictive rules governing the type of securities that asset managers may deal in; and competitive safeguards in the telecommunications sector.[78] Reforms in each of these areas would not only increase Japan's attractiveness as a destination for FDI, but would also help to promote competition and increase social welfare through greater consumer choice and/or lower prices.

In this context, one should not ignore the fact that, in calling for certain changes, foreign firms are of course also pursuing their own particularistic interests, while government policy should aim at maximizing the welfare of society overall. For instance, complaints about falling reimbursement prices in the health care sector and claims that this hinders the introduction of innovative drugs and equipment, even if justified, have to be balanced against the need to keep health care expenditures in check. However, generally speaking, demands by foreign multinationals are concerned with regulations that skew market access, and the health care sector provides a host of other examples where regulations (such as the structure of the reimbursement system or product approval processes) do create a bias against foreign products.[79]

Therefore, if the government is serious about attracting more FDI, on the whole, it would be well advised to take the issues raised by the foreign business community in the country into account. Annual reports, position papers, and public statements by organizations such as the ACCJ, the EBC,

[77] European Business Council in Japan (2005: 16).
[78] See, e.g., European Business Council in Japan (2005).
[79] See Chapter 6.

and other foreign business organizations on the business environment in Japan indicate that concerns regarding market structure and access as a result of regulation remain widespread. Addressing these issues would not only dispel the notion that Japan remains a difficult place to do business and make the country more attractive for FDI, it would also contribute to greater competition, not just from foreign firms, and therefore benefit consumers and the economy overall.

Moving on from policies on the functioning and structure of markets, another instrument the government could use to promote inward FDI is tax policy. Reflecting the increasing mobility of multinationals, countries around the world have been lowering corporate tax rates to keep domestic firms from moving abroad and to attract foreign firms. Although this trend has raised concerns about a "race to the bottom," failing to follow suit would clearly put Japan at a disadvantage. Against this background, effective corporate tax rates were cut in 1999 from 46 percent to 40 percent. However, since then, countries in Europe and East Asia have continued to lower or were in the process of lowering corporate tax rates further. In Europe, the Netherlands reduced the effective corporate tax burden to 20 percent in 2007, Germany decided to lower rates in 2008 from around 38 to 29 percent, and France was considering to cut rates from roughly 34 to 20 percent over a five-year period.[80] Similarly, in Asia, Malaysia and Singapore were in the process of lowering, or were planning to lower, corporate taxes.[81] Consequently, at about 40 percent, the level of corporate taxes in Japan seems increasingly out of tune with tax rates of 20 to 30 percent in other parts of the world and there has been a growing debate on lowering corporate taxes to enhance the country's international competitiveness. Given that Japan continues to have large budget deficits, the Ministry of Finance has been cautious about lowering taxes, but, as in other countries such as Germany, the government sooner or later probably will have to redistribute the tax burden by cutting corporate taxes and raising taxes on consumption.

Other tools to encourage FDI are trade policy, international investment agreements, and measures to encourage the free flow of resources, people, and ideas. Trade frequently serves as a springboard for FDI, since firms targeting a new market typically start by relying on exports and increase their presence in the country only gradually. However, Japan's level of import penetration remains the lowest in the OECD, and tariff and nontariff barriers as well as product market regulations are partly responsible for this.

---

[80] Nikkei, "Slow to cut corporate taxes, Japan risks losing global edge," February 3, 2007.
[81] Nikkei, "Slow to cut corporate taxes, Japan risks losing global edge," February 3, 2007.

According to a recent study, the Overall Trade Restrictiveness Index, which measures the combined effect of tariff and nontariff barriers, is 14.3 percent for Japan, compared with 12.6 percent for the European Union and 8.2 percent for the United States.[82] To some extent, the higher trade restrictiveness may reflect the fact that, unlike other advanced economies, Japan is a relative latecomer when it comes to bilateral or regional trade agreements to complement multilateral trade negations. Yet, while this may explain why Japan's import penetration is low, it also illustrates that there remains ample room for further trade liberalization which would help to boost FDI, too.

Investment agreements, which aim to strengthen the standards of protection and treatment of foreign investors and establish mechanisms for dispute settlement,[83] represent another way to promote FDI. Having for many years relied solely on multilateral trade and investment negotiations, Japan has been actively pursuing bilateral arrangements in the form of Economic Partnership Agreements (EPAs) since 2002. So called because they cover a range of issues from the removal of tariff and nontariff barriers to bilateral investment, flows of human resources, and economic and technical cooperation, Japan has entered EPAs with a number of countries. As of April 2007, EPAs had been concluded or agreement had in principle been reached with Singapore, Malaysia, Thailand, Indonesia, the Philippines, Mexico, and Chile. In addition, negotiations were under way or about to start with India, Australia, Vietnam, Brunei, ASEAN as a whole, and the Gulf Cooperation Council, while preliminary discussions were being held with Switzerland.[84] Although EPAs with these countries represent first steps in the right direction, conspicuously absent from this list are Japan's main trading partners: Korea, with which negotiations, as already mentioned, reached a deadlock in 2004, as well as China, the United States, and the European Union. Yet, it is with the United States and the European Union that bilateral agreements would have the greatest immediate effect on trade and, in its wake, investment, while agreements with China and Korea would promote investment in the longer term.[85]

---

[82] Kee, Nicita, and Olarreaga (2006), cited in OECD (2006:183).
[83] See UNCTAD (1998: chapter IV).
[84] Ministry of Foreign Affairs, website on "Free Trade Agreement (FTA) and Economic Partnership Agreement (EPA)" (sic), <http://www.mofa.go.jp/policy/economy/fta/> (accessed April 14, 2007).
[85] Japan and China did agree to hold high-level economic talks by the end of year during Chinese Prime Minister Wen Jiabao's visit to Tokyo in April 2007. While this represents a start, such talks are unlikely to yield any tangible results quickly.

Finally, in his 2007 New Year speech, Prime Minister Abe said he would promote the "Asia Gateway Vision" – a collection of measures "with a view to make Japan a place where human resources from Asia and from all around the world gather, enabling Japan to become a center of communication to the world, thereby making Japan an attractive place for Asia and other parts of the world."[86] To achieve these goals, ten priority issues were identified, including the liberalization of air travel in Asia, the revision of customs clearance procedures to facilitate trade, promoting student exchanges and opening Japan's university to the world, and so on.[87] Such measures could contribute to addressing some of the challenges Japan needs to overcome to attract more FDI, such as the low import penetration, the shortage of qualified personnel with an international outlook, and cultural issues more generally, but as is so often the case, the "Vision" is short on detail and unlikely to be implemented quickly. Moreover, even then, many of the measures would contribute to an improved investment climate only in the long run.

Business Facilitation Measures
In addition to economic factors and the policy framework, a third potential determinant of FDI is government measures to actively attract foreign firms. Such measures may range from advertising campaigns to change unfavorable perceptions regarding the investment climate to investment incentives and the reduction of "hassle costs."[88] In Japan, measures to promote inward FDI date back as early as 1984, when the government-owned Development Bank of Japan commenced a loan program specifically aimed at attracting foreign firms. Various other measures followed: in 1992, the Import and Inward Investment Promotion Law was passed, offering foreign firms tax incentives and credit guarantees, and a year later, the Foreign Investment in Japan Development Corporation (FIND) was set up to provide foreign companies with investment services and support. The measures were gradually enhanced in the years that followed, but it was only under Koizumi that the promotion of inward FDI became more visible.

Efforts in that direction consist of an information and public relations campaign to signal that Japan is serious about attracting foreign business.

[86] Prime Minister of Japan and His Cabinet, "New Year's reflection by Prime Minister Shinzo Abe," online: <http://www.kantei.go.jp/foreign/abespeech/2007/01/01shokan_e.html> (accessed April 16, 2007).
[87] Prime Minister of Japan and His Cabinet, "Asia Gateway kiso: Chukan ronten seiri" [Asia Gateway Vision: Interim report on issues"], online: <http://www.kantei.jp/jp/singi/asia/070322ronten.pdf> (accessed April 16, 2007).
[88] See UNCTAD (1998: chapter IV).

The Japan External Trade Organization (JETRO), for example, has held seminars and symposiums in countries around the world on investing in Japan, while Koizumi appeared in a TV spot promoting inward FDI that was aired around 130 times in the United States and Europe.[89] The goals set by Koizumi to double inward FDI, first in 2003, and then again in 2006, could also be regarded as public relations measures indicating the government's determination, since they serve no other real purpose. Other measures have aimed at clarifying, streamlining, and speeding up administrative procedures: JETRO Invest Japan Business Support Centers were established across Japan and one-stop shops in ministries and agencies were set up to provide information and expedite administrative procedures dealing with foreign firms. Moreover, the government has introduced a no-action letter system, which helps to improve the transparency of administrative decisions by providing a written reply to inquiries from companies and individuals about the government's interpretations of laws affecting them. Finally, the government has attempted to create more favorable employment and living conditions by changing visa regulations, introducing support measures for international schools, and concluding bilateral agreements on pension contributions.[90]

These certainly are useful measures, but more could be done. Advertising that Japan is keen to attract investment may help to change perceptions grown over decades that the country only reluctantly accepts foreign business; but such campaigns are easily undermined when actual policies contradict this message – as in the case of the postponement of the triangular merger scheme, for example. Similarly, measures to streamline and increase the transparency of administrative procedures and the introduction of the no-action letter system address a long-standing concern of the foreign business community in Japan and therefore have been widely welcomed. Yet, it has also been highlighted that replies are not considered legally binding, oral replies are in some cases still allowed, and the ministries have not actively encouraged its use, so that few no-action letters have actually been issued in areas where they are most needed.[91] There is also further room

[89] JETRO (2004c: 31).

[90] See Japan Invest Council, "The follow-up of the Program for Promotion of Foreign Direct Investment in Japan," Expert Committee Report, April 2006, online: <http://www.investment-japan.go.jp/statements/files/20060401–1.pdf> (accessed April 14, 2007).

[91] European Business Community in Japan memo, "Response to queries from OECD on regulatory reform in Japan," February 18, 2004, online: <http://ebc-jp.com/news/OECD%20Briefing%20(18Feb2004).pdf> (accessed April 14, 2007).

for improvement when it comes to employment and living conditions. For example, foreigners with a valid visa are still required to obtain a reentry permit if they wish to leave and reenter the country; while doing so is little more than a formality, it imposes an unnecessary burden on foreign residents. Another issue is that social security agreements have been entered with only a few countries and mandatory contributions to the Japanese public pension system are refunded to departing expatriates only in part,[92] making working in Japan less attractive than it could be.

An element that governments around the world often rely on to attract FDI, but that plays only a negligible role in Japan, is investment incentives. Investment incentives typically consist of measures to either increase the return of a particular FDI undertaking or to reduce its costs or risks, for example, through reductions in corporate income tax rates, tax holidays, accelerated depreciation, exemption from import duties, and so on. In Japan, central government measures are limited to minor tax incentives[93] and loan guarantees.[94] Japan's regions, on the other hand, are increasingly competing to attract FDI, although the incentives offered, such as six-month rent subsidies, are also relatively minor in international comparison.

Generally speaking, this lack of fiscal and financial FDI incentives is probably a good thing. Although a theoretical case for investment incentives focusing exclusively on foreign firms can be made, research suggests that it is rarely a good way to increase national welfare.[95] Moreover, companies are likely to choose a country on the basis of economic determinants and the policy framework for FDI, and incentives can at best play a marginal role. A survey of multinationals covering 74 investment cases, for example, indicates that incentives were frequently not even considered and simply made an already attractive country more attractive.[96]

Conclusion

Based on the foregoing considerations, the medium- to long-term outlook for FDI in Japan seems rather mixed. On the bright side, the country's economy has finally recovered from its decade-long recession and, despite

---

[92] See European Business Council in Japan (2005).
[93] Designated inward investors are allowed to carry over losses for a period of up to ten years compared with a period of five years for other companies.
[94] See METI, "Details of aid measures," online: <http://www.meti.go.jp/english/report/data/cFDI230e.html> (accessed April 14, 2007).
[95] See, e.g., Blomström and Kokko (2003).
[96] See UNCTAD (1998: 103).

the demographic challenges, there is considerable potential for (catch-up) growth at fairly respectable rates to continue for years to come. Given that the large majority of foreign investments in Japan appear to be of the market seeking variety, improved economic performance should further raise the country's attractiveness, help to raise profit rates, and, moreover, facilitate market entry and survival. What is more, the surge in investment seen in recent years in itself may have contributed to lifting the trajectory of FDI inflows into Japan: research suggests that foreign firms learn not only from their own previous investment experience in a foreign country but also from the experience of other firms, helping to raise the likelihood of investment survival.[97] Thus, it is conceivable that the recent wave of FDI may have triggered a positive feedback loop, where the growing presence of foreign firms in Japan helps to attract more multinationals in the future.

Yet, it also needs to be borne in mind that the surge in inward FDI witnessed around the turn of the millennium benefited from a combination of exceptional circumstances, including the global boom in FDI and far-reaching deregulation in Japan. Another significant acceleration in investment inflows, it seems, would require substantial further structural change and deregulation. Because of its high costs, the country is unlikely to become a regional production or operations base for foreign multinationals. However, it may attract more market-seeking FDI, especially if the government continues to deregulate industries and product markets. In addition, there also appears to be greater potential for FDI of the asset-seeking variety, and in particular the acquisition of firms that possess technological and production capabilities as well as other intangible assets. Japan certainly does not lack firms that would make potentially attractive investment targets for foreign multinationals – be it for market-seeking or asset-seeking reasons. But foreign investors still face a range of obstacles when trying to acquire a Japanese firm – ranging from lingering suspicion toward foreign investment to corporate antitakeover measures and government policies on M&As that still make it much more difficult to acquire a firm in Japan than in other advanced economies.

Against this background, the most likely scenario for future investment inflows into Japan is one of moderate increases. Overall, the country's economy continues to gradually open up, as is illustrated by the lifting of the ban on triangular mergers, which goes some way toward facilitating the acquisition of Japanese firms and thus raise inward FDI. At the same time, however,

---

[97] Shaver, Mitchell, and Yeung (1997).

Japan is embracing globalization only reluctantly and remains wary of the economic forces unleashed by reforms and structural change. It therefore seems unlikely that the country will be ready any time soon to accept the kind of cross-border M&A activity seen in Europe and the United States. Inward FDI penetration therefore is bound to continue to trail significantly behind that of any of the other major advanced economies.

EIGHT

Conclusion

Globalization through the international movement of goods, services, and factors of production is a key force driving economic growth. Japan's own historical experience provides ample illustration of this observation. Foreign direct investment (FDI) played a vital role in the country's early industrialization, providing not only capital but, crucially, also much of the technology, know-how, and managerial skills that underlie the development of the electrical machinery, motor vehicle, and machine tool industries during the first decades of the twentieth century. Similarly, exports (incidentally largely concentrated in these industries) were a main engine of growth in Japan's postwar economic miracle, with imports supplying the necessary raw materials. More recently, the relocation of production through overseas direct investment has helped Japanese firms to bolster their international competitiveness, first as a way to mitigate the impact of rapid yen appreciation during the 1980s and, more recently, as a means to take advantage of lower production costs in China and other parts of the world.

Although Japan has clearly benefited from globalization, the country's attitudes toward economic integration with the rest of the world have always been ambivalent. With the exception of that brief period of relative openness at the beginning of twentieth century, Japan has been reluctant to open its economy to imports and inward FDI, viewing them, in general, as a threat rather than as a boon. When official barriers were gradually dismantled during the 1970s and 1980s, imports and inward FDI continued to face severe obstacles in the form of economic policies and structural features. However, as this study sought to illustrate, this situation has begun to change. Triggered by the long-term economic stagnation following the burst of the bubble economy, economic reforms and structural change removed many of the obstacles that had hitherto hindered inward FDI, and helped by a global boom in cross-border mergers and acquisitions (M&As), FDI flows into Japan experienced a significant boost.

Yet, even today, Japan remains an outlier among developed economies in terms of import penetration and stock of inward FDI relative to gross domestic product (GDP), not to mention the share of foreign workers in total employment. Thus, there remains ample room for further strengthening Japan's integration into the world economy, allowing the country to benefit more fully from globalization. The purpose of this concluding chapter is to take a wider look at the issue of Japan's globalization based on the findings of this study. In particular, the aim is to return to the two broad questions on the *level* and the *impact* of inward FDI and consider these in the context of long-term economic and political trends in Japan.

Trends in Japanese Inward FDI
Looking at developments since the early 1990s, there is plenty of evidence that Japan's economic, political, and social structures as well as the interplay between them have undergone a wide-ranging transformation. At the same time, however, as in any country or period, for every example of genuine change a counterexample illustrating continuity can be found. This is also very much the case with regard to inward FDI in Japan and attitudes toward globalization more generally. Thus, although the economy has become more open to foreign investment, whether this represents a real "turning point" signaling that Japan is beginning to truly embrace globalization remains to be seen.

In this context, examining and explaining the level of FDI in Japan – the issue on which most research to date has concentrated – remains an important task. Chapter 2 suggested that Japan's economic size, geographic location, and other similar factors alone cannot account for the low level of inward FDI and that therefore government regulations and structural factors played an important role. The historical overview in that chapter indicated that, until the 1970s, government policy indeed presented various explicit barriers to FDI, which, following gradual "liberalization," were replaced by implicit barriers in the form of economic structures as well as government policies regulating competition and product markets. Added to this may be the institutional setting created by the interplay of government policies and economic structures.

The industry studies in Chapter 6 provided concrete examples of how these factors shaped the environment for FDI. In the financial sector, for instance, industry structures and patterns of competition to a large extent were fashioned by the "convoy system." Aiming to ensure stability in the financial system, government policies restricted the activities banks and insurers could engage in, the products they could offer, and the terms on which such products could be offered. In addition, the government occasionally intervened directly to prevent bankruptcies by "persuading" stronger institutions to absorb weaker ones. This convoy system contributed to impeding market access by foreign firms in at least three ways. First, the convoy system provided banks and insurance firms with an incentive for long-term shareholdings as a basis on which to compete for customers, thus limiting the availability of acquirable firms both in the financial sector and beyond. Second, product regulations prevented foreign entrants from competing on the basis of product differentiation and costs, thus canceling out any advantage that they might have had vis-à-vis domestic rivals. And third, by strongarming larger banks into absorbing weaker ones, the policy ensured that there were no acquisition targets for foreign firms.

The pharmaceutical industry provided another example. Although foreign firms have operated in this sector for decades, a similar interplay between government policies and market structure and their limiting effect on FDI penetration can be seen here too. In the case of the pharmaceutical industry, policies were formulated as a result of interactions among the Liberal Democratic Party (LDP), the Japan Medical Association, and the Ministry of Health and Welfare. One of the outcomes of this institutional setting was product regulations in the form of a clinical trial system and drug approval procedures that posed significant hurdles for foreign firms. Given the added challenge of navigating the country's complex distribution system (or building one from scratch), foreign firms' options were severely restricted, typically leaving them little choice but to tie up with a local Japanese partner.

Against this background, it required a severe economic crisis to provide the impetus for deregulation, structural change, and a transformation in government–business relations. The government's initial response to the collapse of the bubble economy, mounting bad loans, and economic slowdown was either to hope that the problem would go away (as in the case of nonperforming loans) or to rely on measures that largely cemented the status quo, such as the numerous fiscal stimulation packages providing funds to the ruling LDP's constituency in the construction sector. It was not until the economic malaise had deepened further that the government in the second half of the 1990s embarked on economic reforms to make the economy more flexible through deregulation in the service sector (telecommunications, financial services, wholesale and retail), by bringing accounting rules in line with international practice and introducing measures to facilitate

M&As, by introducing measures to simplify drug approvals, and so on, as shown in Chapters 3 and 6. It was also during this period that the situation in the financial sector came to a head, forcing the government to abandon the convoy system and producing takeover targets in the banking and especially the insurance sector. In addition, partly as a consequence of government measures and partly because of the deepening economic problems themselves, structural changes gathered pace, resulting in the unwinding of cross-shareholding, which in combination with falling costs and weak companies made acquisitions by foreign firms and hence the substantial increase in inward FDI possible.

Significantly, attitudes toward inward FDI have generally become much more positive. The clearest indication of this are the various goals set by Prime Minister Koizumi. Although the policies that played the greatest role in facilitating foreign investment in Japan – those just mentioned – were largely introduced by his predecessors, Koizumi, who became prime minister in 2001, most clearly pursued a policy platform of economic reform, in which FDI figured prominently – as illustrated, for example, by the "Invest Japan" campaign. Public opinion has also become more favorable. Surveys among ordinary Japanese indicate that considerably more saw foreign firms in Japan in a positive than in a negative light and thought that foreign firms had a positive rather than a negative effect on the economy (Chapter 7).

Yet, in the Japanese business community itself, apprehensions remain widespread. This is seen most clearly in the response to the lifting of the ban on triangular mergers in May 2007: widely portrayed as paving the way for a wave of hostile takeover bids by foreign firms and posing a threat to national interests, the step has led numerous Japanese firms to adopt antitakeover measures, including the increase of cross-shareholdings, and sparked calls by the powerful Keidanren (Japan Business Confederation) for changes to M&A requirements that would have rendered the triangular merger scheme largely ineffectual. In an encouraging move, however, proposals for tougher requirements have been rejected by the LDP on the grounds that they would give too much protection to domestic companies and prevent changes to the status quo.

The triangular merger scheme has been eagerly awaited by the foreign business community in Japan and how it operates in practice is likely to play an important role in determining future inward FDI flows. Although the FDI environment and, with it, multinationals' perceptions of Japan as an FDI destination have substantially improved, there have also been several setbacks. Apart from the postponement of the triangular merger scheme and the increase in cross-shareholdings as part of antitakeover measures, these include a renewed rise in "strategic" shareholding by banks and several prominent withdrawals, resulting in a net decrease in inward FDI in 2006. Against this background, the extent to which the triangular merger scheme provides an effective tool for foreign investment will not only have a direct impact on the level of inward FDI flows, but will also provide an important signal of Japan's preparedness to accept foreign capital and hence shape multinationals' perceptions of the country as an investment destination.

Moreover, the concerns about hostile takeovers and the "threat" that the acquisition of domestic firms by foreign counterparts may pose to national interests indicate that, despite the recent changes in the investment environment, traditional attitudes remain strong. To some extent, such concerns, when voiced by the business community, may be motivated more by entrenched managers' interest in self-preservation than by any concern for the national interest. At the same time, however, it also reflects a deep-seated suspicion of the competitive forces unleashed by globalization. Although unease about globalization can be found in most countries, this suspicion with regard to competitive forces seems to run deeper in Japan, where it runs like a thread through postwar economic history. The Ministry of International Trade and Industry's (MITI's) famous industrial policy, for example, was as much concerned with reigning in "excessive competition" and maintaining industrial order as it was with picking winners. Similarly, the convoy system under the auspices of the Ministry of Finance severely restricted competition in the financial sector, putting stability ahead of the efficient allocation of capital. Moreover, even today, many sectors of the economy remain "sanctuaries" in which competition is severely restricted. Given this environment, the corporate practices and industry structures that evolved over the decades have been shaped as much by cooperation and collusion as by competition. Cross-shareholdings within the *keiretsu*, for example, ensured that struggling firms were bailed out by other group members, managers were isolated from shareholder pressure, and competition over ownership control was absent.

Under these circumstances, globalization, and especially inward foreign investment, not only challenge particularistic interests but also, in the form of alien business practices, Japan's "economic culture." This may explain why the country appears to find it more difficult than others to adapt to globalization. Yet, there are also voices that clearly recognize both the opportunities offered by globalization and the price Japan would pay if it fails to take advantage of them. The *Nikkei Shinbun*, for example, editorialized:

The postwar world is experiencing a period of unprecedented prosperity thanks to economic globalization. But Japan does not appear to be fully enjoying the fruits of this magical growth. While it has managed to emerge from years of slump, its recovery lacks strength. This is probably because it is not taking full advantage of the benefits brought about by the globalized economy.

While Japanese companies are expanding operations worldwide, the nation as a whole has yet to experience inner globalization. Its economy will not have a bright future unless the people learn to look toward outside and the markets are open to foreign investment. There will be no economic growth without openness.[1]

In sum, despite the surge in inward FDI around the turn of the millennium, Japan's integration into the world economy continues to be very lopsided, with "inner globalization" lagging behind not only that in other countries but also relative to "outer globalization." Although the stock of inward FDI relative to GDP has risen more than fivefold, from 0.4 percent in the mid-1990s to 2.2 percent in 2005, this pales in comparison with the outward stock, which has also continued to increase and in 2005 reached 8.5 percent (Figure 8.1). Given this persisting imbalance, the level of inward FDI not only remains a pertinent issue for scholars and business practitioners, but – considering the economic implications – should also be cause for concern for Japan's policy makers.

Inward FDI and Economic Growth

Following the "lost decade" from the early 1990s to the early 2000s, Japan's economy has finally managed to regain its poise. Thanks to a buoyant world economy and a weak yen, exports have been strong. Enjoying bumper profits, firms have grown increasingly confident and are expanding business fixed investment, replacing worn capital equipment, and investing in new facilities. In addition, although improved business conditions have yet to fully filter through to wages and private consumption, it should be only a matter of time until the recovery spreads to households as well. It therefore appears that the economic expansion, which began in 2003, may still have a few years to run. Yet, to a large extent, this recovery represents a catch-up process following the long period of slack. At an annual rate of about 2 percent, growth is already close to what many economists regard as Japan's potential rate, and from a long-term perspective, the country continues to face serious economic challenges.

[1] *Nikkei Net*, "Make Japan a global nation of lofty aspirations," January 3, 2007.

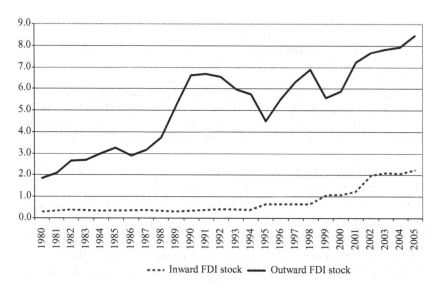

Figure 8.1. Japan's inward and outward FDI stock as a percentage of GDP
Source: UNCTAD, *Key Data from WIR Tables*, Tables 11 and 18; online: <http://www.
unctad.org/Templates/Page.asp?intItemID=3277&lang=1> (accessed May 2, 2007).

Chief among these, as shown in Chapter 4, are population trends – the
shrinking and aging of the population – which mean that any future growth
in Japan will have to come from gains in productivity, especially total factor
productivity (TFP). However, one important reason for the slowdown in
Japan's economic growth since the 1980s has been its disappointing TFP
performance, particularly during the 1990s. In fact, during that decade,
TFP in the manufacturing (excluding electrical and optical equipment)
and construction sectors actually fell, while TFP growth in market services (excluding post and telecommunications) decelerated substantially.
The overall stagnation in Japan's TFP since 1990 is particularly disappointing when seen against the acceleration in TFP growth experienced by the
United States and Britain, although even Germany and France, both with
their own economic problems, continued to register TFP growth during this
period. That being said, TFP growth has picked up more recently, in part
thanks to the modernization of capital as a result of increased investment
activity. Nevertheless, productivity levels in Japan continue to significantly
lag behind those in the major Western economies, especially in services and
other "domestic" sectors of the economy.

It is against this background that FDI can make an important contribution to economic growth in Japan. Multinational companies invest abroad

on the strength of firm-specific intangible assets, such as managerial skills, technological knowledge, and marketing know-how. The transfer of these assets from parent firms to their overseas affiliates is expected to contribute to TFP growth in the host country through a variety of channels. These include the direct effect on host country affiliates benefiting from the transfer of intangible assets as well as the indirect effects on local firms and industries through technological spillovers and the impact on competition. Empirical evidence, presented in Chapter 5, suggests that such direct technology transfer effects can indeed be observed in practice. Japanese firms acquired by foreigners tend to enjoy higher TFP and TFP growth than their domestically-owned counterparts. Although part of this difference is due to the fact that foreigners tend to choose firms for acquisition that already perform better than other local firms, comparing the performance of target firms of cross-border (out–in) and domestic (in–in) M&As shows that the former registered substantially higher TFP growth than the latter two and three years after the acquisition.

The impact of FDI on the performance of individual industries or the economy overall unfortunately is difficult to assess, given the paucity of data and the fact that, despite the increase since the turn of the millennium, the level of inward FDI still remains low and any macroeconomic effects would therefore be small and hard to detect. However, simulation of the macroeconomic impact using various assumptions based on the TFP improvement effect suggested by empirical analysis and the government target for the stock of inward FDI indicates that the contribution to GDP and gross national product (GNP) is potentially substantial. Thus, assuming that the government target of an inward FDI stock of 5 percent of GDP by 2010 is reached and assuming, moreover, that foreign acquisitions raise target firms TFP by 5 percent in the long run, the simulation suggests that the increase in FDI would lift Japan's GDP by an estimated 0.24 percent. This, however, is likely to be a conservative scenario, given that the estimate of the TFP improvement effect is based on the manufacturing sector, where productivity differentials with other advanced economies are likely to be relatively small. In the service sector, which is where most FDI has in fact been concentrated, the gap in productivity, and hence the potential improvement in TFP as a result of foreign investment, is probably considerably greater. Assuming, therefore, that the improvement in target firms' TFP as a result of foreign acquisition is three times as large, that is, 15 percent, the increase in GDP, at an estimated 0.68 percent, would also roughly be three times as large. Even if spread over several years, this would provide a lift to economic growth that, given Japan's potential growth rate, is certainly not negligible.

But the most instructive simulation results are obtained when combining the assumption of a quite plausible TFP improvement in the order of 15 percent with the assumption of a substantially greater increase in FDI. Supposing an increase in FDI that would leave foreign firms' share in employment and output at levels still well below those in other advanced economies, this could lift Japan's GDP by an estimated 2 percent, which would be roughly equivalent to an extra year of economic growth. However, assuming an increase in FDI that is substantially greater than the government target does not mean that this is probable – in fact, given current circumstances, it appears rather unlikely. But it does provide an illustration of the substantial contribution FDI *could* make to overall economic growth, highlighting the costs to Japan of resisting "inner globalization."

What is more, the simulation results most likely underestimate the effect of FDI on TFP growth and hence overall economic growth, because they consider only the direct impact of foreign acquisitions on target firms' performance. Not taken into account, again because of the lack of adequate and up-to-date statistical data, are the indirect effects – such as technology and knowledge spillovers and effects on market and industry structure. Yet, such indirect effects clearly can be observed, and the industry studies in Chapter 6 provide concrete examples not only of the many forms that the transfer of intangible assets takes and how this helps to raise the performance of acquired firms, but also how this generates knowledge spillovers and contributes to reshaping market and industry structures.

One of the clearest, and most spectacular, instances of how the transfer of intangible assets has helped to improve target firm performance is the acquisition of Nissan by Renault. The management team dispatched by Renault and headed by Carlos Ghosn provided the Japanese carmaker with leadership, financial expertise, and a clearer international orientation in its operations. In addition to managerial expertise, Renault also brought to the table access to its network of suppliers, helping Nissan to streamline its parts-purchasing operations. Another example are the four banks (Long Term Credit Bank of Japan, Kofuku Bank, Tokyo Sowa Bank, and Nippon Credit Bank) that had failed during Japan's financial crisis and were purchased and subsequently revived by foreign investors. In all four cases, the management teams that were installed introduced more focused business models and customer services that differed from the Japanese norm.

But although most FDI in developed economies these days takes the form of M&As, transfers of intangible assets naturally also occur in the case of "greenfield" investment and can make an important contribution to productivity growth in Japan. A prime example is investment banking, a field that requires advanced technology, high levels of expertise, and global presence – areas in which domestic banks generally lag behind the global players operating in Japan. Of the industry studies in Chapter 6, investment banking also provides the most concrete example of knowledge spillovers to domestic firms, that is, the imitation of innovative financial products developed by foreign investment banks.

However, the aspect that most clearly stands out from the case studies is the way that foreign firms have contributed to changes in market and industry structures in those areas where their presence has reached sufficient critical mass. Prime examples are the insurance sector and the pharmaceutical industry. In the insurance sector, foreign firms were able to acquire a considerable number of failed or struggling Japanese insurers and have gained substantial market share thanks to the introduction of innovative products and more sophisticated sales and marketing operations based on the experience gained in markets elsewhere. Such competition has forced domestic insurers to raise their game by intensifying efforts to develop new products and services and restructure their sales and marketing operations. In the pharmaceutical sector, where foreign drug firms have acquired domestic manufacturers, bought out former joint ventures with local counterparts, and invested in their own distribution channels, the onslaught of foreign competition has led to industry consolidation in both manufacturing and wholesaling.

As the dynamics in the insurance and pharmaceutical sectors illustrate, the impact of FDI on domestic firms can be negative and quite severe. However, where this is the case, it also highlights that the gap in competitiveness must be substantial. Hence, from the viewpoint of the industry or economy as a whole, the entry and/or increase in market share of more productive firms and the exit and/or decline in market share of less productive firms raises the productivity level overall. On the other hand, in the car industry, for instance, Toyota has continued to go from strength to strength despite Nissan's resurgence following the acquisition by Renault. What is more, as the retail banking and telecommunication sectors show, it is not a foregone conclusion that foreign firms will make a significant impact on their respective industries.

It is also important to note that, with the exception of health care services, the industries considered in Chapter 6 are those in which foreign investment has been substantial. Yet, many sectors remain that have seen little inward FDI. Consequently, while technology and knowledge transfer effects and foreign firms' role in industry dynamics may have made important contributions to productivity growth in a few select sectors, the impact on the economy as a whole is likely to have been very limited, taking into account that even an increase in the ratio of the FDI stock to GDP from roughly 2 percent in mid-2006 to 5 percent, as assumed in the simulation, would generate only a modest increase in GDP (0.24 percent or 0.68 percent, depending on the assumption regarding the TFP improvement effect). Therefore, the conclusion to be drawn from both the macroeconomic simulation and the industry studies is similar: while the "surge" in inward FDI since the late 1990s represents an important new development, this can only be the beginning of a process of "inner globalization" if Japan is to fully benefit from the contribution that foreign firms can make to its economy.

Failure to achieve such inner globalization may be particularly damaging because Japan's own firms at the same time are continuing to press ahead with "outer globalization." Since the early 1990s, the relocation of production by Japanese firms has given rise to recurring concerns over the "hollowing out" of the domestic economy, especially as it is the country's most successful and productive firms, led by those from the car and electronics industries, that are at the forefront of taking advantage of the opportunities available overseas. Although at present it is still primarily labor-intensive processes that are shifted abroad, the experience of other countries suggests that once such bridgeheads are established, it is often only a matter of time until more skill-intensive activities follow. In fact, failure to take advantage of the skills offered abroad, often at lower costs than at home, such as in the case of engineers and software specialists in China and India, may weaken the competitiveness of Japanese multinationals. Thus, the imbalance in Japan's globalization indicated by Figure 8.1 highlights the danger that, as the country's most productive firms continue to expand abroad, there are no corresponding inflows of knowledge, skills, and other resources that could help to raise productivity at home.

It is against this background and Japan's disappointing TFP performance that concerns over the potential harm to the "national interest" posed by M&As seem particularly misplaced. Calls for measures that would help to block M&A attempts to prevent the outflow of technology ignore the fact that erecting obstacles to M&As also hinders the inflow of knowledge and technology, of which FDI is a major conduit. Yet, Japan's own history demonstrates the important role that the inflow of foreign knowledge has played throughout the country's cultural, political, and economic development.

Such inflows can be traced back more than a thousand years, starting with the absorption of Chinese culture. Even during the period of "national seclusion" (*sakoku*) in the Tokugawa era, foreign knowledge filtered in through *rangaku* ("Dutch learning" and, by extension, "Western learning").

Following the Meiji Restoration, study missions abroad and the hiring of foreign specialists brought Western knowledge and techniques to Japan. And in the early twentieth century, foreign capital and expertise played a key role in the country's early industrial development and the establishment of some of the country's most successful companies today (as seen in Chapter 2).

The absorption of Western technology also provided a key ingredient in Japan's "economic miracle" during the early postwar period, when, with FDI strictly controlled, it took the form of reverse engineering and the licensing of foreign patents. But whereas this form of knowledge imports served Japan well during this phase of economic development, it has clearly run its course. Traditional technology licensing remains an import source of knowledge transfer, but it is no longer likely to provide the same kind of economic boost: in many industries where technology licensing is particularly important, such as the car, electronics, optical, and machine tool industries, Japanese firms have closed the technology gap and operate near the technology frontier and Japan in fact now is a net exporter of technology, registering large surpluses in the technology balance of payments in most manufacturing industries.[2] Moreover, foreign firms may have been willing to engage in technology licensing at favorable terms when Japanese firms were not perceived as a competitive threat and licensing was the only way to make money in the Japanese market, but this is no longer the case today and foreign manufacturers with advanced technologies always have the option of serving the Japanese market directly – either through exports or FDI as, for example, is the case in the pharmaceutical industry.

Another important reason is that technology licensing represents only one avenue of the transfer of a particular type of knowledge, codifiable knowledge, typically in the manufacturing sector, that can be separated from other types of knowledge and capabilities. But in many cases, the creation of wealth depends on the combination of a variety of different types of knowledge, capabilities, and technology, some codifiable, some not, that are embodied in people, organizational structures, business processes, and products, and as such can only be transferred as a "package," that is, through FDI. In the case of Nissan, for example, it was not technology in the narrow sense that helped to turn the company around, but a much broader set of knowledge and capabilities in the form of management ability, financial expertise, and so on. It is even conceivable that technology in the narrow sense may have flowed from Nissan to Renault. Yet, few would argue that the

---

[2] Ministry of Education, Culture, Sports, Science and Technology (2006: 193), Figure 2–3–16.

Renault–Nissan alliance has been damaging to Japan and those purporting to be concerned about the country's national interest would do well to consider that the risks of losing out on the transfer of knowledge, capabilities, and technology that FDI entails weigh far greater than the potential danger of the outflow of technology.

This line of reasoning carries even stronger force in the service sector: many services can be provided only as such a "package" and Japan would stand to gain even more because it is in the service sector where the country is most in need of a boost. Whereas Japan was very successful in the rapid accumulation of technology in manufacturing, this sector (in terms of employment) is now shrinking, in part as a result of the relocation of production abroad. It is therefore the service sector that will have to generate most of Japan's economic growth, but this is an area in which Japan has never been particularly innovative or produced internationally competitive companies. Consequently, what the country most needs for its future economic prosperity is a vibrant, innovative, high-value-added service sector – and FDI can make an important contribution to this.

Ensuring that this can happen, however, does not mean that the government should single out and promote foreign investment. Instead, what is important is a fair and favorable environment that provides opportunities for innovative businesses – domestic and foreign alike. In an increasingly complex and interdependent world, it is not the nationality of a company that matters, but the contribution it can make to national welfare. Or to use an analogy: for Osaka, good companies are companies that create productive jobs, introduce new knowledge and technology, generate income, and pay taxes – whether the company was established in Osaka or Tokyo makes little difference. In today's global economy, Japan is Osaka and Tokyo is the rest of the world. To Japan's detriment, these new realities are slow to sink in.

References

Ahmadjian, C. L. and J. R. Lincoln (2001) "*Keiretsu,* governance, and learning: Case studies in change from the Japanese automotive industry," *Organization Science* 12 (November–December), 683–701.

APEC (1999) Committee on Trade and Investment, *Guide to the Investment Regimes of the APEC Member Economies,* Singapore: Asia-Pacific Economic Cooperation.

A. T. Kearney (2004) *FDI Confidence Index,* Global Business Policy Council, A. T. Kearney, Inc. Online: <http://www.atkearney.com/shared_res/pdf/FDICIOct_2004_S.pdf> (accessed March 12, 2007).

A. T. Kearney (2005) *FDI Confidence Index,* Global Business Policy Council, A. T. Kearney, Inc. Online: <http://www.atkearney.com/shared_res/pdf/FDICI_2005.pdf> (accessed March 12, 2007).

Baily, M. N. and R. M. Solow (2001) "International productivity comparisons built from the firm level," *Journal of Economic Perspectives* 15(3), 151–172.

Bank of Japan (2006) "The new estimates of output gap and potential growth rate" (sic), *Bank of Japan Review* 2006-E-3. Online: <http://www.boj.or.jp/en/type/ronbun/rev/data/rev06e03.pdf> (accessed April 2, 2007).

Bayoumi, T. (2001) "The morning after: Explaining the slowdown in Japanese growth in the 1990s," *Journal of International Economics* 53(2), 241–259.

Belderbos, R. A. (1998) "FDI and licensing strategies by Dutch multinationals in Japan," *Research Memoranda* NIBOR/RM/98/02, Netherlands Institute of Business Organization and Strategy Research, Maastricht University.

Bergsten, C. F., T. Ito, and M. Noland (2001) *No More Bashing: Building a New Japan–United States Economic Relationship,* Washington, DC: Institute for International Economics.

Blomström, M., B. Gangnes, and S. La Croix (2001) *Japan's New Economy: Continuity and Change in the Twenty-First Century,* New York: Oxford University Press.

Blomström, M. and A. Kokko (2003) "The economics of foreign direct investment incentives," *NBER Working Paper* No. 9489, National Bureau of Economic Research, Cambridge, MA.

Blomström, M. and F. Sjöholm. (1998) "Technology transfer and spillovers? Does local participation with multinationals matter?" *NBER Working Paper* No. 6816, National Bureau of Economic Research, Cambridge, MA.

Christensen, L. R., D. Cummings, and D. W. Jorgenson (1995) "Economic growth, 1947–1973: An international comparison," in D. W. Jorgenson (ed.), *Productivity*, Volume 2, Cambridge, MA: MIT Press.

Corrado, C., C. Hulten, and D. Sichel (2005) "Measuring capital and technology: An extended framework," in C. Corrado, J. Haltiwanger, and D. Sichel (eds.), *Measuring Capital in the New Economy*, Chicago: University of Chicago Press.

Corrado, C., C. Hulten, and D. Sichel (2006) "Intangible capital and economic growth," *NBER Working Paper* No. 11948, National Bureau of Economic Research, Cambridge, MA.

Council on Economic and Fiscal Policy (2005) "Toward the realization of a dynamic, stable society," Economic and Fiscal Prospects Working Group, Japan's 21st Century Vision, Cabinet Office. Online: <http://www.keizai-shimon.go.jp/english/publication/pdf/050419visionprospects_report.pdf> (accessed March 29, 2007).

Council on Economic and Fiscal Policy (2007) "Nihon keizai no shinro to senryaku ni tsuite" [Course and strategy for the Japanese economy], Cabinet Office. Online: <http://www.keizai-shimon.go.jp/cabinet/2007/decision0125_01.pdf> (accessed April 2, 2007).

David, S. (2006) "Good-bye Japan? Market withdrawals 1999–2005: Reasons, barriers, and company-specific factors," Results of a survey conducted at the Department of Business Studies, East Asian Economic Studies, University of Duisburg-Essen, *mimeo.*

De Vecchi, A. F., M. Dratwa, and M. E. Wiedemann (1999) "Healthcare systems and end-stage renal disease (ESRD) therapies – an international review: Costs and reimbursement/funding of ESRD therapies," *Nephrology Dialysis Transplantation* 14 [Suppl 6], 31–41. Online: <http://ndt.oxfordjournals.org/cgi/reprint/14/suppl_6/31> (accessed March 12, 2007).

Development Bank of Japan (2000) "Trend of international reorganization affecting the Japanese automobile and auto parts industries," *Development Bank of Japan Research Report* No. 8.

Doms, M. E. and J. B. Jensen (1998) "Comparing wages, skills, and productivity between domestically and foreign-owned manufacturing establishments in the United States," in R. E. Baldwin, R. E. Lipsey, and J. D. Richardson (eds.), *Geography and Ownership as Bases for Economic Accounting*, Chicago: University of Chicago Press.

Dunning, J. H. (1993) *Multinational Enterprises and the Global Economy*, Wokingham: Addison-Wesley.

Eaton, J. and A. Tamura (1994) "Bilateralism and regionalism in Japanese and U.S. trade and direct foreign investment patterns," *Journal of the Japanese and International Economies* 8(4), 478–510.

Economic and Social Research Institute (2005) "Heisei 17-nen M&A kenkyukai kiji yoshi, heisei 17-nen 2-gatsu 18-nichi kaisai" [Transcript of the 2005 M&A research meeting, 18 February 2005], M&A Kenkyukai Salon. Online: <http://www.esri.go.jp/jp/mer/kenkyukai/050218-03.pdf> (accessed March 12, 2007).

Economic Planning Agency (1998) *Economic Survey of Japan (1996–1997)*, Tokyo.

Encarnation, D. (1992) *Rivals Beyond Trade: America versus Japan in Global Competition*, Ithaca: Cornell University Press.

European Business Community in Japan (2004) *Trade, Investment and the Reform Nexus: The EBC Report on the Japanese Business Environment 2004*, Tokyo.

European Business Council (2005) *Key Moment for Reform: The EBC Report on the Japanese Business Environment 2005*, Tokyo.

Fairbank, J. K., E. O. Reischauer, and A. M. Craig (1973) *East Asia: Tradition and Transformation*, Boston: Houghton Mifflin Company.

Feenstra, R. C. (1998) "Facts and fallacies about foreign direct investment," *Working Paper* 98–04, Department of Economics, University of California, Davis. Online: <http://www.econ.ucdavis.edu/faculty/fzfeens/pdf/fdi2.pdf> (accessed January 15, 2007).

Flath, D. (2003) "Regulation, distribution efficiency, and retail density," in M. Blomström, J. Corbett, F. Hayashi, and A. Kashyap (eds.), *Structural Impediments to Growth in Japan*, Chicago: University of Chicago Press.

Fukao, K. and K. Ito (2003) "Foreign direct investment and service trade: The case of Japan," in T. Ito and Anne O. Krueger (eds.), *Trade in Services in the Asia-Pacific Region, National Bureau of Economic Research – East Asia Seminar on Economics*, Volume 11, Chicago: University of Chicago Press.

Fukao, K., T. Inui, H. Kawai, and T. Miyagawa (2004) "Sectoral productivity and economic growth in Japan, 1970–98: An empirical analysis based on the JIP Database," in T. Ito and A. Rose (eds.), *Growth and Productivity in East Asia (National Bureau of Economic Research – East Asia Seminar on Economics)*, Volume 13, Chicago: University of Chicago Press.

Fukao, K., K. Ito, and H. U. Kwon (2004) "Characteristics and effects of Japan's inward FDI," Paper prepared for the CGP Conference 'International Economic Relations and Structural Change: Issues and Policy Options for Japan and the United States.' Online: <http://www.fordschool.umich.edu/rsie/Conferences/CGP/May2004Papers/Fukao.pdf> (accessed January 15, 2007).

Fukao, K., K. Ito, and H. U. Kwon (2005) "Do out-in M&As bring higher TFP to Japan? An empirical analysis based on micro-data on Japanese manufacturing firms," *Journal of the Japanese and International Economies* 19(2), 272–301.

Fukao, K., Y. G. Kim, and H. U. Kwon (2006) "Plant turnover and TFP dynamics in Japanese manufacturing," *Hi-Stat Discussion Paper Series* No. 180, Hitotsubashi University. Online: <http://hi-stat.ier.hit-u.ac.jp/research/discussion/2006/pdf/D06–180.pdf>.

Fukao, K., H. U. Kwon, and M. Takizawa (2006) "Tainichi kokunai kigyokan M&A to hibaishu kigyo no performance" [Out-in and in-in M&As and target firm performance], *Hi-Stat Discussion Paper Series* No. 133, Hitotsubashi University. Online: <http://hi-stat.ier.hit-u.ac.jp/research/discussion/2005/pdf/D05–133.pdf>.

Fukao, K. and T. Miyagawa (2007) "Productivity in Japan, the US, and the major EU economies: Is Japan falling behind?" Paper prepared for the Third International Workshop of the Joint Research Study Group 'EU Economy,' EUIJ Tokyo Consortium, Hitotsubashi University, Tokyo, March 25, 2007. Online: <http://www.cm.hit-u.ac.jp/~euij/pdf/Fukao.pdf> (accessed April 2, 2007).

Fukao, K. and Y. Murakami (2005) "Do foreign firms bring greater total factor productivity to Japan?" *Journal of the Asia Pacific Economy* 10(2), 237–54.

Genda, Y. (1998) "Japan: Wage differentials and changes since the 1980s," in T. Tachibanaki (ed.), *Wage Differentials: An International Comparison*, Basingstoke: Macmillan Press and New York: St. Martin's Press.

Ghosn, C. and P. Riès (2005) *Shift: Inside Nissan's Historic Revival*, New York: Currency/Doubleday.

Globerman, S., J. C. Ries, and I. Vertinsky (1994) "The economic performance of foreign affiliates in Canada," *Canadian Journal of Economics* 27(1), 143–56.

Godo, Y. (2001) "Estimation of average years of schooling by levels of education for Japan and the United States, 1890–1990," *mimeo*, Tokyo: FASID. Online: <http://www.fasid.or.jp/english/surveys/research/program/research/pdf/database/2001–001.pdf> (accessed January 17, 2007).

Godo, Y. and Y. Hayami (2002) "Catching-up in education in the economic catch-up of Japan with the United States," *Economic Development and Cultural Change* 50(4), 961–78.

Goldman Sachs (2003) "Dreaming with BRICs: The path to 2050," *Global Economics Paper* No. 99. Online: <http://www.gs.com/insight/research/reports/99.pdf> (accessed March 10, 2007).

Good, D. H., M. I. Nadiri, and R. C. Sickles (1997) "Index number and factor demand approaches to the estimation of productivity," in M. H. Pesran and P. Schmidt (eds.), *Handbook of Applied Econometrics, Volume 2: Microeconometrics*, Oxford: Basil Blackwell.

Griffith, R. and H. Simpson (2001) "Characteristics of foreign-owned firms in British manufacturing," *IFS Working Papers 01/10*, Institute for Fiscal Studies, London.

Harner, S. M. (2000) *Japan's Financial Revolution and How American Firms are Profiting*, Armonk, NY: M. E. Sharpe.

Harrigan, J. and R. Vanjani (2003) "Is Japan's trade (still) different?" *Journal of the Japanese and International Economies* 17(4), 507–19.

Hayashi, F. and E. C. Prescott (2002) "The 1990s in Japan: A lost decade?" *Review of Economic Dynamics* 5(1), 206–35.

Høj, J. and M. Wise (2004) "Product market competition and economic performance in Japan," *Economics Department Working Papers* No. 387, OECD. Online: <http://www.olis.oecd.org/olis/2004doc.nsf/linkto/eco-wkp(2004)10> (accessed January 18, 2007).

Horiuchi, A. (2004) "Ginko kiki to kinyu system no saikochiku" [The banking crisis and the reconstruction of the financial system], *Financial Review* 73 (September), Policy Research Institute, Ministry of Finance. Online: <http://www.mof.go.jp/f-review/r73/r_73_041_069.pdf> (accessed March 6, 2007).

Hoshi, T. and A. K. Kashyap (2001) *Corporate Financing and Governance in Japan: The Road to the Future*, Cambridge, MA: MIT Press.

Howe, C. (1996) *The Origins of Japanese Trade Supremacy: Development and Technology in Asia from 1540 to the Pacific War*, Chicago: University of Chicago Press.

Ikeda, M. and Y. Nakagawa (2002) "Globalization of the Japanese automobile industry and reorganization of *keiretsu*-suppliers," *Actes du GERPISA* No. 33 (March), Université d'Evry. Online: <http://www.univ-evry.fr/labos/gerpisa/actes/33/33-3.pdf> (accessed April 27, 2007).

IMF (1993) *Balance of Payments Manual*, Fifth Edition, Washington, DC: International Monetary Fund. Online: <http://www.imf.org/external/np/sta/bop/BOPman.pdf> (accessed March 10, 2007).

IMF (1998a) *World Economic Outlook*, October, Washington, DC: International Monetary Fund.

IMF (1998b) *Japan: Selected Issues*, IMF Staff Country Report 98/113, Washington, DC: International Monetary Fund.

Ito, K. (2002) "Are foreign multinationals more efficient? Plant productivity in the Thai automobile industry," *ICSEAD Working Paper Series* 2002–19, The International Centre for the Study of East Asian Development, Kitakyushu.

Ito, K. (2004a) "Foreign ownership and plant productivity in the Thai automobile industry in 1996 and 1998: A conditional quantile analysis," *Journal of Asian Economics* 15(2), 321–53.

Ito, K. (2004b) "Foreign ownership and productivity in the Indonesian automobile industry: Evidence from establishment data for 1990–99," in T. Ito and A. Rose (eds.), *Growth and Productivity in East Asia*, Chicago: University of Chicago Press.

Ito, K. (2004c) "Plant productivity, *keiretsu*, and agglomeration in the Japanese automobile industry: An empirical analysis based on micro-data of *Census of Manufactures 1981–1996*" (sic), *Hi-Stat Discussion Paper Series* No. 51, Hitotsubashi University. Online: <http://hi-stat.ier.hit-u.ac.jp/research/discussion/2004/pdf/D04-51.pdf> (accessed March 12, 2007).

Ito, K. and K. Fukao (2001) "Jidosha sangyo no seisansei: 'Kogyo Tokei Chosa' kohyo data ni yoru jissho bunseki" [The productivity of the automobile industry: An empirical analysis based on the establishment-level data of the *Census of Manufactures*], *RIETI Discussion Paper Series 01-J-002*, Research Institute of Trade and Industry, Tokyo. Online: <http://www.rieti.go.jp/jp/publications/dp/01j002.pdf> (accessed March 12, 2007).

Ito, K. and K. Fukao (2004) "Physical and human capital deepening and new trade patterns in Japan," *NBER Working Paper* No. 10209, National Bureau of Economic Research, Cambridge, MA.

Ito, T. and M. Tsuri (2003) "Macroeconomic impacts of aging in Japan on the balance of current accounts," *Discussion Paper* No. 170, Project on Intergenerational Equity, Institute of Economic Research, Hitotsubashi University. Online: <http://www.ier.hit-u.ac.jp/pie/Japanese/discussionpaper/dp2003/dp170/text.pdf> (accessed January 17, 2007).

Japan Center for International Finance (2004) "Assessment and strategies of foreign financial institutions in Japan regarding the Tokyo financial/capital market," Japan Center for International Finance, Tokyo. Online: <http://www.jcif.or.jp/pdf/asff200407.pdf> (accessed April 3, 2007).

Japan Research Institute (2000) "The impact of foreign direct investment (FDI) in Japan on the Japanese economy," *Monthly Review*, September. Online: <http://www.jri.co.jp/english/thinktank/research/monthly/pdf/MRe200009fdi.pdf> (accessed February 16, 2007).

Japan Small Business Research Institute (2003) *White Paper on Small and Medium Enterprises in Japan 2003*, Ministry of Economy, Trade and Industry, Tokyo. Online: <http://www.chusho.meti.go.jp/pamflet/hakusyo/h15/download/2003haku_eng.pdf> (accessed January 22, 2007).

JETRO (2002) "The survey on actual conditions regarding access to Japan: Health care services." Online: <http://www.jetro.go.jp/en/stats/survey/access/e_iryofukushi.pdf> (accessed March 12, 2007).

JETRO (2004a) "Retail business," *JETRO Japanese Market Reports* No. 72. Online: <http://www.jetro.go.jp/en/market/reports/jmr/072.pdf> (accessed March 8, 2007).

JETRO (2004b) "The 9th survey on attitudes of foreign-affiliated companies toward direct investment in Japan." Online: <http://www.jetro.go.jp/en/stats/survey/surveys/foreign_companies04.pdf> (accessed April 14, 2007).

JETRO (2004c) *2004 JETRO White Paper on International Trade and Foreign Direct Investment*, Tokyo: JETRO. Online: <http://www.jetro.go.jp/en/stats/white_paper/2004.pdf> (accessed April 14, 2007).

References

JETRO (2005a) "Automobile assembly parts," *JETRO Japanese Market Reports* No. 76. Online: <http://www.jetro.go.jp/en/market/reports/jmr/076.pdf> (accessed March 8, 2007).

JETRO (2005b) "Ongoing change in Japan's life insurance industry," *Japan Economic Monthly*, August. Online: <http://www.jetro.go.jp/en/market/trend/jem/0508_jeme.pdf> (accessed March 8, 2007).

JETRO (2005c) "Trends in the pharmaceutical industry," *Japan Economic Monthly*, August. Online: <http://www.jetro.go.jp/en/market/trend/jem/0508_jeme.pdf> (accessed March 8, 2007).

JETRO (2005d) "Corporate participation in medical facility management," *Japan Economic Monthly*, July. Online: <http://www.jetro.go.jp/en/market/trend/jem/0507_jeme.pdf> (accessed March 8, 2007).

JETRO (2005e) "Attractive sectors: Medical care." Online: <http://www.jetro.go.jp/en/market/attract/medical/med.pdf> (accessed March 12, 2007).

JETRO (2005f) "Facilitating the movement of people across national borders: Revitalizing international business exchange." Online: <http://www.jetro.go.jp/en/stats/survey/surveys/20050511_movement.pdf> (accessed April 14, 2007).

JETRO (2005g) "More foreign students remain in Japan to work," *Japan Economic Monthly*, August. Online: <http://www.jetro.go.jp/en/market/trend/index/pdf/jem0508-3e1.pdf> (accessed April 14, 2007).

Jordan, T. F. (1996) "The future of foreign direct investment in Japan," in M. Yoshitomi and E. M. Graham (eds.), *Foreign Direct Investment in Japan*, Cheltenham: Edward Elgar.

Jorgensen, D. W. and K. Motohashi (2004) "Potential growth of the Japanese and U.S. economies in the information age," *ESRI Discussion Paper Series* No. 88, Economic and Social Research Institute, Cabinet Office. Online: <http://www.esri.go.jp/jp/archive/e_dis/e_dis090/e_dis088a.pdf> (accessed April 14, 2007).

Kawai, M. and S. Urata (1997) "Foreign direct investment in Japan: An empirical analysis," *CJES Research Paper* 1997–3, Macquarie University, Sydney.

Kee, H. L., A. Nicita, and M. Olarreaga (2006) "Estimating trade restrictiveness indices," *CEPR Discussion Paper Series* No. 5576, Centre for Economic Policy Research, London.

Keizai Doyukai (Japan Association of Corporate Executives) (2002) *How to Make Japan a Place Where Non-Japanese People Want to Visit, Study, and Work.* Online: <http://www.doyukai.or.jp/en/policyproposals/articles/pdf/021023.pdf> (accessed March 29, 2007).

Kimura, F. and K. Kiyota (2007) "Foreign-owned versus domestically-owned firms: Economic performance in Japan," *Review of Development Economics* 11(1), 31–48.

Komiya, R. (1972) "Direct foreign investment in Japan," in P. Drysdale (ed.), *Direct Foreign Investment in Asia and the Pacific*, Canberra: Australian National University Press.

Krugman, P. (1998) "It's baaack: Japan's slump and the return of the liquidity trap," *Brookings Papers on Economic Activity* No. 2, 137–205.

Kushida, K. (2002) "The Japanese wireless telecommunications industry: Innovation, organizational structures, and government policy," *Stanford Journal of East Asian Affairs* 2, 55–70. Online: <http://www.stanford.edu/group/sjeaa/journal2/japan1.pdf> (accessed March 12, 2007).

Kushida, K. (2006) "Japan's telecommunications regime shift: Understanding Japan's potential resurgence," in A. Newman and J. Zysman (eds.) *How Revolutionary was the Digital Revolution? National Responses, Market Transitions, and Global Technology in the Digital Era*, Stanford, CA: Stanford University Press.

Lawrence, R. Z. (1993) "Japan's different trade regime: An analysis with particular reference to *keiretsu*," *Journal of Economic Perspectives* 7(3), 3–19.

Lawrence, R. Z. (1994) "Japan's low levels of inward investment: The role of inhibitions on acquisitions," in K. A. Froot (ed.), *Foreign Direct Investment*, Chicago: University of Chicago Press.

Lipsey, R. E. and F. Sjöholm (2004) "Host country impacts of inward FDI: Why such different answers?" *EIJS Working Paper Series* No. 192, The European Institute of Japanese Studies, Stockholm School of Economics. Online: <http://swopec.hhs.se/eijswp/papers/eijswp0192.pdf> (accessed April 26, 2007).

Magee, D. (2003) *Turnaround: How Carlos Ghosn Rescued Nissan*, New York: Harper Business.

Mahlich, J. (N.D.) "The impact of globalization on the Japanese pharmaceutical industry." Online: <http://www.oru.se/oru-upload/Institutioner/Ekonomi%20statistik%20och%20informatik/Dokument/Forskning/Nationalekonomi/Mahlich.pdf> (accessed April 27, 2007).

Mason, M. (1987) "Foreign direct investment and Japanese economic development, 1899–1931," *Business and Economic History* 16, 93–107.

Mason, M. (1992) *American Multinationals and Japan: The Political Economy of Japanese Capital Controls, 1899–1980*, Cambridge, MA: Council on East Asian Studies, Harvard University.

Mason, M. (1995) "Japan's low levels of inward direct investment: Causes, consequences and remedies," in E. K. Chen and P. Drysdale (eds.) *Corporate Links and Foreign Direct Investment in Asia and the Pacific*, Sydney: Harper Collins.

McKinnon, R. and G. Schnabl (2003) "China: A stabilizing or deflationary influence in East Asia? The problem of conflicted virtue," *Working Paper* 03–007, Economics Department, Stanford University. Online: <http://www-econ.stanford.edu/faculty/workp/swp03007.pdf> (accessed January 17, 2007).

McKinsey Global Institute (2000) *Why the Japanese Economy is not Growing: Micro Barriers to Productivity Growth*, Washington, DC.

METI (2000), "Summary of the 1999 Survey of Overseas Business Activities," Ministry of Economy, Trade and Industry, Tokyo. Online: <http://www.meti.go.jp/english/statistics/downloadfiles/h2c400be.pdf> (accessed January 22, 2007).

METI (2006a) "The 39th Survey of Trends in Business Activities of Foreign Affiliates (Main Points)," Ministry of Economy, Trade and Industry, Tokyo. Online: <http://www.meti.go.jp/english/statistics/downloadfiles/h2c200he.pdf> (accessed March 12, 2007).

METI (2006b) "Summary of the 35th Survey on Overseas Business Activities," Ministry of Economy, Trade and Industry, Tokyo. Online: <http://www.meti.go.jp/english/statistics/downloadfiles/h2c400he.pdf> (accessed March 12, 2007).

Ministry of Education, Culture, Sports, Science and Technology (2006), *White Paper on Science and Technology 2006*, Tokyo.

Mitsui Kaijo Kiso Kenkyujo (2001) *Tainichi chokusetsu toshi zoka no riyu to Nihon keizai ni motarasu eikyo ni kan suru chosa* [Survey on the reasons for the increase in FDI

262

References

in Japan and the impact on the Japanese economy], Mitsui Kaijo Kiso Kenkyujo [Mitsui Kaijo Basic Research Institute], Tokyo. Online: <http://www.investment-japan.go.jp/research/index_h12.htm> (accessed March 12, 2007).

MITI, Tsusho Sangyo Seisakushi Hensan Iinkai Hen [MITI and Editing Committee of the History of Trade and Industrial Policy (eds.)] (1991) *Tsusho sangyo seisakushi* [The history of trade and industrial policy], Volume 8, Ministry of International Trade and Industry, Tokyo.

Miyajima, H., K. Haramura, and Y. Enami (2003) "Sengo nihon kigyo no kabushiki shoyu kozo: Antei kabunushi no keisei to kaitai" [The ownership structure of Japanese firms after the war: The emergence and dissolution of stable shareholdings], *Financial Review* 68, Policy Research Institute, Ministry of Finance, Tokyo. Online: <http://www.mof.go.jp/f-review/r68/r_68_203_236.pdf> (accessed January 15, 2007).

Motonishi, T. and H. Yoshikawa (1999) "Causes of the long stagnation of Japan during the 1990s: Financial or real?" *Journal of the Japanese and International Economies* 13(3), 181–200.

Muramatsu, S. (2001) "Foreign capital and the recent M&A environment in Japan," in A. Holzhausen (ed.), *Can Japan Globalize? Studies on Japan's Changing Political Economy and the Process of Globalization in Honour of Sung-Jo Park*, Heidelberg: Physica-Verlag.

Nakamura, Y., K. Fukao, and M. Shibuya (1997) "Tainichi chokusetsu toshi wa naze sukunai ka? Keiretsu, kisei ga mondai ka?" [Why is FDI into Japan so small? Is it because of the keiretsu or because of regulations?], *Tsusho Sangyo Kenkyusho Kenkyu Series [MITI Research Institute Study Series]*, No.31, Ministry of International Trade and Industry, Tokyo. Online: <http://www.meti.go.jp/mitiri/downloadfiles/m4331-1.pdf> (accessed January 15, 2007).

National Institute of Population and Social Security Research (2002) *Population Projections for Japan: 2001–2050*. Online: <http://www.ipss.go.jp/pp-newest/e/ppfj02/ppfj02.pdf> (accessed March 12, 2007).

National Institute of Population and Social Security Research (2006) "Nihon no shorai suikei jinko [Population projections for Japan]," December. Online: <http://www.ipss.go.jp/pp-newest/j/newest03/newest03point.pdf> (accessed March 29, 2007).

NLI Research Institute (2002) "Cross-shareholdings decline for the 11th straight year (FY2001 Survey)." Online: <http://www.nli-research.co.jp/eng/resea/econo/eco021001.pdf> (accessed February 16, 2007).

NLI Research Institute (2003) "The relationship of companies and banks as cross-shareholdings unwind – Fiscal 2002 cross-shareholding survey." Online: <http://www.nli-research.co.jp/eng/resea/econo/eco031118.pdf> (accessed February 16, 2007).

NLI Research Institute (2004) "Mochiai jokyo chosa: 2003 nendo ban" [Survey of cross-shareholdings: FY 2003 Edition]." Online: <http://www.nli-research.co.jp/doc/mochiai03.pdf> (accessed February 16, 2007).

Nomura Soken Kenkyujo (2005) "Waga kuni ni okeru tainichi shinshutsu gaikoku kigyo no image ni kan suru chosa kenkyu [Survey regarding the image of foreign companies in Japan]." Online: <http://investment-japan.go.jp/research/H16-2/h16-2.pdf> (accessed April 14, 2007).

OECD (2001) *Measuring Globalisation: The Role of Multinationals in OECD Economies*, Paris: Organisation for Economic Co-operation and Development.

OECD (2003) *OECD Economic Outlook*, No. 73, June, Paris: Organisation for Economic Co-operation and Development.

OECD (2005a) *Measuring Globalisation: OECD Economic Globalisation Indicators*, Paris: Organisation for Economic Co-operation and Development.

OECD (2005b) *Education at a Glance: OECD Indicators 2005*, Paris: Organisation for Economic Co-operation and Development.

OECD (2006) *OECD Economic Surveys: Japan*, Paris: Organisation for Economic Co-operation and Development.

Okabe, K. (2001) "Are cross-shareholdings of Japanese corporations dissolving? – Evolution and implications," *Nissan Occasional Paper Series* No. 33, Nissan Institute of Japanese Studies, Oxford University. Online: <http://www.nissan.ox.ac.uk/nops/nops33.pdf> (accessed February 16, 2007).

Poe, M., K. Shimizu, and J. Simpson (2002) "Revising the Japanese Commercial Code: A summary and evaluation of the reform effort," *Stanford Journal of East Asian Affairs* 2, 71–95. Online: <http://www.stanford.edu/group/sjeaa/journal2/japan2.pdf> (accessed February 16, 2007).

Posen, A. S. (1998) *Restoring Japan's Economic Growth*, Washington, DC: Institute for International Economics.

Posen, A. S. (2001) "Recognizing Japan's rising potential growth," *NIRA Review*, Winter. Online: <http://www.nira.go.jp/publ/review/2001winter/posen.pdf> (accessed April 2, 2007).

Posen, A. S. (2004) "What went right in Japan?" *Policy Briefs* 04–6, Institute for International Economics. Online: <http://www.iie.com/publications/pb/pb04–6.pdf>.

Pyo, H. K. and K. Nam (1999) "A test of the convergence hypothesis by rates of return to capital: Evidence from OECD countries," *CIRJE Discussion Paper* CF-51, Center for International Research on the Japanese Economy, Faculty of Economics, University of Tokyo.

Ramstetter, E. D. (2001) "Labor productivity in foreign multinationals and local plants in Thai manufacturing, 1996 and 1998," *ICSEAD Working Paper Series* 2001–31, The International Centre for the Study of East Asian Development, Kitakyushu.

Ramstetter, E. D. (2002) "Does technology differ in local plants and foreign multinationals in Thai manufacturing? Evidence from translog production functions for 1996 and 1998," *ICSEAD Working Paper Series* 2002–04, The International Centre for the Study of East Asian Development, Kitakyushu.

Rapp, W. V. (1999), "Foreign firms in Japan's securities industry in the 1980s and post-bubble economy", in R. Aggarwal (ed.), *Restructuring Japanese Business for Growth: Strategy, Finance, Management and Marketing Perspectives*, Boston: Kluwer Academic Publishers.

RECOF (2003), *Nihon Kigyo no M&A Databook [M&A Databook of Japanese Companies]*, Tokyo: RECOF.

Riku, J. (2005) "Current situation for generic drugs in Japan", *Journal of Generic Medicines* 2(3), 219–31.

Samuels, R. J. (1987) *The Business of the Japanese State: Energy Markets in Comparative and Historical Perspective*, Ithaca: Cornell University Press.

Sangyo Kenkyusho [Industry Research Institute] (1983) "Gaishikei seizogyo no ritchi no jittai ni kan suru chosa hokokusho" [Report on the actual situation of the location of foreign-owned manufacturing firms], Sangyo Kenkyusho.

Saxonhouse, G. (1993) "What does Japanese trade structure tell us about Japanese trade policy?" *Journal of Economic Perspectives* 7(3), 21–43.

Shaver, M. J., W. Mitchell, and B. Yeung (1997) "The effect of own-firm and other-firm experience on foreign direct investment survival in the United States, 1987–92," *Strategic Management Journal* 18(10), 811–24.

Steindel, C. and K. Stiroh (2001) "Productivity: What it is, and why do we care about it?" *Staff Report* 122, Federal Reserve Bank of New York.

Stiroh, K. (2001) "What drives productivity growth?" *Federal Reserve Bank of New York Economic Policy Review* 7(1), 37–60.

Tachibanaki, T. and R. Nagakubo (1997) "Kabushiki mochiai to kigyo kodo" [Shareholdings and enterprise behavior], *Financial Review* 43, Policy Research Institute, Ministry of Finance. Online: <http://www.mof.go.jp/f-review/r43/r_43_158_173.pdf> (accessed January 15, 2007).

Thomas III, L. G. (2001) *The Japanese Pharmaceutical Industry: The New Drug Lag and the Failure of Industrial Policy*, Cheltenham, UK: Edward Elgar.

Udagawa, M. (1990) "Business management and foreign-affiliated companies in Japan before World War II," in T. Yuzawa and M. Udagawa (eds.), *Foreign Business in Japan Before World War II: Proceedings of the Fuji Conference*, Tokyo: University of Tokyo Press.

UNCTAD (1998) *World Investment Report 1998: Trends and Determinants*, Geneva: United Nations.

UNCTAD (2002) *World Investment Report 2002: Transnational Corporations and Export Competitiveness*, Geneva: United Nations.

UNCTAD (2003) *World Investment Report 2003 – FDI Policies for Development: National and International Perspectives*, Geneva: United Nations.

UNCTAD (2004) *World Investment Report 2004: The Shift Towards Services*, Geneva: United Nations.

UNCTAD (2005) *Prospects for Foreign Direct Investment and the Strategies of Transnational Corporation, 2005–2008*, Geneva: United Nations.

UNCTAD (2006) *World Investment Report 2006 – FDI from Developing and Transition Economies: Implications for Development*, Geneva: United Nations.

Wakasugi, R. (1994) "Why is FDI in Japan so small? An examination of the entry of foreign firms," *Yokohama National University Discussion Paper Series* 94-4, Yokohama National University.

Wakasugi, R. (1995) "On the causes of low levels of FDI in Japan," in E. K. Y. Chen and P. Drysdale (eds.), *Corporate Links and Foreign Direct Investment in Asia and the Pacific*, Sydney: Harper Collins.

Weinstein, D. (1996) "Structural impediments to investment in Japan: What have we learned over the last 450 years?" in M. Yoshitomi and E. M. Graham (eds.), *Foreign Direct Investment in Japan*, Cheltenham: Edward Elgar.

Weinstein, D. (1997) "Foreign direct investment and *keiretsu*: Rethinking U.S. and Japanese policy," in Robert C. Feenstra (ed.), *The Effects of U.S. Trade Protection and Promotion Policies*, Chicago: University of Chicago Press.

Wilkinson, E. (1990) *Japan versus the West: Image and Reality*, Harmondsworth: Penguin.

Yamamura, K. (1986) "Japan's deus ex machina: Western technology in the 1920s," *Journal of Japanese Studies* 12(1), 65–94.

Yoshino, M. Y. (1970) "Japan as host to the international corporation," in C. P. Kindleberger (ed.), *The International Corporation: A Symposium*, Cambridge, MA: MIT Press.

Yoshitomi, M. and E. M. Graham (eds.) (1996) *Foreign Direct Investment in Japan*, Cheltenham: Edward Elgar.

Yuzawa, T. and M. Udagawa (eds.) (1990), *Foreign Business in Japan before World War II: Proceedings of the Fuji Conference*, Tokyo: University of Tokyo Press.

Index

Printed in the United States
By Bookmasters